The globalization of human rights

The globalization of human rights

Edited by Jean-Marc Coicaud, Michael W. Doyle, and Anne-Marie Gardner

**United Nations
University Press**

TOKYO · NEW YORK · PARIS

United Nations University Press
The United Nations University, 53-70, Jingumae 5-chome,
Shibuya-ku, Tokyo, 150-8925, Japan
Tel: +81-3-3499-2811   Fax: +81-3-3406-7345
E-mail: sales@hq.unu.edu (general enquiries): press@hq.unu.edu
http://www.unu.edu

United Nations University Office in North America
2 United Nations Plaza, Room DC2-2062, New York, NY 10017, USA
Tel: +1-212-963-6387   Fax: +1-212-371-9454
E-mail: unuona@ony.unu.edu

United Nations University Press is the publishing division of the United Nations University.

Cover design by Jean-Marie Antenen

Printed in Hong Kong

UNUP-1080
ISBN 92-808-1080-4

Library of Congress Cataloging-in-Publication Data

The globalization of human rights / edited by Jean-Marc Coicaud,
Michael W. Doyle, and Anne-Marie Gardner.
    p.   cm.
"The product of a research project conducted under the auspices of the
Peace and Governance Programme of the United Nations University"—
Ack. Includes bibliographical references and index.
ISBN 92-808-1080-4
1. Human rights. 2. Civil rights. 3. Political rights. 4. Globalization.
I. Coicaud, Jean-Marc. II. Doyle, Michael W., 1948– III. Gardner,
Anne-Marie.
JC571 .G5855 2003
323—dc21   2002154215

Contents

Acknowledgements   vii

Introduction: Human rights and international order   1
Michael W. Doyle and Anne-Marie Gardner

Part 1: The construction of human rights at the domestic level

1 On the relationships between civil and political rights, and
social and economic rights..   23
Ruth Gavison

2 The incorporation of civic and social rights in domestic law   56
Claire Archbold

Part 2: The practice of human rights at the regional level

3 Comparative practice on human rights: North-South   89
James Mouangue Kobila

4 Human rights and Asian values..................................   116
Tatsuo Inoue

**Part 3: Human rights at the international level: Implementation
and distributive justice**

5 The politics of human rights..................................... 137
  Pierre de Senarclens

6 Global accountability: Transnational duties towards economic
  rights... 160
  Henry Shue

Conclusion: Human rights in discourse and practice: The
  quandary of international justice................................ 178
  Jean-Marc Coicaud

Acronyms... 201

List of contributors... 202

Index.. 203

Acknowledgements

This book is the product of a research project conducted under the auspices of the Peace and Governance Programme of the United Nations University (UNU). In the course of the project, the editors and authors benefited from the hospitality offered by the Center on Human Values, from Princeton University, at the occasion of a workshop organized in October 1999. The editors and authors wish to thank the commentators of the chapters and the participants to the workshop. Their comments were instrumental in helping to give a better focus to the chapters brought together in the book. The authors would also like to thank the anonymous reviewers of the manuscript for their helpful suggestions. In Tokyo, Ms. Yoshie Sawada of the UNU provided administrative support with efficiency and care. In the office of the United Nations University Press, Gareth Johnston, Janet Boileau, and the copy-editor Juliet Sydenham, helped tremendously to bring the book to life and in finalizing it.

Introduction: Human rights and international order

Michael W. Doyle and Anne-Marie Gardner[1]

Reflecting on the costly conflicts and international interventions in Kosovo and East Timor, UN Secretary-General Kofi Annan recently declared: "State sovereignty, in its most basic sense, is being redefined ... States are now widely understood," he went on to say, "to be instruments at the service of their peoples, and not vice versa ... [while] individual sovereignty – by which I mean the fundamental freedom of each individual, enshrined in the Charter of the United Nations and subsequent international treaties – has been enhanced by a renewed and spreading consciousness of individual rights."[2]

The Secretary-General is clearly identifying a powerful stream in the rethinking of legitimate international order. He also highlights a serious tension between increasingly influential global principles, on the one hand, and the practical difficulty, on the other hand, of implementing them in the face of states reluctant either to abide by the principles of human rights or to commit the resources needed to give those principles impartial and general effect when they are violated. But before these practical dilemmas arise, there are conceptual challenges that should be addressed first.

Is there a sufficient consensus on the content of "individual sovereignty"? What is, what should be, the relation between civil and political individual sovereign rights and social and economic individual sovereign rights? Can individuals suffer desperate material deprivation and still be fully sovereign? Do states across various regions and in different stages

1

of development – east and west, north and south – share enough of a consensus on the content of those rights to call them legitimate and universal? And if states do share a consensus, is it strong enough to incorporate duties of international distribution to the materially desperate or global obligations to assist in the enforcement of those duties against claims of national sovereignty? These are the questions this volume addresses. But before we do so, we would like to introduce the debate on human rights and address how a concern with international human rights, viewed practically in world politics, fares against the criticisms typically made by the influential, sceptical tradition of realist thought on international relations. Are human rights and international relations compatible?

The evolution of global human rights

The 1948 Universal Declaration of Human Rights (UDHR), which outlined a "common standard of achievement" for the future of human rights, has become the cornerstone of a burgeoning international human rights regime. The number, scope, and implementation strategies of international human rights treaties and conventions has increased over the past half-century, creating a vast body of human rights law at the heart of a robust regime. Three trends highlight the increased prominence of human rights in international relations and the difficult questions the regime faces for the dawn of the new millennium. First is the proliferation in the number and scope of human rights instruments, expanding across three "generations" of rights. A second trend traces the regime's increased attention to implementation – evidenced both by mechanisms included within instruments as well as by activities of new actors in the regime. Finally, most scholars agree that the concept of human rights places limits on state sovereignty, but the exact relationship between state sovereignty and human rights, or individual sovereignty, remains a matter of intense debate and continued evolution.

The UDHR was not a binding treaty, but rather a declaration of principles and aspirations. The most visible trend in the development of human rights over the past decades has been in the increased number and range of treaties which elucidate or add to the principles of the UDHR. Most notable are the two international covenants – the International Covenant on Civil and Political Rights and the International Covenant on Economic, Social and Cultural Rights – which transformed many of the principles of the UDHR into binding treaties when the covenants came into force in 1976. These are supplemented by a vast number of more specific instruments (e.g. the Convention against Torture and

Other Cruel, Inhuman or Degrading Treatment or Punishment; the Convention on the Elimination of all Forms of Discrimination against Women; the Convention on the Rights of the Child) and regional conventions (the European Convention on Human Rights in 1953, the American Convention on Human Rights in 1978, and the African Charter on Human and Peoples' Rights in 1983). Scholars often describe three "generations" of rights according to the order in which types of rights gained prominence in the regime: civil and political rights (e.g. right to free speech); economic, social, and cultural rights (e.g. right to education); and group rights (e.g. from minority protection within states to rights to national development within a global order). These generations of rights are illustrated by their inclusion in the three regional conventions – the European Convention includes only civil and political rights, the later American Convention covers first and second generation rights, and the most recent African Charter contains all three.[3]

Another important evolution in the international human rights regime has been its change of emphasis from promotion of rights (articulation in declarations and conventions) to active protection of rights (mechanisms for monitoring and enforcement).[4] Many of the conventions specified above establish a special commission or committee designated to monitoring the treaty's provisions (e.g. the Committee on Torture). New actors – in addition to the regional intergovernmental organizations which drafted the regional conventions – have also joined the regime. National governments like the Carter administration in the United States have made human rights an element of foreign policy. A host of new non-governmental organizations such as Amnesty International or Human Rights Watch provide information and lobby governments, highlighting violations and contributing to global protection efforts.

But the most transformative aspect of the human rights regime for the international system is found not in its growth in scope, instruments, implementation, and players but in its impact on a fundamental principle of international relations: state sovereignty. The foundation of the current state system – and a key feature of international relations since the seventeenth century Treaty of Westphalia – is the notion that states enjoy sovereign equality: no state has the right to interfere in the domestic affairs of another state; this is preserved as Article 2(7) of the UN Charter. However, many scholars agree that by granting rights to individuals, the conception of human rights limits state sovereignty – human rights abuses within state borders, even perpetrated by a government against its own people, are no longer matters solely within the purview of domestic affairs. Many noted experts agree with Secretary-General Annan that a state's legitimacy is tied to proper treatment of its citizens and an offending state can no longer hide behind a mantle of sovereignty alone.

This issue – the nature of the relationship between human rights and state sovereignty – lies at the core of many contemporary debates in the field: the cultural relativity of rights, international humanitarian intervention, human rights abuses as underlying causes of conflict, and how to address past abuses in post-conflict peacebuilding.

International scepticism and human rights

Despite the growth of human rights over the past 50 years, much of the discourse on international relations theory is deeply sceptical of the normative weight and practical force of not merely global human rights, but all claims to rights and duties across borders. Some even dispute the role of ethics in politics in general. Statements such as Vaclav Havel's that the war in Kosovo was a (perhaps, he says, *the* first) humanitarian war, a war motivated by ethical concern, strike many scholars and realist practitioners of international politics as strange and mistaken.[5] Many are much more likely to endorse the words of William Wordsworth, that great earlier poet of democratic revolution, with his ever-so-devastating comment on his times: "Earth is sick; And Heaven is weary, with the hollow words; Which states and kingdoms utter when they talk; Of truth and justice."[6] Even though Arnold Wolfers, Michael Walzer, Stanley Hoffmann, Hedley Bull, Richard Ullman, and a new generation of international relations scholars have identified important markers for the role of ethical judgment in international relations, the default scepticism must still be addressed.[7] We need to explore the sceptics' view and explain why international ethics should not and need not be evaded through three classic but dangerous simplifications, each of which serves as an excuse for dismissing ethical judgment.[8]

- Ethics should be limited to private life; supposedly because public political life is necessarily a separate world of dirty hands. This is the Machiavellian problem.
- Ethics should be domesticated, seen as fit only for domestic politics and judged to be inherently absent from, and irrelevant to, international politics, which is the Hobbesian problem.
- Ethics can be dismissed as being inherently a set of hypocritical or merely self-serving political slogans. We could call this Wordsworth's problem.

The first and most prevalent reason why we are told that ethical judgment can be ignored is that it is inapplicable to political decisions. As Dean Acheson, former US Secretary of State, once said, "Moral Talk was fine preaching for the Final Day of Judgment, but it was not a view I would entertain as a public servant."[9] This is often called the ethics of public responsibilities. Engaging in politics means, and requires, "learning to be cruel to be kind" (as Shakespeare's Hamlet intoned).[10] In political theory, this is the Machiavellian problem. "A wise prince," Machiavelli said, "knows how to do wrong when it is necessary." And it is often, very often, necessary to act, he adds: "... contrary to truth, contrary to charity, contrary to humanity, contrary to religion – if the Prince wishes to sustain his government."[11]

Ethics, it is said, is for stay-at-homes, those happy men and women who till their own gardens, secure in the knowledge that they are able to do so safely. But princes, it is added, have no choice but to be like the "ferocious beasts," for the moral life available to private men and women is neither safe nor sufficient for them. "Princes must be like a very savage lion and a very tricky fox." But why "must"? First, for themselves: for without beast-like force and fraud, they will be overthrown. And, second and more tragically, for us: for without the political order of government we would all have to be beasts, too, or perish under the attacks of thieves and murderers. Our making ethical judgments of specific political acts is therefore inappropriate and an act of bad faith, so many realists have said.

But this is too simple. Machiavelli knew it was, and so should we. Princes can and should be making moral choices. Not every prince is the leader of a threatened coup, everywhere and with everyone at war. Old, traditional princes would do themselves harm if they acted like new princes, the successful coup masters. Rules and traditions are the bulwarks of traditional princes.

As importantly, we private men and women in our gardens can hardly claim the virtue the political amoralists grant us. Are we, in fact, free from moral conflict? Are we free from contrariness with respect to truth, charity, humanity, and religion? Machiavelli, author of the *Mandragola*, knew we were not. In that racy, sexual comedy, the wily Callimaco, deeply in love, tricks old Nicia into allowing him to sleep with his beautiful young wife Lucrezia. With Lucrezia's connivance, Callimaco invents a curse that the first man to sleep with her will suffer a painful death. Gullible Nicia allows Callimaco to "suffer" for him. Private men and women – Callimacos and Lucrezias – are as crafty and ruthless as any fox-like public prince.

Machiavelli thus says private life, too, is not without moral corruption and authentic moral conflict. So should we. Moreover, we do. We do not grant our politicians a moral hunting licence. Indeed, we may hypocritically hold them to standards we rarely meet. In short, we share a moral universe with politicians. If we endorse their ability to punish or even kill in the name of the state, it is because we allow ourselves to use force in self-defence. They can be said to do it for us, because we are prepared to do it for ourselves. We hope they will do it more impartially – for public ends – and are often disappointed. But both public and private individuals can make moral choices and often face dreadful trade-offs. The world often requires some very hard trade-offs where rules of moral conduct confront the moral value of public survival and these are choices both we and our leaders understand.

If all politicians are not inherently different, inherently absent from moral judgment, maybe, say the second set of critics, it is the *international* politicians who fall outside the ethical standard. The minister of health and the town mayor are in the ethical world; Bismarck, Kissinger, the foreign minister, and the secretary of defence are out. This is the Hobbesian problem.

Hobbesians argue that nation states exist in a condition of international anarchy with no superior world state to provide law and order. There follows a general struggle for power – all against all – fuelled by competing desires for scarce goods, by fear of what others might do, by hunger for glory. Internationally, nations have no choice but to compete, because the competition is for survival. Domestically, ethics can be established once a state establishes law and order. Then promises will be enforced, social norms will be decreed, and those norms will be taught to the young. Lacking an international government of law and order, all is uncertain. Anything goes in the struggle for survival. This is the condition of complete struggle that Sherman had in mind when he told the citizens of Atlanta, after he burned their city, "War is cruelty and you cannot refine it."[12]

But again moral life is not so simple. International politics is not an absolute struggle of all against all. Contemporary relations between the UK and France, Germany and Belgium, and the United States and Canada bear no similarity to that Hobbesian model. Relations are safe from war and shaped by international law.[13] Even the genuine representation of citizens becomes mixed. Both the US Midwest and Canada cause acid rain, but Ottawa's greater concern for the consequences may better represent a downwind New Englander than does Washington. Even in war, most states have come to accept the principle that the struggle is not "against all." Rules of war forbid struggle against non-combatants, against children, against the ill in hospitals. And some modern Hobbesians fail to ask what is the meaning of survival – national or state survival. States are artificial beings, not natural ones. They exist, as Wolfers has noted, for the purposes of their inhabitants, not their inhabitants for states.[14] Some citizens shuck off their sovereign Leviathans as the British did in 1688, the American colonists did in 1776, and the former Soviets did in 1991. Moreover, the moral meaning of survival is frequently contested – up for domestic political competition – as it was in France in the 1940s. Was France to survive physically and conservatively as it did under Marshall Pétain's Vichy regime or be risked, grandly, as it would be under General de Gaulle's Free French Resistance?[15]

States represent, or can represent, not merely our fears (as Hobbes argues) but also our hopes and our ethical commitments. Goals and values therefore define what normal survival means, what is worth protecting in both domestic and international politics. US civilian and military officials, for example, swear to preserve the constitution, a set of principles. Our ends define what is worth sacrificing for and shape even the international behaviour of states.

The third objection to international ethics accepts the view that politicians can be as ethical as we are (or no worse) whether they are engaging in foreign or domestic affairs. But, as the sceptics like Wordsworth have said, politicians regularly – just about always – choose not to be. Their international ethics is all ordinary cynical hype and nothing more. They can be ethical. They choose to be hypocritical, paying the small tribute vice pays to virtue. Preaching ethics to them is thus like preaching chastity in a bordello. In 1949, the Navy decried the A-bomb, then the sole property of the Air Force, as immoral. By 1951, two years later, as the Navy started to assemble its own atomic arsenal and plans for a nuclear submarine force, atomic bombs suddenly became necessary to the survival of the free world. Of course, neither their criticism nor defence was thought convincing.

Again we should hesitate to generalize the hypocrisy. Ethical arguments need not be altruistic to be convincing and some seem even to masquerade as self-serving advantage. At the Teheran Conference in 1943, Stalin suggested to Churchill that after the defeat of Hitler, all 50,000 of the German Officer Corps should be summarily shot by the Allies. Churchill replied, "The British Parliament and public will never tolerate mass executions. They would turn violently against those responsible after the first butchery had taken place."[16] Churchill's fear of reprisals from the British public does not wash. Indeed, shouldn't we suspect hypocrisy in reverse? Appalled by the indiscriminate slaughter Stalin proposed, Churchill invents the self-serving logic of electoral advantage and political survival to appeal to the ruthless Stalin and, perhaps, soothe his own discomfort with "moral talk."

A grammar of international ethics and rights

International ethics are therefore not impossible because politicians – unlike us – must be beasts, nor because international politics is a universal jungle, nor because nothing but hypocrisy and partisan advantage can influence a politician. What then is international ethics? How do human rights incorporate those ethical principles?

Human rights, like all ethical claims, are part of the inescapable judgment that precedes action. Not all judgment, however, is or need be ethical. Prudential judgment prescribes productive strategies in the pursuit of given ends for a given person. Aesthetic judgment asks what is best, good, or beautiful. Ethical judgment combines prescription (like prudence); over-ridingness (what is best like aesthetics), and impartiality – what should be done not just by or for me, but by or for anyone in the same position. You should, as I should, fulfil an ethical duty because it is designed to apply to us all, like the "golden rule" of doing unto others as you would have them do to you.

Three concerns shape ethical judgment. In a fine book on *Nuclear Ethics*,[17] Joseph Nye calls them motives, means, and consequences. Let us call them ends, means, consequences.[18]

An ethical end is necessary. Only ends justify, if anything can, the means we employ. In simple terms, it is ends that make some wars just: for example, defensive wars when they seek to protect the borders, the territorial integrity and political independence that allow people to determine their own lives freely. Related ethical arguments can justify some humanitarian interventions across borders to rescue peoples from genocide and other grievous and systematic violations of their basic rights. People can not shape their lives collectively if they are being repressed and slaughtered.

Good ends, however, are not sufficient to justify our acts. The theologian Paul Ramsey has shown why not in a striking parable. If we really, truly, sincerely, deeply wanted to end, once and for all, the deaths and injury to tens of thousands each year in auto accidents – a worthy end surely – there is a simple and sure-fire means. All we have to do is tie, in as comfortable way as possible, babies to the front and rear of our automobiles. Can anyone doubt that, slowed to a fully moral crawl, our cars would successfully avoid thousands of traffic accidents?[19]

The problem here is in the means: the anguish to innocent infants, and perhaps even more the anguish to parents, none of whom is individually responsible for the collective tragedy of auto fatalities. Some ethicists have condemned nuclear deterrence for just these reasons: deterrence terrorizes innocent civilians.

Third, even with good ends and acceptable means, we need to consider and anticipate consequences. Our sense of ethical ends (e.g. national self-defence, national self-determination) and ethical means (e.g. in war, respecting non-combatant immunity because non-combatants pose no direct threat) are powerful and inherited and learned intuitions. They are taught by parents, learned at our mother's knee (or, as Acheson once said, some other low joint). They are part of now-traditional, evolved social conventions.

We need to govern these intuitions or rules by a consideration of consequences. It is wrong to lie in ordinary morality, but only a fool would tell a known murderer the location of his prospective victim. Similarly, even if Kissinger is correct that the United States fought in Vietnam in order to prevent South Vietnam from falling prey to a totalitarian communism from the North[20] and if the United States had fought the war justly, minimizing where possible civilian non-combatant casualties; the war could and would have been morally flawed if the United States had failed to consider the suffering that would result from trying to win against a guerrilla movement supported by a large fraction of the population in a culture that the United States did not understand for a local government that had little support from too few of its own people.[21] A similar moral wasteland was emerging in Serbia in the spring of 1999 when NATO looked at the prospect of destroying, by October or November of that year, tens of thousands of non-combatant Serbs through the disease and medical deprivation that in a modern society accompanies the destruction of electricity, transportation, and trade – all traditionally legitimate targets for bombing. The ends and means were justifiable: rescuing and returning thousands and thousands of non-combatant Albanian Kosovars "ethnically cleansed" from their homes and avoiding in the process as much as was feasible the bombing of non-combatant Serbs. It was the indirect consequences on the ability of the Serb population to provide essential services needed for health that were becoming morally unacceptable. Goals and means become disproportionate when warriors find themselves destroying villages in order to save them or killing more non-combatants in order to save fewer non-combatants. Unavoidably violent means need to be proportionate to legitimate ends. And to do this, we need to consider all the available alternatives and weigh the consequences of each.

How are these ethical principles related to human rights concerns? In order to understand the role of human rights in the international system and the importance of the trends outlined earlier, it is not enough to defuse sceptical arguments and to conceptualize the nature of ethical judgment more generally. One must also delve into the notion of rights. What makes human rights deeply similar to the broad principles of international ethics, yet "strikingly different from the rest of international law," is that individuals, rather than their states or governments, have *rights*.[22] This shifts the focus from state sovereignty to individual sovereignty. What, then, are "rights"? How are they distinguished from other moral norms? What is the nature of the relationship between rights and duties?

Three aspects distinguish rights from other moral norms: they are expressed in general terms, prescriptive, and non-contextual. First, rights can be expressed in general terms. Following in the tradition of natural rights, rights are usually articulated in a bill or declaration of rights. In the international human rights regime, the UDHR and the two international covenants are collectively referred to as the International Bill of Rights. Though the debate rages over specific hierarchies of rights (do civil-political rights have precedence over social-economic-cultural rights or vice versa), states can agree and articulate in conventions what rights exist and what the gravest breaches are (e.g. genocide, torture).

Second, rights are prescriptive. They grant the rights-holder an entitlement, an empowerment to press claims, or grounds to demand action.[23] They are not favours bestowed by others; they invoke indignation when not upheld or honoured. Human rights specifically may connect to the legitimacy of a state: traditional notions of state sovereignty alone are not enough to confer legitimacy if a state ignores the prescriptions of the human rights regime and offends the basic rights of its citizens.

Finally, rights are to some extent non-contextual. Under classic theories of natural rights, any human being, by virtue of his/her potential to exercise rational choice, has rights.[24] Rights are thus grounded in human dignity and are only limited primarily by others making similar rights claims. One scholar goes so far as to describe rights as trumps, which outrank any other interests and override utilitarian calculations of community benefit.[25] Human rights are rights of the highest order – the final resort in the realm of rights.[26]

If rights are expressed in general terms, prescriptive, and non-contextual, what can we conclude about their relationship to duties? While some early political and legal philosophers argued that every right had a correlative duty, most scholars now agree that the relationship is more complex than this simple reflexivity. Some rights do have a correlative duty; however, some rights (like the right to pick up a dollar bill off the sidewalk) have no corresponding duty and some duties (like giving to charity) are not reflected in a reciprocal right.[27] One noted scholar argues that basic human rights escape this intellectual morass because they always trigger three kinds of correlative duty: the duty to avoid depriving, the duty to protect from deprivation, and the duty to aid the deprived.[28] It is the role of ethical judgment in international relations to determine when and how to enforce universal human rights principles and to determine what duties – and to whom – are attendant with individuals possessing rights.

International human rights and international order

If the arguments above hold water, then international ethics and international human rights are not impossible intrusions in international relations. Ordinary ethical judgment, moreover, is identifiable and applicable and, following the arguments of two authors in the volume (Ruth Gavison and Claire Archbold), necessary to decide on the just content of human rights. Why then, so regularly, do we find such a gap between human rights principles and actual behaviour in foreign relations?

The simplest reason is that the behaviour may or may not in particular instances be motivated by human rights. More troubling is that even when it is (and we often have little reason to assume not) it does not have the same civilizing effects as ethical behaviour in domestic politics. It is much more constrained because international politics is conflictual, confused, and uncontrolled. There are at least four reasons for this unfortunate outcome:[29]

(a) anarchy – no enforcement
(b) moral diversity – conflicting values
(c) uncertainty – as to adversary, intentions
(d) uncertainty and lack of control over our responses.

International anarchy does not make ethical behaviour impossible. As noted, statesmen are moral and immoral beings like the rest of us, but it does make ethical behaviour difficult and the international good problematic. The lack of a world government capable of enforcement means unethical behaviour lacks adequate punishment, and evil is insufficiently deterred. Many criticized the US war in Vietnam as an unjust war, one that was either a violation of the independence of a singular Vietnamese people fighting a local civil war or a disproportionately conducted campaign in an interstate war between North and South Vietnam, or a complicated mix of both. And Idi Amin met with widespread moral condemnation in Africa in the 1970s for his human rights violations. But as long as Washington was a superpower and Amin controlled the Ugandan army, arresting war criminals or correcting wrongs meant war. Intervention against the United States was suicidal. Intervention against Uganda was unacceptable as long as invading Uganda was unacceptable to Ugandans and to Uganda's African neighbours. Until 1979, that is, when Amin finally provoked Tanzania – provoking in the process international enforcement by an African neighbour.

International enforcement is not totally absent. The tribunals for the former Yugoslavia and Rwanda are enforcing international norms on the perpetrators of gross abuses. The problem is that international enforcement is not comprehensive. It rarely impacts the powerful or their friends and therefore suffers from charges of bias even when the case in point (as with the two tribunals) is fully justified. Another effect of international anarchy is that even ethically motivated states need to take measures of self-help to defend themselves. These measures restrict the resources that might be otherwise spent in aiding the poor economically – upholding social and economic rights – or helping to enforce just behaviour among states.

Second, complicating international anarchy is moral diversity. There is not a practical international consensus on right and wrong. There are some nearly universally recognized values, including human dignity; various human rights specified in the UDHR; and, in practice, avoiding nuclear war. But they are thin. States have diverse ideologies and values and these lead to conflicts.[30] Fundamentalist Islam is said to be in a "clash of civilizations" with the Christian West.[31] Even if exaggerated in its impact, differences between Islam and the West over women's rights and freedom of the press clearly occasion strife. How extensive these differences in fact are and how consequential for international order are the subjects of the papers by Tatsue Inoue and James Mouangue Kobila in this volume.

Even with a wider consensus on principles, ethical conflicts over application of human rights can be extreme, when social and environmental circumstances differ and when power and authority become involved. Traditionally, when a group of desperately poor immigrant farmers seeks to settle in the seemingly less than fully used lands of a society of nomadic hunters, both have and, perhaps, justly can claim group social rights: the farmers to settle and hunters to resist the destruction of their hunting and way of life. As Locke once said, in these circumstances one "appeals to heaven" and thus wars ensue. In much less extreme circumstances, the differences between the two International Labor Organization (ILO) Conventions on the rights of indigenous peoples are telling. The first (No. 107 in 1957) focused on "progressive integration" of indigenous peoples into the larger state structure while the second (No. 169 in 1989) urged governments to "protect rights and guarantee respect." This marked an evolution in application from stressing assimilation and equality as the ultimate right to emphasizing the right to preserve the indigenous culture; but conflicts continue between these first and third generation rights.

And despite a broad consensus on basic human rights and the efficacy of market economies, the threat of foreign imposition – Washington dominance or neocolonialism, as many rights are argued to be of Western origin – sometimes leads to strife over national honour and independence. In the contemporary international economy, large and (some say) growing inequalities present significant moral challenges (as our authors

Pierre de Senarclens and Henry Shue argue) to the practical fulfilment of duties of just distribution.

Third, international politics, even more than domestic politics, is full of uncertainty. In one gruesome example, the casualties at Hiroshima and Nagasaki were five times more than expected partly because US planners expected that the cities would take the protective measures other Japanese cities had taken when they were first bombed. But the lone atomic bombers failed to trigger the protections.[32] Given the wartime passion, the United States probably would still have bombed, but the arguments made at the time in favour of a warning explosion were weakened by the false lower estimates of Japanese casualties. Given the actual outcome, some have clamoured for the action to be declared a war crime, as the destruction wrought disproportionately affected defenceless civilians.

Sometimes we do not know whether to support or oppose or ignore possible human rights abuses not merely because other principles may be disputed, but also because the facts are unclear. Neither states nor individuals who violate human rights readily volunteer evidence against themselves; witness the difficult task of war crimes investigators in the former Yugoslavia attempting to reconstruct events in order to identify, indict, and prosecute offenders. Non-governmental organizations (NGOs) have been particularly active in some cases trying to overcome this obstacle. The activities of Amnesty International in Argentina helped bring political disappearances and other violations of human rights to light and spurred other states to take enforcement action.[33]

Even when the facts are known, outsiders are often uncertain how to interpret them. Liberal observers can wonder whether Cuba or China or Eritrea are people's democracies (as some of their apologists claim) suffering trying times and tolerating restrictions on freedom such as those that characterized US politics between 1776–1781 and 1861–1865. Or are they dictatorships of the left consolidating autocratic rule by abusing civil and political rights? Or something else altogether? In order to address human rights issues in a particular context, policy makers must wade through sometimes scant and sometimes conflicting information regarding a state's actions and the political context in which those actions occurred.

And fourth, states do not control their internal responses or coordinate their international actions very well. When states wind up trying to punish the behaviour of other states that elements of their own bureaucracies have provoked, ethical behaviour loses its effectiveness, even its meaning. If the US Congress supported aid to the Contras in Nicaragua because and only because the Contras could help deter the Nicaraguans from external attacks on Honduras (where the Contras were based) and if it did not know that a CIA operation funded the Contras and directed the Contras in cross-border raids against Nicaragua, then the first action (supporting Honduras), justifiable as it may be on its own terms, is undermined ethically by the covert actions that accompanied and preceded it; for the Nicaraguans were engaged in just reprisals when they crossed the Honduran frontier. In addition, if one assumes that eliminating Iraq's nuclear, biological, and chemical arsenal is a legitimate response to Iraq's aggression against Kuwait, who is at fault for trampling on the social and economic rights of ordinary Iraqi citizens? Is it the United States and United Nations for instituting sanctions and tolerating covert operations against Iraq, the Iraqi government for withholding allowable aid, or Hussein himself for hiding biological and chemical weapons programmes?

Plan of the volume

As a step toward clarifying the debate over human rights and international order, we have invited the authors to address the relation between civic and political rights on the one hand and social and economic rights on the other. They will investigate whether the first set of rights entails the second and whether duties and obligations extend across borders. The project will examine these issues at three different levels: domestic, regional, and international.

We have commissioned authors for two papers to address these questions at the domestic level and both emphasize that particular human rights regimes are politically constructed. Ruth Gavison of Tel Aviv University in the first paper focuses on philosophical issues such as whether the political and civil and economic and social sets of rights are linked in theory and whether they entail each other. According to Gavison, three issues underpin the human rights debate: (1) which civil-political or socio-economic concerns rise to the level of rights, (2) which of those rights constitute the basic core of human rights, and (3) what, if any, measures ought to be taken to protect those rights. These issues should be decided on the basis of normative and political considerations, *not* analytic ones. She suggests that rights claims, and in particular human rights claims, are inherently controversial – the subject matter of rights accommodates a variety of different legitimate positions on the core issues above. She rejects several common arguments which give primacy to either civil and political or economic and social rights and argues that whether or not intervention on behalf of human rights is justified is something to be determined by the nature of particular cases, not by an a priori philosophical analysis of the concept of a human right.

In the second paper, Claire Archbold examines the current practice of incorporating various combinations of rights in domestic law. She analyses the distribution of three classes of rights (civil and political, social and economic, and group rights) in the constitutions of Canada and South Africa, and the United Kingdom and Northern Ireland. Comparison across the three examples highlights differences in the political process of constitution writing, in the generations of rights included in the final document, and in the role of the constitution in reflecting an existing or defining a new human rights consciousness. From this survey, Archbold concludes that the form and content of a Bill of Rights will reflect the political and social history of the nation for which it was written and the document will arise from a process of compromise between fundamentally opposed points of view as to the value of various rights. As a compromise it is imperfect, but she concludes that "the document's significance is that it is agreed. The nation-building power of a widely-agreed Bill of Rights was acknowledged in South Africa and in Canada, and has yet to be tested in Northern Ireland."

At the regional level of analysis, our focus is on the comparative practice of human rights. The volume makes two different cross-regional comparisons: North-South and East-West. James Mouangue Kobila addresses the first theme and Tatsuo Inoue tackles the second.

James Mouangue Kobila's paper compares the evolution and practice of human rights in the North and South, and describes obstacles to the implementation of human rights in the South as well as offering some recommendations for surmounting these obstacles. He looks specifically at various human rights commissions, human rights courts, and domestic practices and as well as responses to calls for regional arrangements. Kobila argues that both civil and political rights as well as economic, cultural, and social rights have seen greater implementation in the North than in the South. In advocating the universality of human rights, he rejects particularistic claims and argues for progressive development of universal human rights in the South, paralleling his description of how such rights developed in many Northern countries. Kobila concludes with an extensive list of obstacles to implementation of human rights in the South (including the lack of public order or weakness of the rule of law) and proposes some recommendations to overcome the obstacles – such as the development of democratic institutions, greater and more efficient development aid, greater protections for the press, ratification of human rights instruments, and more rapid development of regional human rights arrangements.

In his chapter, Tatsuo Inoue presents two main criticisms of the "Asian values" critique of civil and political rights. The first criticism is that this critique is, ironically, dominated by "West-centrism" in that it borrows the Western vocabulary of political morality, namely state sovereignty and socio-economic rights. Inoue argues that sovereignty is invoked as a trump against rights when, in fact, the two are inextricably intertwined in the history of the West. He also disagrees with the view that Asia can and/or should pursue socio-economic rights prior to personal, civil, and political ones; rather, civil-political rights should come first on practical rather than moral grounds. Backing his charge of West-centrism, Inoue also notes that the very categories of "Orient" and "Occident" are Western constructions. Inoue's second criticism of "Asian values" is his view that Asia has "endogenous" reasons to accept civil and political rights. Not only is constitutional democracy superior to any non-democratic method of managing Asia's ethnic tensions (e.g. authoritarianism), but civil-political rights are necessary for achieving communitarian as well as liberal ends. Civil rights, he concludes, are a pre-condition for civil society and for the rich communal life valued by communitarians, whether East or West.

Finally, a third section focuses on two issues at the international level: implementation and distributive justice. The first paper, by Pierre de Senarclens of the University of Lausanne, highlights the status of international human rights and their enforcement since the World Conference on Human Rights in Vienna (1993). His analysis stresses the fundamental linkage between economic, social, and political aspects of human rights, noting that they must be addressed in concert in order to achieve real progress. He also recognizes that the structure of the international system, in the form of state sovereignty and power politics, limits the effectiveness of mere paper agreements – the world is still ideologically and politically divided when it comes to the interpretation and practical implementation of human rights norms. Implementation of human rights through institutional reforms and projects, de Senarclens argues, should be grounded in a better understanding of international political economy – recent global economic trends have done very little to bring prosperity to the least developed nations while neither rich Western industries nor the autocratic governing elites of poorer nations find the protection of basic economic rights to be in their immediate interests. Thus, problems faced by the poorest nations might be best addressed by states working in regional unions and by the institution of more effective regulatory structures at the international level, of which he offers several examples. He concludes that the political sovereignty of states must be defended in order to provide opportunities for social protection, economic regulation, and distributive justice that are "the foundations of our modern conception of citizenship."

Henry Shue explores whether there is a right and duty of humanitarian economic assistance across borders. Shue begins with the assumption that there are economic rights and that someone must bear the concomitant duties to ensure that those rights are fulfilled. He argues that such duties are, or can be, transnational in nature because of the "deep indirect connections through the institutional structure of the international system in which all human individuals live." He dismisses "causal dissipation" (that one bears no responsibility toward most of humanity because one does not touch most of humanity) by noting that individuals do not exist in asocial space, but are embedded in thick transnational webs of institutions and the underlying principles that shape the institutions. We have a transnational duty to stop imposing severe economic distress caused by shared institutions that produce and maintain radical inequality. Shue concludes by challenging the idea of principled communitarianism (under which transnational duties can be rejected in favour of higher priority duties owed to fellow members of more limited communities), arguing that the inhabitants of rich states bear transnational duties because they are beneficiaries of an international system which has disabled the bearers of the "primary duties."

Together the volume's authors struggle with the most controversial questions of fundamental human rights and human dignity. In the conclusion by Jean-Marc Coicaud of the United Nations University we draw the strands of controversy together to assess where "individual sovereignty" and global differences stand today.

Notes

1. This introduction draws on material delivered as the Benjamin Meaker Professorial Lecture at the University of Bristol, UK, on 6 June 1999, by Michael Doyle. We want to thank Ruth Gavison and the anonymous reviewers of the volume for their suggestions on an earlier draft of this chapter.
2. Kofi Annan, "Two Concepts of Sovereignty," *The Economist*, 18 September 1999.
3. The African Charter is also unique in that it articulates individual duties – to the state and to family – as well as rights.
4. See David P. Forsythe, *The Internationalization of Human Rights*, Lexington Books, Lexington, MA, 1991.
5. Vaclav Havel, President of the Czech Republic, commented, "This is probably the first war that has not been waged in the name of national interests but rather in the name of principles and values. Kosovo has no oil fields to be coveted ... [NATO] is fighting out of the concern for the fate of others." *Boston Globe*, 5 July 1999, p. A14. And in a speech before the Canadian Parliament, he added, "Decent people cannot sit back and watch systematic, state-directed massacres of other people. Decent people simply cannot tolerate this, and cannot fail to come to the rescue if a rescue action is within their power." *Toronto Sun*, 2 May 1999, p. 38.
6. William Wordsworth, *Excursion*, London, Edward Moxon, 1836.
7. The group is becoming increasingly substantial. Among these contributions are Mervyn Frost, *Ethics in International Relations*, Cambridge, Cambridge University Press, 1996; Andrew Linklater, *Men and Citizens in the Theory of International Relations*, London, Macmillan, 1990; David Lumsdaine, *Moral Vision in International Politics*, Princeton

NJ, Princeton University Press, 1993; Christopher Brown, *International Relations Theory, New Normative Approaches*, Columbia, NY, Columbia University Press, 1992; Roger Spegele, *Political Realism and International Theory*, Cambridge, Cambridge University Press, 1996; Martha Finnemore, *National Interests in International Society*, Ithaca, NY, Cornell University Press, 1996.

8. For extensive discussions of scepticism in international relations see Marshall Cohen, "Moral Skepticism in International Relations," *Philosophy and Public Affairs* 13(4), Fall 1984, and Charles Beitz, *Political Theory and International Relations*, Princeton, Princeton University Press, 1979, chs. 1–2.

9. As quoted in Amy Gutmann and Dennis Thompson, *Ethics and Politics*, Chicago, Nelson Hall, 1997, p. xi.

10. This is also Max Weber's argument from "Politics as a Vocation. For this issue see Michael Walzer, "Political Action, The Problem of Dirty Hands," *P&PA* 1, Winter, 1972, pp. 160–180.

11. Machiavelli, *The Prince*, translated by Harvey Mansfield, Jr., Chicago, University of Chicago, 1985, p. 14.

12. William T. Sherman, *Memoirs*, New York, 1875, pp. 119–120 and see Michael Walzer, *Just and Unjust Wars*, New York, Basic Books, 1977, pp. 32–33 for discussion.

13. Anne-Marie Slaughter, "Law among Liberal States, Liberal Internationalism and the Act of State Doctrine," *Columbia Law Review* 92(8), December, pp. 1907–1996; and Richard Ullman, *Securing Europe*, Princeton, NJ, Princeton University Press, 1991.

14. Arnold Wolfers, "Statesmanship and Moral Choice," in *Discord and Collaboration*, Baltimore, Johns Hopkins University Press, 1962, ch. 4.

15. Marc Bloch, *Strange Defeat*, London, Oxford University Press, 1949, translated by Gerard Hopkins.

16. As quoted by Hans Morgenthau, "Human Rights and Foreign Policy," in Kenneth W. Thompson, ed., *Moral Dimensions of American Foreign Policy*, New Brunswick, Transactions Press, 1984.

17. Joseph Nye, *Nuclear Ethics*, New York, Free Press, 1986. Other valuable introductions to the topic include *Ethics and International Affairs* by J. E. Hare and Carey Joynt, New York, St. Martins, 1982.

18. Motives are crucial for assessing moral character, but they are not quite the same as ends. My dentist may be motivated only by money when he drills my teeth, but what distinguishes him from the torturer also motivated by a generous salary is the end of the act he is performing – fixing cavities rather than coercing confessions.

19. The example is Paul Ramsey's from *The Just War*, New York, Scribner's, 1968.

20. Henry Kissinger, *The White House Years*, Boston, Little, Brown, 1979, p. 228; and see William Shawcross, *Sideshow*, New York, Simon and Schuster, 1979, for an extensive moral criticism of US policy in Southeast Asia.

21. This is part of Michael Walzer's criticism of US intervention in Vietnam, from *Just and Unjust Wars,* New York, Basic Books, 1977, pp. 188–196.

22. Roslyn Higgins, *Problems and Process in International Law*, Oxford, Clarendon Press, 1993, p. 95.

23. See Jack Donnelly, *Universal Human Rights in Theory and Practice*, Ithaca, NY, Cornell University Press, 1989, pp. 9–12.

24. David Sidorsky in Henry J. Steiner and Philip Alston, eds., *International Human Rights in Context*, Oxford, Oxford University Press, 2000, p. 170.

25. Ronald Dworkin, as explained in R. J. Vincent, *Human Rights and International Relations*, Cambridge, NY, Cambridge University Press, 1986, p. 17.

26. Donnelly, p. 12.

27. Vincent, p. 9.
28. Vincent, p. 11.
29. We draw these distinctions from Locke and his discussion of the troubled "state of nature"; for discussion see Doyle, *Ways of War and Peace,* New York, Norton, 1997, ch. 6. For a thoughtful analysis raising similar points see Stanley Hoffmann, "International Law and the Control of Force," in *The Relevance of International Law,* ed. Karl Deutsch and Stanley Hoffmann, New York, 1971, and his recent essay, "The Politics and Ethics of Military Intervention," in *World Disorders,* Lanham, MD, Rowman and Littlefield, 1998, pp. 152–176.
30. Michael Walzer discusses the implications of thin and thick moral conventions in *Thick and Thin, Moral Disagreements at Home and Abroad,* University of Notre Dame Press, 1996.
31. Samuel Huntington, *Clash of Civilizations and the Remaking of World Order,* New York, Touchstone, 1996.
32. Hare and Joynt, p. 90.
33. See Kathryn Sikkink, "Human Rights, Principled Issue-Networks, and Sovereignty in Latin America," *International Organization* 43(3), Summer 1993, pp. 411–441.

Part I

The construction of human rights at the domestic level

1

On the relationships between civil and political rights, and social and economic rights

Ruth Gavison[1]

In this chapter, I propose to deal, summarily, with the relationships between interests usually classified as civil and political (CP) rights, and those usually classified as social and economic (SE) rights.[2]

On the face of it, the issue of the relationships between groups of claims does not appear to be one of great importance. The need to address it comes from the fact that a bewildering variety of positions on this issue have been advanced. The controversy centres around two related, but distinct, issues: the relationships between the types of concerns involved, and whether they should be recognized as basic human rights. Some argue that both groups of interests are equally important to human welfare, so they should both be considered human rights, equal in importance and status. This is the vision that "won" in the Universal Declaration of Human Rights in 1948.[3] The vision that the groups are and should be kept separate and distinct won when the Declaration was translated into the two 1966 covenants,[4] and is a vision argued for within many theories of political philosophy. The question of which cluster of rights deserves primacy has been answered in a variety of ways: Some seek to give priority – logical, normative, and political, to CP rights. They are either indifferent or hostile to SE rights, while voicing different attitudes towards SE concerns. The legal system of the United States is an example of this attitude. Most importantly, many Western theories of political justice and liberalism make CP rights a necessary component of the liberal, democratic state, but do not include SE benefits in the order of rights. Moreover, some such theories present the taxation required for efforts of redistribution seeking to address SE concerns as a violation of CP rights, specifically the rights to liberty and property. Others claim that without satisfaction of SE needs, CP concerns are secondary and meaningless and therefore the former have priority over the latter and at times justify non-protection of CP claims by the need to guarantee SE ones. These are the facts that make the discussion of the relationships between these concerns one of both theoretical and practical importance, and they will dictate the structure of this chapter.

The twentieth century is often described as "the age of rights." Against this background, I do not need to go into the debate whether rights talk is desirable. This decision has been made.[5] In fact, the great success of rights talk explains current tendencies such as the attempt to identify everything one sees as desirable as a "right," to warn that policies deemed very undesirable are not only bad but also inconsistent with rights, and to deny the status of rights to concerns which one thinks are not legitimate. My main argument in this chapter will be that these tendencies are often misleading and even dangerous. Rights are very important, but they should not be allowed to pre-empt, confuse, or impoverish practical discourse. On the other hand, the practical difficulties should not impede the recognition as rights of the appropriate concerns.

In a nutshell, my argument will be this: rights are special normative entities. Human rights are a sub-class of rights. Rights have moral, political, and legal functions. Basic interests required for human dignity and flourishing should be the subject of rights, and these interests include both CP and SE concerns. In this sense, CP and SE concerns reinforce each other as ingredients for basic human dignity. The satisfaction of both is required by the unifying concept of human dignity. There is no historical, logical, political, or moral reason for thinking that only CP concerns can and should be the subject of rights.

However, this is just the beginning, not the end, of the road. The mere recognition of a right does not say much about the scope and the nature of the duties that may legitimately and wisely be imposed in order to protect it. Since rights conflict among themselves, and since rights do not necessarily defeat all other interests, the specific scope of rights is often a matter that should be decided by the political processes of each society. There is a wide range of such arrangements, which may be compatible with a general commitment to human rights. The choice between these arrangements should be based on moral, political, and empirical considerations, and is not a matter of conceptual or analytical moves. More specifically, recognition of a right to liberty or to property does not inherently support a sweeping rejection of taxation and redistribution for the purpose of guaranteeing some level of SE welfare to all. Similarly, a right to equality cannot, by itself, require major redistribution. We need first to clarify what we mean by a "right to equality," and discuss the way such a right may compete with other rights and interests.

Finally, the relationship between the types of rights is complex. CP rights and SE rights can both derive from the unifying notion of human dignity. They complement each other. CP rights may also promote the ability to fight effectively for SE rights, and to minimize SE catastrophes. On the other hand, there may be tensions between rights, both within each of the clusters (e.g. the tension between the right to free speech and the rights to reputation and privacy) and between them.

Before elaborating on some of these themes, two preliminary comments are called for. First, the scope of this chapter is huge, and the literature written on each of the theses mentioned here is immense and constantly growing. My discussion will often have to be extremely skeletal, with major points presented as assertions rather than as conclusions of arguments. All I can say for this choice is that it is inevitable to keep the chapter within reasonable limits, and that I believe all the assertions can indeed be supported more fully, and often have been supported extensively in the relevant literature.

Second, if we accept the claim that human rights are universal, then they are especially befitting to international regimes. Constitutional and legal rights may well be more particularistic, and limited to particular societies.[6] Moreover, they all have strong institutional support, which is related to institutions of the states and the societies within which they operate. I was asked to cover the functioning of rights within municipal systems. Naturally, I concentrate on internal mechanisms of enforcement and elaboration of rights. I will therefore move back and forth between analytical and international discussion of human rights, and their recognition within municipal systems.

The nature of human rights

Human rights are a sub-class of rights. The debate about the nature of rights is complex and persistent. We will limit ourselves to questions related to rights functioning as human rights.[7] Human rights are rights that "belong" to every person, and do not depend on the specifics of the individual or the relationship between the right-holder and the right-grantor. Moreover, human rights exist irrespective of the question whether they are granted or recognized by the legal and social system within which we live. They are devices to evaluate these existing arrangements: ideally, these arrangements should not violate human rights. In other words, human rights are moral, pre-legal rights. They are not granted by people nor can they be taken away by them. They can only be respected or violated by them.

Human rights are often complexes of the types of benefits listed by Hohfeld (claim rights, liberties, immunities, and powers). Whatever their type, their special function is to justify the imposition of duties on others.[8] These duties, in turn, make meaningful the sense in which the right-holder has entitlement. Demanding that a right be protected, or that a duty corresponding to it be performed, is thus not a matter of charity or even of justice. The right-holder is entitled to the performance of the corresponding duty.[9]

Furthermore, rights are strong entitlements. This is an additional, and a distinct, feature of rights. Even if one does not accept Dworkin's position that rights act as trumps,[10] precluding their violation for reasons of prudence or utility, or Nozick's conception of rights as side-constraints, rights do provide more than regular reasons for action. For instance, they confer the right to do wrong, i.e. they protect the right-holder against interference, even if the particular instance of exercising of the right cannot be justified by an all-things-considered judgment.[11]

All rights – natural, moral, constitutional, and legal – enjoy this peremptory nature.[12] Only human or natural rights have the additional feature that they exist irrespective of any social or institutional endorsement, based only on moral justification and the humanity of the right-holder. This distinct combination is the source of both the great appeal of the notion and of its weakness. It also explains the unease often felt when courts play out the institutional implications of this combination, giving priority to claims of human rights, as such, over practical judgments made by legislatures or communities.

Human rights, in themselves, do not come with either an authoritative tribunal for deciding their scope, or with the mechanism to make sure that they are in fact protected. The de facto success of claims of human rights depends on enforcement, and when the decision-making mechanism is not accepted, there may well be a debate about the legitimacy of this invocation of rights. This debate signifies the tension between the pure justificatory element of human rights, and the ingredient seeking to stress its special strength and its effectiveness, the special claim to be respected.[13] The pre-political, pre-legal nature of human rights is what permitted the allies to put Nazi leaders on trial, disregarding their claim that the German law under which they acted either permitted or demanded what they did. NATO invoked the same notion to justify its intervention in Kosovo. In both cases, however, military and political might was needed. In both cases, those who opposed the intervention claimed that it was an unjustified use of force, violating their rights rather than protecting the rights of those under their jurisdiction.[14]

The picture becomes clearer when we move into municipal legal systems. The pre-political nature of human rights suggests that they do not require social endorsement for their recognition. Ideally, all societies should voluntarily abide by these constraints. However, wise societies know that there are forces which systemically seek to undermine the rights of others. They therefore construct institutional mechanisms to protect the rights of inhabitants even against legislatures and executives. These mechanisms often include granting constitutional status to some rights, enforceable by independent (constitutional) courts. Presumably, their nature as pre-legal rights influenced the decision to accord them constitutional status, but in turn their effectiveness within the system depends on that status.[15]

We see here an important implication of the institutional nature of law, and the way it affects "pure" practical reasoning. Human rights justify the imposition of duties, and thus have moral import. Legal rights benefit from the general legitimacy enjoyed (in stable societies) by the state and its decision-making processes. But within the state and the legal structure, different branches derive their legitimacy from different sources. These different sources of legitimacy (in the Weberian sense) affect the primary role of the different branches. The "political" branches owe at least some of their legitimacy to their periodic accountability to the public. Legislatures and executives are allowed to pursue policies that do not enjoy universal acceptance, because they have a political mandate to make decisions about policies for their constituencies. Courts usually derive their legitimacy from their independence within the state structure, which is in turn based on their primary role as expounders of the law, and as those who ensure that in its application to individual cases the rule of law will be maintained. They are primarily appliers of pre-existing laws (including laws conferring rights) to individual situations. The elaboration of the duties derivable from rights is a part of the judicial function, so judicial creativity in these matters is legitimate and even desirable and indispensable. Nonetheless, courts must be no less responsive to social mores than legislatures.

When all the courts do is indeed enforce rights accepted by all – the structure does not raise a problem, and the rights protected are both human and legal. However, when courts defeat the preferences of majorities in the name of human rights, the legitimacy of their action is often contested. The threat to judicial legitimacy does not stem from the mere fact that courts "create" laws as they adjudicate. It stems from the fact that some such decisions are deeply controversial. The groups offended by the decision then claim that the courts transcended their role, which requires – according to the challengers – that they should have deferred to the judgment of the political branches. Courts may then be accused of acting as philosopher kings, impoverishing political discourse and destabilizing the political order, which, we are then reminded, is ultimately required for the protection of all human rights themselves.[16] In other words, courts are seen as institutions designed to protect those rights that have acquired social and political endorsement. However, they are challenged when they seek to impose duties that they considered mandated by the unmediated recognition of pre-political human rights.[17]

Tensions between the political process (and democracy) and the judicial protection of human rights are thus relevant to all human rights. They owe as much to the nature of the judicial process as to the pre-legal feature of human rights. This can be seen clearly when we remember that debates about the judicial interpretation of rights exist even when there is no serious debate about the legal or constitutional origin of the rights involved. Nonetheless, the vaguer and more abstract the formulation of the right, the more vulnerable any attempt to derive or to invalidate specific arrangements by invoking it becomes.

So here is the dilemma: the appeal of the notion of human rights is precisely its ability to defeat specific arrangements by particular legal systems, and to provide an external criterion of evaluating them.[18] However, the enforcement of human rights requires political force. When the implications of human rights are controversial, the legitimacy of using such force is reduced. And in fact, social institutions may well only enforce those rights that they deem acceptable to their societies. They may invoke the rights, with their evaluative power, only to serve their own conventional morality. If it follows that human rights can be effective only when they are not controversial, their original appeal almost disappears. Human rights are then seen to depend on their enforceability, which seems to contradict the idea that their force is moral and pre-legal. So we want to reject this interpretation and this description of social and practical reality. On the other hand, the effective strength of rights in actual political discourse does depend also on their enforceability. It sounds empty to say that I have a right if there is no effective way in which I can enforce the obligations of others either not to interfere in my exercise of it or to actively assist me to do so.

I cannot treat this issue directly and systematically in this essay. I will simply assert that the tension is real, and that human rights scholars (and activists) should attend to it. The appeal of the ideal of human rights within a generally just society, governed by the rule of law, is important. It can be maintained only if a serious effort is made to minimize the extent to which the protection of rights repeatedly leads to the defeat of the products of its regular political deliberations. This notion has become quite central in discussions of rights and of judicial activism.

One way of going about it is to distinguish between "thin" and "thick" readings (or conceptions) of rights.[19] "Thin" readings are the ones truly shared by all, or at least rights that can seriously claim universality. Basic rights to human dignity and freedom are obvious candidates. Torturing, killing, or persecution of political dissidents, or of members of a certain race or religion, are unjustified violations of human rights. The courts of a political system should declare such activities illegal, and make the perpetrators accountable. But care should be taken when we move into arrangements, which may be presented as unjustified violations of human rights only under "thicker" readings of such rights. An example is the refusal to adopt a generous welfare policy. The decision may be presented as a violation of rights to life and dignity. But it may also be presented as required by the ethos of liberty and personal responsibility. These issues should be discussed on their merits and decided by the political process, and not given the protection and the institutional implications of "human rights." The details of these arrangements are a matter to be elaborated by that society, and should not be seen as being determined only by an analysis of the rights concerned. Arrangements within particular societies may become "thicker" in different ways. Once an arrangement gets the required support, it may well become a right within that system. Nonetheless, this is a right within the system, but it is not a human right. Another system may decide not to adopt it, and still not be violating the rights of those subject to it.

Accepting a "thin" reading of human rights suggests that, within particular societies, human rights discourse should focus on persuading the political branches of the need to promote the relevant concerns by defining them as rights within the system. This approach is superior, for both moral and institutional reasons, to trying to "force" them to legislate and implement these policies through international and external pressures, invoking the duty of these countries to protect and promote human rights.[20]

Lest I be misunderstood, I do not claim that all human rights should be reduced to claims which in fact enjoy the support of social forces within one's society. This position would indeed negate the pre-legal moral force of human rights. Human rights are unique in that they justify the imposition of duties, even if social and political powers reject such duties. However, the protection of rights will be effective only if this moral force is backed by actual acceptance. Since all political authority is based on a claim to legitimate authority, moral arguments inevitably feature in the deliberations of all power holders. A system of checks and balances is designed to make sure that the perception of moral justification of more than one agency will be taken into account in political decisions.

Nor do I argue that courts (or other branches of government) should never make controversial decisions. There are cases in which a basic

human right, under its "thinnest" reading, is blatantly violated. And there
are situations in which declaring such action illegal may be extremely
controversial. In such cases, we hope the courts will have the courage
and the integrity to save society from itself. Clear cases of this sort are
when the court is asked to stop a serious violation of rights in a semi-
lynching situation.[21] Many feel that the case of the massive detention of
Japanese-Americans during World War II is a case in point. Administrative detention is clearly a violation of people's rights to freedom, due
process, and freedom of movement. The reasons advanced to justify the
detention were not persuasive. This is precisely the type of case in which
we hope the court will protect rights and give them their moral force.[22]

A case exemplifying an invocation of rights to invalidate legislation
that does raise an issue of legitimacy is that of the alleged "right to
abortion." We all agree that freedom of movement should not be systematically denied without due process of law. The controversy about
the legitimacy of the restrictions imposed on Japanese-Americans during
World War II is thus not about the principle, but about its application
in that particular case. Abortion, on the other hand, raises very different
issues. We all agree that murder is a serious crime, and that it violates
the right to life. Some people think abortion is murder. For them, laws
permitting it are laws legitimating murder, and consequently patently
immoral. Others, myself included, disagree with their classification of
abortion as murder. We believe that women should have the liberty to
decide whether or not to bear a child even after they got pregnant. I
want the laws of my country to give them this liberty. I do not think,
however, that such liberty is required by women's human rights. I would,
therefore, hesitate to give unelected judges the power to invalidate the
considered preferences of their communities on this issue by invoking
human rights.[23]

I hope these two examples may illustrate what I have in mind when I
talk about the distinction. Needless to say, the question may arise as to
whether a specific alleged implication of a right falls within a "thin"
reading, and should thus be considered a human right, or whether it be-
longs to the "thick" reading, so that the political system has more liberty
in regulating it. The mere fact that someone opposes the right does not in
fact render it controversial in the sense I refer to. By "controversy" I
mean the existence of a serious public debate within society about the
principles governing the way the question should be decided. The fact
that there would always be borderline cases does not undermine the
usefulness of the distinction.

Institutionally, when there is no real controversy about rights, it is not
very important who should make the decisions. Presumably, all decision
makers will tend to make similar decisions. When a controversy exists,

the identity of the decision maker empowered to make the decision may determine the outcome. In some cases of controversy we want the court to hand down the decision. These are mainly the cases in which interested parties or powerful organs violate norms accepted by society. The independence of the courts is then an essential part of their ability to decide well and correctly. However, when the controversy is about the general conception of the good, about what is required by public interest, about what the norm should be, judges seem less attractive candidates. It seems better for these decisions to be made through the political processes. In our discussion we saw a connection between human rights talk and the identification of the optimal decision maker. Human rights talk suggests the suitability of courts. Therefore, expansive human rights talk tends to enlarge the jurisdiction of courts, and legitimate judicial activism. Insistence on "thin" readings of human rights relegates more of the responsibility for articulating the implications of rights and the duties they generate to the political organs.

I can now reformulate the purposes of this chapter. In all societies, debates about the desirable scope of protection of human rights and the interests protected by them will be central features of political deliberation. These will obviously include debates about both CP and SE concerns. My focus is on the suitability of rights talk to the protection of CP and SE concerns respectively. For each of the groups, I will examine claims that issues relating to them should be fully resolved by analysis of human rights and not through regular political deliberations. I will argue that most of these claims, for both types of concerns, are deeply flawed. The two clusters share the fact that some concerns within them can and should be seen as human rights. Neither of these clusters of rights is logically or normatively prior to the other. Recognition of some concerns in each cluster as rights does not require that the other concerns cannot be seen as rights. The recognition of interests belonging to both concerns as rights does not generally dictate any specific arrangement, or permit the invalidation of such arrangements. The questions are normative and political, and should be decided and challenged as such. Answers do not automatically derive from the nature of rights or even from recognizing them as rights, so the responsibility for their decision does not lie exclusively with a "forum of principle."

In the second section I examine, and reject, some standard arguments against seeing SE concerns as rights. Here I want to emphasize that seeing CP and SE concerns as equal candidates for the status of rights can be derived directly from my analysis of the nature of human rights and the reasons for recognizing certain claims as human rights. The exposition above about the nature of human rights, the tension between their pre-legal nature and the need to enforce them, and the role of the judiciary and the political branches, applies to all human rights, whether they seek to protect CP concerns or SE ones. A closer look reveals that this unity is not accidental. None of the reasons for recognizing human rights leads to a distinction between these concerns which would justify giving one cluster of rights primacy over the other. We "recognize" rights following from one's humanity precisely in order to indicate the moral urgency of not letting political powers exhaust the realm of moral claims. The universality of these concerns seeks to highlight the fact that freedom and dignity are basic human needs in all cultures and in all times.[24] A life of struggling to subsist offends the notion of human dignity much more than a life in which one's freedom to speak is curtailed. We usually care about speech only after our subsistence needs are met. The structural reasons which induce the political powers to ignore rights exist for both CP and SE concerns: rulers may seek to silence their critics in order to perpetuate their power, so they are likely to try and restrict CP rights. Allocation of public resources is often dictated by political powers, and the underclass often has fewer political powers than other groups, so SE rights are also at risk.[25] Some forms of adequate standards of living may be necessary background conditions for exercising civil and political rights. The conclusion is that there are situations in which legal and constitutional entrenchment of rights is needed for both CP and SE concerns.

The legitimacy of imposing particular arrangements on a society in the name of human rights, despite the fact that the society in question did not authorize, or explicitly rejected, that arrangement, is indeed problematic in many ways. But this, too, is as true for CP concerns as it is for SE ones. Suffice it to remind ourselves of the debate about abortion or about religion in the schools. In fact, in many countries, debates over alleged transgressions of the courts on controversial CP rights are more intense than the discussion of their role on SE rights. This may stem from the fact that courts are often more active in their expansive readings of CP rights than they are in their readings of SE ones.[26]

The distinction between "thin" and "thick" readings of rights is also equally applicable to all human (and constitutional) rights, and the distinction between CP rights and SE rights does not affect its applicability. A good example within CP rights is freedom of religion. A law forcing a person to convert is accepted by most to be a blatant violation of this right. A reading of the right that precludes such a law is a "thin" one. But the limits of religious teaching may be drawn in different ways in different societies, or in the same society at different times. Balancing the rights of religious freedom and freedom from religion is usually relegated to the political decision of the societies in question. An example from within SE rights is the human right to free public education. This is a right recognized by the International Covention on Economic and Social and Cultural Rights (ICESCR). Some countries grant a right to free education up to the level of college, while others grant only elementary education. All these countries meet their obligations under the convention, but the former states recognize a broader right to education than the latter ones.

The analysis of the nature of human rights does not support a principled distinction between CP and SE concerns. To the contrary, it supports their unity, as deriving both from the same ideal of human dignity. I shall return to this unity below. Let us now turn to some arguments seeking to suggest that only CP concerns can and should be seen as human rights.

SE interests can be protected as human rights

Let me start by clearing the table of a claim that was made in the 1950s, seeking to reject the possibility of recognizing SE interests as rights, on the basis of the logical features of rights.[27] This argument has run out of favour in recent decades,[28] but I want to reject it explicitly since its residues linger.

The argument is based on distinctions between positive and negative rights and duties, and between liberty rights and claim rights. The two distinctions are often treated as interchangeable, but they should not be confused. Liberty rights create areas of freedom in which individuals are under no duty to act or abstain from acting. A claim right enables the individual to demand that others act or refrain from acting with regard to a particular matter. In terms of the legal system – liberty rights are those areas in which the law does not intervene. A negative claim right is characterized by the fact that co-relative to it there are duties on others not to act in ways that infringe upon it. A positive claim right is a right characterized by the presence of duties on others to act in ways that protect or promote it.

Legal rights can be of all these sorts. The scope of my liberty of speech is determined by the details of the duties imposed on me not to defame or incite. If the constitution is interpreted as limiting the power of legislatures to impose such duties, I also have a constitutional negative claim right, and an immunity right, to speak. My right to vote is a positive personal power, which I have the positive liberty to exercise. The government is under a (negative) duty not to deny me the right, but also under a (positive) duty to allocate the money and to arrange the details required to permit me to exercise it.

It is easier to impose duties of abstention (do not kill, rape, or maim) than it is to impose positive duties of care (pay to support others, save the person drowning in the lake, donate blood to the needy). This is especially true if we speak of duties imposed on everyone, irrespective of special relationships. Some argue that even if we impose a duty to save, this would be an imperfect, unenforceable duty, and that therefore no one can have a right to be saved. The argument then continues upon the assumption that SE rights are positive claim rights that are impossible to enforce. Who has the co-relative duty? What does this duty consist of? Is it possible that these duties should apply universally, without responsiveness to the wealth and abilities of the state and individuals concerned? Children may have a right to support against their parents and guardians (although enforcement is very difficult even in these contexts). But what does it mean to have a human right to adequate conditions of living? Or to an education? They conclude that SE interests may be important ideals, but that they are incoherent as claims of rights, and therefore cannot be identified as human rights.

However, this argument is based on a misconception of the role of human rights in practical reasoning, and on a serious mistake concerning the meaning of the protection given to "classical" CP interests.

First, the logical force of the argument that SE concerns cannot be regarded as rights because of their incoherence rests on a conception of rights very different from the one we have been using. It is a much stronger conception, closer to the one used by adherents of the control theory of rights, whose attractiveness is strongest for legal contexts. Under this conception, a right is not merely the source of justifying the imposition of co-relative duties. It requires, in addition, that the claim is directed at identified individuals or organs, and that the beneficiary can control its enforcement. Clearly, this conception is not applicable to human rights or, more generally, to moral rights. No human right, as such, comes complete with extensive enforcement mechanisms. As we saw, one of its main functions is moral and evaluative. It may well be that some aspects of a human right are not likely to be effectively enforced, or even that it may not be desirable to enforce them against the preferences of other individuals lest their liberty is curtailed without justification. This does not indicate that we should refrain from endorsing and recognizing the interest as a basic human aspiration and ideal, one that in principle may justify the imposition of duties on others. The political debate will then centre on the question of which such duties should indeed be imposed. The right to freedom from hunger, recognized by most, is a good example of just one such right.

Second, the argument is based on the assumption that, by definition, the protection of CP concerns only requires the recognition of liberties or negative claim rights, whereas the protection of SE concerns requires recognition of unenforceable general positive duties, involving great public expenditure and taxation. This, however, is not the case. Not all

CP concerns involve only negative claim rights and not all SE concerns require positive duties of action and financial contribution. The right to vote, for example, is a CP concern requiring action and positive expense, while protecting the privacy of people on welfare requires "only" abstention from monitoring and dissemination of information.[29] A clear case that defeats the claim is the right to non-discrimination, seen as a basic CP right. This right is invoked to justify admitting women and minorities into schools and military units that used to be closed to them. Such integration often requires great expenditure, and clearly goes beyond negative claim rights.

In other words, the protection of CP rights may require the imposition of positive duties and public expenditure no less than that these are required for the protection of SE rights. Another typical example is that of the right to property, seen by some as the paradigmatic CP right. The right to private property is often presented as a liberty right, which requires only the costless abstention of government from acting. However, as a long line of scholars, from M. R. Cohen[30] in the 1930s to Sunstein and Holmes[31] at present show, this is a serious mistake. The protection of private property requires not only abstention but also public decision making about the scope of private property. Property is made "private" by exclusionary rules, which are made and enforced by the public. Like all public enforcement, the protection of property requires public expenditure. We may protect property by using tax money to enforce the right by detecting, indicting, and imprisoning thieves who violate it. We may also think that we can protect private property more effectively by giving youngsters an education, which may give them a way out of thieving to begin with. Private property and a decent education for all are both goods that societies may choose to protect, facilitate, and provide. The decision whether they should be seen as rights, or as interests seeking recognition in the public sphere, is a matter of practical reasoning, not of conceptual analysis. That the problem is not logical is further proven by the willingness of most Western countries to recognize a general right to free public education.[32]

The nature and the extensiveness of the duties that need to be imposed in order to support certain arrangements is an important feature of the discussion of the desirability and feasibility of an arrangement. Admittedly, many SE concerns do require major redistribution, which may be both unfeasible and unjust. This is why the enforcement mechanisms of the ICCPR and the ICESCR are different. However, recognition of this feature of rights talk is very different from the alleged preliminary conclusion that, as a matter of the nature of rights, no SE concerns can or should be recognized as human rights. I return to these differences in enforceability below.

Arguments against seeing SE concerns as rights are sometimes based on different types of claims. One such argument goes thus: CP rights are neutral rules of the game, framework rules within which we can pursue our goals. SE claims are limiting this freedom to pursue our goals through forced collectivization and redistribution. Anyway, SE concerns, like all other debates about the good life, should be discussed within "the game" constructed by CP rights. Consequently, CP rights should be accorded primacy over SE concerns. At times, this feature of the distinction is presented as one of the logical priority of the right to liberty and CP rights in general over SE.[33]

The distinction between the rules of the game and ordinary politics is indeed important. For most practical purposes, debates should be within the rules of the game, and challenges of the rules of the game themselves should be relatively rare. It is also true that drawing this distinction is one of the reasons for constitutional politics. We entrench the rules of the game in the constitution, so that we can have a robust debate within it about desirable arrangements. But basing the priority of CP rights over SE concerns on this reasoning may be circular. It is true that human rights are a strong candidate for inclusion in a constitution, to be seen as a part of the rules of the game. But why should these include just CP rights? Why should some basic SE rights not be included in our "rules of the game"?

A person struggling to subsist does not have any meaningful freedom to pursue any goals. CP rights may well perpetuate a situation in which some people are free to pursue their goals only because others live a life in which this freedom is totally absent. If this is the case, CP rights are far from being neutral. The theory of human rights talks about basic human needs. It does not privilege one social order over another in this way. Social order is indeed necessary to protect all human rights. The content of the social order and the way it defines its basic commitments, however, cannot be privileged through a definitional move under which the present order is protected by "rights," whereas all other interests are seen as mere interests. This is the basic political issue of any society, and we cannot resolve it by invoking the ideal of human rights, or by defining in a certain way what the "rules of the game" are.

An additional argument for restricting the status of human rights to CP rights comes from a certain reading of history: according to this analysis, rights talk started in Western civilization in the seventeenth century. Its main function was to limit the power of governments and kings. This limitation was achieved by classical CP concerns, and had nothing to do with the welfare of individuals under government. One does not need to go into the validity of this historical account.[34] There is no reason why we should be ruled now by the contingencies of the history of ideas. The answer to the question of which concerns should be seen as rights or as human rights should be determined by our analysis of the urgency of the needs, their relation to human dignity, and the need to give them the special protection generated by rights.

We must add that the tendency to claim that SE concerns could not be rights, and that classical CP concerns must be, is itself not neutral, but a result of a specific picture, both descriptive and normative, of the relationships between individuals and the groups to which they belong. It is connected to traditions stressing individualism and the pervasiveness of a distinction between public and private, under which markets are deemed private, and allegedly should be left outside the jurisdiction of states and the law. In that tradition, there is a tendency not to give adequate attention to the relationships between the rights and duties of individuals living in society. The Universal Declaration of Human Rights (UDHR) emphasizes the context of human rights in an attempt to prevent or minimize the threat of great atrocities. But the Declaration is based in a context of a social life in which individuals are members with both entitlements and obligations. Nonetheless, one of the main complaints of critics of rights talk is that in many cultures, especially individualistic ones, the connection between rights and responsibilities is severed. The institutional features of the protection of rights strengthen this tendency: courts typically deal with specific claims of individuals, and cannot deal effectively with the background conditions that often determine one's welfare.

Some claim that the interdependence of rights and duties is more important in the SE context than it is in the CP one. Since our institutional mechanisms are better geared to protect independent claims of rights, without the need to attend to their context, CP rights belong more easily to our known legal and constitutional structure. This is superficially true. The recognition of SE rights does presuppose links of solidarity that are stronger than those assumed by the recognition of CP rights of individuals.

This is why the institutional mechanisms required to protect CP rights are often different from those required to protect SE rights. The difference stems in part from the fact that effective protection of SE concerns requires a richer range of human and social interaction than does the protection of many CP rights. It is relatively easy to provide protection to those advocating unpopular views, or to avoid exposure to such expressions. It is very difficult to send one's child to a school where social tensions make learning difficult. Dealing with the social tensions requires a deeper and more extensive involvement than refraining from punishing a person for his expressions. A court can make it very unlikely that a person be convicted for speech. Its ability to make sure that a black child in the US South gets effective and adequate education or medical care is much more limited.

Notwithstanding the validity of this argument, it can also be applied to CP rights. The effective protection of CP rights may also require the imposition of duties on a large, indeterminate group of people. If these duties are not performed, the effectiveness of protecting CP rights may be seriously hindered. Let us take the most paradigmatic of CP rights – freedom from torture. Effective protection against torture requires a combination of circumstances. First is the duty to refrain from torture (a negative claim addressed to all). Then there is the duty of governments to protect individuals from torture, by imposing the first duty and enforcing it. But history shows only too well that freedom from torture also requires a society that is not willing to tolerate the use of torture. There are societies in which people support torturing others, when they are conceived as threats and as enemies. In such societies, effective protection from torture may also require a long-term educational and legal effort to de-legitimate it. One could also add international organizations to the list of duty-bearers, because they can exert influence on governments to refrain from torture or to protect from it.[35] Despite this variety of duties and duty-bearers that may be required for an effective protection from torture, no one would doubt that freedom from torture should be recognized as a human right.

I want to clarify that I am not suggesting that a commitment to CP concerns protects individuals, while a commitment to SE concerns is more responsive to claims of groups. The indignity of a life of struggling to subsist is an affront to the individuals whose fate it is, and freedom of speech and association are not primarily about the interests of individuals to express themselves, but to the society in which we live. Freedom of association, and even freedom of religion in its group aspects, presuppose social networks and their importance. One of the major justifications of freedom of expression and of democracy is the constraints they put on the nature of social processes, and the stability they enhance. Freedom of expression (or religion) for Jehovah Witnesses is not just an individual right. It is the right of the group to which individuals belong to gain access to the public forum of persuasion. The law against incitement is not a limitation of the right of one person to free speech in order to protect the right of another to life. It is a limitation of the right to speech intended to defend social institutions and structures, which are conditions-precedent of all human welfare and security.

For this reason, I do not need to enter another debate which may be casting doubt on the coherence or intelligibility of SE rights: the idea that the subjects of rights are only individuals, and that all "group rights" are in fact reducible to various kinds of individuals' rights.[36] Human rights are indeed universal and indivisible, and reflect a deep concern with individuals, as they live in societies. Both CP and SE concerns are central to human welfare. Our picture of human rights should not be a tool that disguises the complexity of the constituents of human welfare.

We can conclude that the answer to the question of which concerns should be seen as rights or as human rights should be determined by our analysis of the urgency of the needs, their relations to human dignity, and the need to give them the special protection generated by rights. There is no reason for concluding, at the outset, that SE concerns cannot be the subject of (human) rights.

The hierarchy between CP and SE rights

I mentioned above that most contemporary scholars have dropped the arguments seeking to show that SE concerns should not be seen as human rights. However, the same arguments are used, together with other arguments, to claim that CP rights should be seen as prior and primary. This position is reflected by the fact that liberal theories of democracy often insist on constitutional protection for CP rights only, relegating the protection of SE rights to regular laws and policies. In institutional terms, as we saw, this means that, while SE rights are protected only against arbitrariness or discrimination by the government, CP rights are protected against legislative decisions as well.

In part, this preference for CP rights may be connected to the ideal of democracy. It may be argued that CP rights are critical for the functioning of democracy, and once democracy is in place, coupled with such constitutional protection, the products of the political system are bound to be acceptable in terms of social justice as well. However, this justification is of only limited force: many affluent constitutional democracies continue to live with abject poverty and hopelessness in their midst. CP rights may be necessary, but they are not sufficient as guarantees of human dignity for all.

Against the background noted above of the priority of CP rights in many discussions, the debate about the status of SE concerns as rights, and the relationship between the two, may gain practical and political importance. It is therefore important to emphasize some of the ways in which SE concerns are at least as central to human welfare and to the structure of human societies as are CP concerns. This point is merely an elaboration of my primary thesis above: these issues are not matters of conceptual analysis or of the nature of rights. Their analysis requires a closer look at the background conditions and the presuppositions of life in democracies.

Two different routes lead to the same conclusion. One is the frequently quoted idea that all human rights derive from the concern with human dignity. Among civil rights, the ones most clearly related to dignity are the rights not to be tortured, raped, or defamed. Not allowing a person to express various ideas is a serious limitation of liberty, but its connection to dignity is more remote. Usually, dignity also requires some ability to control one's life and participate in the decisions made in one's political community. As we saw, these are positive rights against the state, which is required to confer the powers and provide the resources needed for the implementation of their exercise. But not being able to survive, or not being able to marry or to have children for lack of ability to support them, or not being able to afford a standard life-saving medicine – these are instances where the threat to human dignity is clear and obvious. In terms of relevance to human welfare and dignity, the need to avoid a life reduced to the struggle for subsistence may often be more primary and central than the need to gain political liberty.

We reach the same conclusion when we look more closely at the ideal of democracy and political participation, which all liberal theories emphasize. The justifying power of democracy stems from its being the regime where individuals are allowed an equal right of participation. However, democratic participation is more than the power and freedom to cast a vote. It is the ability to cast this vote from a position of knowledge and freedom. While no one can be forced to become knowledgeable or free and autonomous, background conditions must be such that people can have effective liberty to gain them. This effective liberty includes freedom from the struggle for subsistence.

In other words: not only can both CP and SE concerns be rights. Not only are some SE needs as central to human welfare as the most important CP interests. It is also that the exercise of CP rights cannot be rich and full without a basic freedom from hunger. The real question is, then, whether societies should use some of their resources to guarantee all their members an adequate level of welfare. Which translates into the question of how the division of resources between state, society, and individual members should be structured, and how much resources a society can and should take from its rich members to enhance public resources and resources used for redistribution.

It should be clear by now that I am not arguing that the recognition of SE rights dictates extensive programmes of redistribution. The resistance to programmes seeking to secure SE concerns is not motivated only by power and self-interest. It is also supported by important moral, social, and political arguments. These need to be seriously addressed when social policies are considered. These real differences between CP and SE rights require creative thoughts about social arrangements, some of which I discuss below. My purpose in this section is to show that these considerations justify neither the exclusion of SE concerns from the realm of rights, nor giving CP rights primacy over SE rights.

Property, liberty, and social justice

Before I move ahead, I want to complement my arguments so far by addressing the powerful and influential argument, made by Robert Nozick, against recognition of SE rights, by invoking the need to protect CP rights. In *State, Anarchy and Utopia*, Nozick cast the age-old argument on the priority of CP concerns explicitly in terms of rights. According to him, any taxation for purposes other than the night-watchman functions of the minimal state is a violation of the rights of individuals to liberty and dignity, since it is akin to slavery: it forces them to work for the welfare of others. Such policies, he claims, are not merely undesirable and should be opposed in democratic deliberations; they should be ruled out by anyone committed to taking the rights of individuals seriously.

Most scholars and politicians in the West do not accept Nozick's argument and his principled stance against taxation designed to achieve redistribution.[37] To succeed, Nozick's critics have to reject both his premise that taxation is inconsistent with respect for rights of liberty and property, and his general position against welfare arrangements that are not based on one's work. For my purposes, the distinction between the two phases of Nozick's argument is crucial. The right to liberty or to property does indeed not rule out taxation or redistribution. But this conclusion, in itself, does not justify any specific redistributive arrangement. Neither, however, does a general right to adequate living conditions. Specific schemes of taxation and redistribution should be discussed on their moral and political merits. They are neither rejected nor mandated by a commitment to human rights.[38]

Nozick's argument is of special relevance to my concerns, because he seeks to base his rejection of welfare laws on the claim that they inherently violate individuals' rights. He presents a person's right to liberty as a side-constraint on one's actions, not as just an additional consideration to be weighed against others while pursuing one's goals.[39] The nature of liberty rights as side-constraints stems from the Kantian insistence on seeing individuals as ends. This perception of the individual, in turn, precludes using one person to gain advantages (or to avert catastrophes) for another. This picture of rights, again, stresses the peremptory nature of rights. Side-constraints reflect the things we may not do to individuals, because by doing them we would violate and undermine the most basic ground for recognition of the others' worth. People have entitlements, and these entitlements impose limits on what can be done to them and their holdings without their consent. This picture of rights, again, seeks to draw practical lessons from the nature of rights and the presuppositions of recognizing them.

The Kantian image of individuals who should not be violated is indeed attractive and important. However, the key question then becomes: what are one's entitlements? Nozick's answer in terms of work and voluntary exchange is only persuasive in part. The literature on this subject is huge. Arguments similar to Nozick's are often made by advocates of the free market analysis of political economy, and by "Law and Economics" scholars. However, there are serious philosophical, economic, and legal analyses expounding the difficulties arising from their premises. All I need to say in this context is that there is no knockout victory in this debate, and that one is unlikely. Once we concede this, the question of social justice cannot be presented as one totally controlled and pre-empted by the recognition of individuals' rights to liberty or property.

Some scholars are content to stop at this point. This is a mistake. The questions of how to strike an acceptable balance between liberty and solidarity, between individual autonomy and social mutual responsibility, are the central political questions of our age. The fact that human rights talk, in itself, does not answer these questions should not allow them to be decided only by political power and conflicting self-interest. The questions often reflect internal tensions between the premises of an allegiance to human rights. Furthermore, various forms of institutional rights, constitutional as well as legal, may well be important elements of the solution.

I cannot of course say much about the substance of this debate in a chapter like this, but I do want to add a few reminders. I argued above that liberty, property, or the distinction between CP and SE concerns could not really decide the relevant issues. Instead, we need to base our analysis on moral and normative considerations going beyond the general commitment to these rights. But we must also attend to facts about human nature, the nature of social and political organization, and the limits of political feasibility.

While Nozick's principled argument against taxation for redistribution must be rejected, some of the sentiments he expresses are indeed central to liberty and dignity, and some of the dangers he points out are very real. The fact that so many of the Communist regimes were oppressive, arguably beyond the necessities dictated by their social aims, and that even their ability to take care of the SE welfare of their population was very limited, should give us pause. The kind of administration that is needed to enforce complicated systems of taxation and redistribution is indeed likely to generate problems. In extreme forms, it may even threaten important aspects of personal and political freedom. A system of redistribution that builds only on coercion of the haves cannot be stable. There are serious limits to our ability to control social processes, and interventions do have unanticipated consequences that may sometimes undermine their desired consequences and make the intervention, all things considered, unjustified.

On the other hand, it is very hard to take seriously the claim that all taxation other than that required to support the minimal state will inevitably lead to the denial of freedom, initiative, and an ethic of responsibility. Or to ignore the fact that intelligent public investments in education and empowerment (i.e. responding to SE needs through taxation) may well contribute to growth and to welfare more than increasing the expenses of policing the have-nots so they cannot effectively threaten the well-being of the haves (i.e. responding to CP needs through taxation). In other words, rights to liberty, dignity, or property cannot decide, on their own, how a society should distribute its resources.

It is significant and fortunate, on the other hand, that in contemporary discussions of these issues, there is hardly an argument that they should be decided summarily by the recognition of the centrality of a right to equality in our commitment to human rights. Equality is recognized as a right only in some limited senses – a right not to be discriminated against, a right to be treated equally by public institutions, including the courts. The implications of the commitment to equality in our system of social justice are usually conceded not to be determinative of specific arrangements.[40] Moreover, the SE rights we are talking about are not primarily rights to equal shares or allocations, but rights to adequate standards of living, health, and education.

This is not to say that the right to equal treatment does not impose important constraints on the arrangements of particular societies. Nonetheless, like liberty and property, equality alone cannot decide these issues.

Grave SE concerns and oppressive regimes

Until now I have examined arguments for the exclusion of SE concerns from the realm of human rights or for seeing SE rights as secondary to CP ones. However, there are also advocates for the superiority of SE rights over CP rights.

Governments and religious leaders in many countries object to international pressures that they should respect the CP rights of their citizens, invoking the primacy of forms of solidarity and control, which are necessary, so they claim, to maintain their culture and to permit life in complicated, poverty-ridden areas. These objections are not usually phrased in terms of the wish to protect SE rights. Rather, they are based on a rejection of the tradition of rights itself, claiming that this tradition is individualistic and Western, and that its claim of universality is mistaken. As mentioned above, I will not deal with this position here.[41]

Other leaders concede the applicability of documents such as the

UDHR to their countries. They argue, nonetheless, that in non-modern countries suffering from systemic poverty, meeting the subsistence needs of the population requires centralist control which is not consistent with respect for the basic CP rights recognized in the industrial West.

If it had been the case that the prevention of famine and starvation require, under some circumstances, the denial of some CP rights – this might have been a serious and tragic dilemma. However, there is absolutely no evidence that this is indeed the case. To the contrary, many argue that democratization and freedom of speech and protest are effective ways of preventing, or at least minimizing, such catastrophes. Sen, for example, points out that India did not have a single major famine since it became a democracy, and that forced silence contributed a lot to the scope and dimensions of the tragedy of the "Great Leap Forward" in China.[42]

I do not want to sound naive, suggesting that SE and CP concerns are two separate realms, each totally autonomous. Clearly they are not. In fact, the complex relationship between them is what I am stressing. In many cases, the rise, or the persistence, of oppressive regimes is facilitated by economic interests, seeking to perpetuate their monopolies and to fight plans of massive redistribution. In such cases, the government does not seek to justify its atrocious violations of CP rights, such as murder, torture, illegal imprisonment and the like, by invoking SE concerns. The argument is that these are necessary to maintain security and order. The denial of CP rights, in these cases, permits the situation of an increasing denial of welfare and subsistence for large parts of the population. Granted, ensuring that the economy is planned and growing and that for people to receive education and acquire skills may require effective government may not always be easy to achieve when one has to struggle against traditional leaders who resist the changes. Nonetheless, these needs do not justify oppression and arbitrary power. In fact, government action that may challenge traditional leadership will be more effective if the population itself is empowered, so that challenges of tradition can come from civil society itself. Protests, dissidence, and trade unions may indeed make moving a society through quick processes of industrialization more difficult. But shortcuts in these processes are likely to be even more dangerous. I repeat my advice concerning thin and thick readings of rights. There may be conditions, which may justify, in one country, less expansive protection of some CP (or SE) rights than in other, more developed and more stable, societies. But this is very different from saying that CP rights are not applicable, or that they are secondary to SE rights.

Rulers of oppressive regimes may not be very interested in the welfare of their population, in either the CP or the SE aspects of it. But an analysis of developing countries may explain why the right to private property is not usually counted among basic human rights. Torture and oppression are not legitimate (or effective) tools in promoting either law and order or economic growth. Prohibitions against them are justly considered strong side-constraints on the conduct of governments and other individuals. On the other hand, some gradual restructuring of the economy, and some agrarian reform, may well be required to adapt the country to modern conditions. Such restructuring may require a certain measure of coerced interference with private property. It may also require some public interference with freedom of contract as well as various structures of public expenditure. I do not think all such interference is made totally unacceptable by a commitment to human rights. On the other hand, I do not think that such interference is automatically justified by the wish to promote social justice or economic growth. Human history shows that wholesale redistribution of property accumulated by few was usually extremely brutal, and did not make an enduring contribution to social justice. Again, this is a question that needs to be deliberated and decided, responsibly, by the society in question. Today's economies depend to a large extent on private and semi-private investment and on international assistance by bodies such as the IMF and the World Bank. It seems that the incentive structure today is biased, if anything, against the willingness of states' leadership to increase the planned aspects, or even the welfare components, of their economies.[43]

We may conclude that it may well be convenient for rulers to invoke SE needs to justify the denial of CP rights, but that this denial is not in fact required to meet such needs. Whenever a claim is made that violations of CP rights is required to protect pressing SE needs of the population, the arguments should be subjected to a penetrating analysis. The burden is on the state or individuals seeking to justify the violation of CP rights for these reasons. In any event, such justification may be based on the conflict and the need to balance between rights and interests. It does not support a general primacy of SE concerns over CP rights.

Enforceability of CP and SE rights

For the reasons mentioned above, individuals might well have a human right to adequate living conditions. In other words, they do have rights to such conditions of life that stem from the mere fact of their humanity, and these rights do not depend on effective recognition by their societies. These rights justify the imposition of duties, on states and on individuals, to act in order to protect and promote them. The main questions are what these duties are and how they should be enforced.

It is of great interest and significance to note that the international community decided to create different enforcement mechanisms for CP and SE rights, primarily in the form of the ICCPR and the ICESCR. While international mechanisms are not very effective even for CP rights, the separation of the two covenants signifies a debate about the status of SE rights. More specifically, there is less willingness to identify and impose the duties, be they on states or other individuals, which are co-relative to the SE rights of individuals. As we mentioned above, there are many practices in human rights discourse that strengthen the prime place of CP rights. In many contexts, only CP rights are discussed under the label "human rights." The choice of two covenants lends great support to the force of the distinction. Against the background of the UDHR decision to treat the two clusters of rights together and as being of equal status, the decision to distinguish between enforcement mechanisms may seem inconsistent. I do not think it is. While the clusters are interconnected in many ways, there is a justification to emphasizing some structural differences between them as well. These differences should not lead, however, to overlooking the indivisibility of the concerns.

In the CP context, the duties are imposed on states. They need to pass laws and to create background realities and institutions that will minimize violations of the rights mentioned in the covenant. In some cases the duties are specified, and some forms of balancing between these rights and other considerations (such as emergency situations) are explicitly excluded.[44] If suspects are subjected to torture or to humiliating treatment under the jurisdiction of a state, if people disappear or do not have a fair trial before an independent judiciary – this is a failure of duty on the part of the state. These duties are both negative – not to infringe upon the right, and positive – to take steps to promote it. In the SE covenant, on the other hand, the duty is only to make efforts to reach an adequate level of protection. Moreover, the SE covenant explicitly allows developing countries not to grant these rights to individuals who are not their nationals.[45]

There is an additional difference of importance. The international community accepts some responsibility for seeing to it that CP rights are not violated, especially when the violations are crimes against humanity. There is no similar commitment in the SE context other than a commitment to cooperation and coordination. It seems that the duty is not imposed on every individual and every state, but only on one's own state. The differences between the two covenants become even more apparent with the establishment of the International Criminal Court and in the aftermath of the Pinochet affair.

It is thus important to remind ourselves that these are differences in enforceability, not in the status of the concerns as rights, or in their importance to human dignity. Massive taxation and redistribution does raise serious moral and political issues. These are best decided by the societies in question. International supervision (and possibly supervision by domestic courts as well) should be careful and delicate. Developing standards, thresholds, and guidelines is a better way to approach these issues than outright decisions and condemnations of failures. A country that is forced to prevent child labour, or is condemned as a human rights violator because it does not, when its economy is still based on this institution – is not likely to become a supporter of human rights. More likely, it will feel that human rights are indeed a form of Western imperialism. However, the same caution is recommended on issues which belong to CP rights, such as the status of women and the role of religion in public life.

The differences between the enforcement mechanisms of CP and SE rights on the international level exist for most domestic legal systems, irrespective of the way these concerns are recognized in the systems. However, a closer look at the details of legal and political decisions suggests that the difference is not in the nature of the rights, but in the differences in the typical co-relative duties that need to be imposed in order to protect and promote them. Courts hesitate to impose heavy budgetary burdens on their governments. Their reluctance is based on considerations of institutional competence, separation of powers, and effectiveness. They also hesitate to make policy decisions on matters that are ordinarily assigned to the political branches. It is important to see that these legitimate and weighty considerations should not lead us to distort the role of SE rights in our thinking and in our political action.

A look at the comparative law of human rights may be useful. The Indian constitution and that of South Africa both include SE rights. However, in India SE concerns are given the status of guiding principles, and in South Africa they are full-fledged rights. In both countries, some parts of the population argue for judicial activism in promoting SE rights, while others warn against it. In both, the courts' performance gets contradictory assessments from parts of the population. Yet in both countries, the courts end up not giving expansive interpretations to SE claims. The reason is that such interpretations would have involved the courts in making policy decisions which might not be enforceable. The UN has decided to reflect this reality in the structure of the covenants. No doubt, the decision was also a result of political negotiations between states.[46] But it reflects more than differences of power within the UN decision-making bodies. A large majority of states did not want a possibility of international determination of their social and economic policies. The choice was between diluting the enforcement of all rights or giving CP rights a stronger enforcement mechanism. I believe the choice to do the latter is amply justified.

Protection of rights vs. protection as rights

In the US there are hardly any SE rights protected by the Constitution. All welfare arrangements, in principle, are within the power of regular legislatures. Once some scheme is adopted, there is a constitutional right to due process and equality in benefiting from it. But the entitlements themselves are not protected. This fact has been illustrated quite powerfully by the dramatic change in the welfare regime over the last few years. In this narrow sense the US compares badly with other countries whose constitutions contain explicit commitments to SE rights (e.g. India and South Africa). Furthermore, there is a stark difference between the way the US treats CP rights – which are constitutional rights protected by the courts – and the way it treats SE concerns.

Does it follow that the US violates the SE rights of its population? The absence of a constitutional protection for SE rights does not in itself lead to a positive answer to this question. Recognition of SE constitutional rights is neither a sufficient nor a necessary condition for a finding that a given country respects these rights. This feature is not unique to SE concerns. Bills of Rights, in general, are neither sufficient nor necessary for the effective protection of the rights listed in them. Suffice it to remind ourselves of the fact that England still does not have an entrenched Bill of Rights with full judicial review,[47] and that the former USSR had a very advanced Constitution. In the US, the existence of a Bill of Rights in itself, including specific commitments to equality and freedom of expression, was not enough to generate either desegregation, extended freedom of expression, or equality for women. On the other hand, the existence of a Bill of Rights and a tradition of judicial review may facilitate extended recognition of rights through judicial law making that may push the legislative branches in the direction of additional protection.

It is more important that the concerns are addressed effectively than that they are recognized as rights. However, we saw that one of the main reasons for recognizing rights is precisely the wish to make their protection more effective. The institutional features of rights, and the international power of recognizing them as such, do provide some help in making claims of rights more effective. The US Bill of Rights, in itself, did not guarantee full protection of the rights mentioned in it, but it did provide the tools that permitted better protection when the courts felt they were willing and able to undertake it. I have argued above that over-expansive rights talk may be dangerous, and harm the legitimacy of the courts. This danger should be heeded, but it does not serve as a conclusive argument against insisting that both CP and SE concerns, when appropriate, should be protected as rights. The necessary balance between protection and flexibility should be achieved by the institutional checks and balances and by their careful use.

The implications of globalization

My analysis was based on a world order in which there are sovereign states that bear primary powers and responsibilities in the life of their populations. Within this order, human rights are constructs designed to evaluate municipal arrangements by invoking a universal set of standards. There is a growing tendency to seek international mechanisms of enforcement, but these are still the exception rather than the rule. The protection of the welfare of individuals, in most cases, depends on what their states do and refrain from doing much more than on international pressures or resolutions.

Interestingly, exceptions to the principle of sovereignty have centred to date on attempts to prevent and punish atrocities resulting from the violation of CP rights. While the world seeks to give humanitarian and medical relief to areas of the world stricken by starvation, there has been no attempt to use force to change the system of government that leads to such catastrophes. This is as it should be. But international law has also been very slow to adjust to the fact that in the SE realm, the implications of globalization are immense, seriously affecting the power of states to relieve the SE concerns of their populations. In the confines of this chatper, I cannot do justice to these issues. I do want, however, to point out some structural features, which make globalization upset some "old" connections between CP and SE concerns within municipal systems.[48]

In the past, states had some incentive to deal with social justice and a feeling of social cohesion within their borders, since states enjoyed relative autonomy. While there were always great differences between communities, states, and nations, there was a sense in which the responsibility for the balance between individual liberty and social justice could be placed on the state. While states did not and could not obliterate the differences between families and communities, they did provide a framework within which the resources of the state as a whole could be mobilized to provide for the population. Furthermore, democratization meant that, in principle, this same population had a say in determining the identity of national decision makers. In principle, the have-nots could influence government in such a way that their main SE concerns would be met.[49] I mentioned above that democratization in itself cannot guarantee social justice, but it could be relied upon to express a reasonable balance between individual rights and social solidarity. Bluntly, the rich and the powerful had to give adequate response to the poor of their states and communities, for a variety of moral and prudential reasons. Their own welfare required that most of their population would be satisfied, and that levels of hopelessness would not end up with rioting or even revolution. Finally, democratization meant that at least some protection of welfare and education would gain the respectability of rights, not just that of political arrangements or of charity. Consequently, within states, rulers and elites alike learned that they cannot ignore the welfare of their population.

Globalization seems to undermine some of the presuppositions of this ideal picture. This is one of the reasons why the hope that protection of CP rights would generate, in itself, acceptable resolution of the SE concerns, did not materialize. On the global level, this relationship between vote and product was never obtained. There seems to be a growing gap between voice, responsibility, and power. Many factors contribute to this gap. One is the interdependence of markets and the mobility of industry, labour, and capital. The other is the great divergence of the cost of labour in different parts of the world. A third is the vulnerability of third world leaders and peoples, who depend on Western technologies and capital they do not have. As a result, there is a serious detachment between markets and centres of life for many industries and industrialists.

This situation creates problems for both the developed and the undeveloped parts of the world. Unskilled labour in the developed world cannot compete with labour from the undeveloped world. It is threatened by the fact that production moves elsewhere and that its own country attracts foreign workers, legal as well as illegal, who are willing to work in conditions no longer acceptable to natives. Furthermore, the decision-making processes by which international economic structures are decided are not accountable to municipal political processes. They are conducted by international fora in which quite often the affluent classes of a number of countries decide on agreements that are good for them but bad for their countries as a whole.[50] These developments contribute to the present predicament of the welfare state in the industrial West. In the undeveloped parts of the world, international pressures and internal corruption make a gradual move towards modernization, combining growth with structures responsive to the education and SE concerns of all, extremely difficult.

Some of these issues are discussed in the chapters by Shue and de Senarclens in this volume. I mention them here because they highlight the growing fragility of processes that until now secured, to some extent, a balance between CP and SE concerns in many societies. Any modern attempt to deal with these rights will have to be sensitive to these facts.[51]

Notes

1. I thank Paul Safier and the participants in the UNU workshop in Princeton, October 1999, for useful comments on a previous draft. Yael Ronen helped me in preparing the draft for publication.

2. In the first group, I include rights to life and bodily integrity, the right not to be tortured or humiliated, the basic freedoms of conscience, religion, opinion, speech, assembly, association; political rights of participation; freedom of movement and freedom from imprisonment; and the right to non-discrimination and the right to trial and due process. It is interesting and relevant that the right to property is sometimes numbered among CP rights in some documents, but is absent in others. The second group includes the rights to education, accommodation, an adequate standard of living, healthcare, freedom from poverty, work and leisure, in short – welfare rights.

3. Adopted by UNGA Resolution 217, III, 10 December 1948.

4. International Covenant on Civil and Political Rights, International Covenant on Economic, Social and Cultural Rights, both adopted by UNGA Resolution 2200A, XXI, 16 December 1966.

5. I take it that this is also the position of most of the literature critical of rights talk, such as Glendon's book. The critique is not a general condemnation of the utility of rights, but an exposition of the dangers of an over-imperialistic rights talk. Mary Ann Glendon, *Rights Talk: The Impoverishment of Political Discourse*, Cambridge, MA, Harvard University Press, 1991.

6. Moral rights may be in an intermediate situation. Some say they are, by definition, universal and timeless. Others invoke notions, which are more contextualized and culture-relative. The latter position is clearly applicable for positive morality.

7. Thus we do not need to get into the interest vs. the will theory of rights, since human rights clearly do not require "control" of the individual for them to exist. Human rights are clearly justificatory, not descriptive, entities. For the interest vs. the control debate see Matthew Kramer, N. E. Simmonds, and Hillel Steiner, *A Debate over Rights*, Oxford, 1998.

8. In this characterization I follow the influential analysis of rights put forward by Joseph Raz.

9. I thus accept Shue's general characterization of human rights, although the normative implications I draw from the existence of such rights are different from his.

10. For a classic exposition see his "Rights as Trumps," in Jeremy Waldron, *Theories of Rights*, Oxford, OUP, 1984, pp. 153–167.

11. For a discussion of this feature of rights see Waldron, "The Right to do Wrong," in *Liberal Rights*, Cambridge, CUP, 1993, p. 63. An obvious example is the right to freedom of speech. In many cases, the right will protect a speaker who injured another's reputation or privacy even though the violation of these rights is not justified in that particular case.

12. It is important to distinguish this peremptory force of rights from the question whether rights are or can be absolute. A right is absolute if it defeats all other possible reasons or considerations. The right not to be tortured is often brought as a paradigmatic, and rare, illustration. But all rights, even those that are conceded not to be absolute, have this peremptory power.

13. This tension is the one captured by the persistent debate between interest and control theories of rights. Interest theories of rights give rights a moral peremptory force, while control theories emphasize the institutional effectiveness.

14. The two cases are similar in general structure, invoking human rights and international standards to justify the use of force. There are, of course, many differences. After World War II, the force used was "Victors' Justice," i.e. an international tribunal, enjoying widespread international support, where alleged war criminals were put on trial. In Kosovo, they were invoked to justify military actions, done without UN approval.

15. Constitutional rights are often as abstract and general as are international formulations of human rights. In such cases, the transition from human rights to constitutional rights does not mean added concreteness and determinacy. In fact, the First Amendment

guaranteeing freedom of speech in the US is even less specific that the guarantees of free speech in the Covenant on CP Rights.

16. These modern critiques, like Glendon's, echo Bentham's earlier statement that natural rights were both incoherent and dangerous.

17. My chapter deals with the relations between moral justificatory force and effectiveness in municipal legal systems. The international human rights regime was developed in order to remedy to some extent the failure of states to protect the human rights of their own citizens. Naturally, they rely more heavily on moral force, as a way of increasing effectiveness. Inevitably, sanctions in international law are usually less effective than in municipal courts. It can be expected that international human rights jurisdiction may therefore be more coherent than that of municipal courts, because it is less limited by political constraints. On the other hand, the international system cannot replace state power in effective protection of rights. States can do much more for the human rights of their inhabitants than international declarations. The interrelations between international and municipal human rights jurisdictions are therefore complex, and it cannot be assumed that international law interpretations are necessarily superior to these made by municipal systems.

18. For a classical formulation of this appeal see MacDonald's essay. Margaret MacDonald, "Natural Rights," *Proceedings of the Aristotelian Society 1947–48*, pp. 35–55, reprinted Waldron, 1984, pp. 21–40.

19. For the distinction see e.g. Michael Walzer, *Thick and Thin, Moral Disagreements at Home and Abroad,* University of Notre Dame Press, 1996, and Mark Tushnet, *Taking the Constitution Away from the Courts*, Princeton, NJ, Princeton University Press, 1999.

20. In the text I draw a distinction between internal political activity within a state and international pressures. But within the state there is also the possibility of seeking to promote human rights by litigating test cases in the courts. Litigation is in an intermediary position here. It invokes a national institution, which is a partner in elaborating the society's social norms. Litigation is therefore a form of internal political persuasion. On the other hand, it invites the court to invalidate laws in the name of universal human rights. This is indeed an example of complex internal dynamics, which seek to strengthen the evaluative power of human rights. We should recall that, while the authoritative decision or interpretation is made by the court – the other branches of government are also partners to this elaboration of internal political norms against the background of external ones.

21. I describe a situation as semi-lynching when the motivation behind the violation is acute anger, frustration or fear that leads to a tendency not to respect inhibitions and laws prohibiting violence or requiring due process.

22. It may well be that this is, on the part of many, wisdom after the event. Some may still argue that courts should not second-guess the decisions of the executive in war-like situations. The structure of the argument is important, this is the type of case in which our judgment is distorted by passion and the wish for revenge. Rights and institutional constraints are designed to help us from succumbing to the temptation to lose our judgment.

23. See my "The Role of Courts in Rifted Democracies," *Isr. L. Rev.*, 1999.

24. I cannot enter here the important and fascinating debate about the cultural relativity of human rights, and the argument that the West is imposing its own system of values on the East. Different forms of social organization may indeed structure relationships between individuals and societies in different ways, allowing different modes of freedom and dignity to individuals. Nonetheless, I do not know of any great human civilization that does not include respect for the dignity and the freedom of individuals, nor do I know of any society in which people did not strive for them. See the powerful discussion

of Panrikar. Panrikar Raimando, "Is the Notion of Human Rights a Western Concept?" 120 *Diogenes*, 1982, pp. 75–102.

25. It should be noted that the effectiveness of courts as defenders of rights is much higher in CP concerns, because judges inevitably belong to those parts of the population for whom subsistence is not an issue. The insulation of judges from populism may act against the effective protection of the human rights of the weak. This is one of the explanations suggested for the ineffectiveness of courts in redressing racial discrimination in the US.

26. The US Supreme Court first invoked the constitutional right to liberty to invalidate laws granting rights to workers. This may be a case in which a civil right to liberty was invoked to defeat SE rights. In modern times, however, the liberty clause in the Constitution is invoked in order to expand liberty in issues such as abortion. SE arrangements are left almost free of judicial review.

27. M. Cranston, *What Are Human Rights?* London, Bodley Head, 1973.

28. By 1984 Waldron dismisses such arguments in his *Introduction to Theories of Rights*, p. 11, see note 10 above.

29. See also the right to form trade unions, Article 8 of the SE Covenant. One may respond that the "location" of rights should not affect their classification. The right to form trade unions, under this argument, should be seen as a CP right despite the fact that it is mentioned in the ICSECR. But then it seems that the distinction is reduced to that between negative and positive rights, and not to the context in which these rights arise and are central. The right to form trade unions is an SE right despite the fact that it may well be seen as a private instance of the more general right to free association. The reason is historical; forming trade unions is a central aspects of the process in which workers sought to improve their negotiation position vis-à-vis employers.

30. M. R. Cohen, *Property and Sovereignty*, 13 *Cornell L.*, 21, 1927.

31. Stephen Holmes and Cass R. Sunstein, *The Cost of Rights, Why Liberty Depends on Taxes*, W. W. Norton and Co., 1999.

32. This is the only right in the ICESCR for which states are explicitly required to institute a specific arrangement – compulsory free primary education. If they do not have such education in place, they are required to prepare a plan that will guarantee such a system within a specified short period, Articles 13–14.

33. This is the impact of Nozick's construction of rights as side-constraints. I discuss his analysis below. A similar move is made by H. L. Hart in an early paper, which he appears to have modified, "Do We have Natural Rights?" And see his comments on Bentham's *On Rights*. H. L. Hart, "Are There Any Natural Rights?" *Essays on Bentham*, Oxford, OUP, 1982. For a claim that logically there is a priority to claim rights see Golding's analysis. Martin Golding, "The Primacy of Welfare Rights," *Social Philosophy and Policy* 1, 1984, p. 119; Robert Nozick, *State, Anarchy and Utopia*, New York, Basic Books, 1974.

34. The tradition of human rights exemplified by Locke does centre on the question of the limits of government. However, one may counter that the novelty was the rights talk, but that concerns with welfare are much older than those with freedom. See e.g. Golding.

35. James Nickel, "How Human Rights Generate Duties to Protect and Provide," *Human Rights Quarterly* 15, 1993, p. 77.

36. On this controversy I agree with the conception endorsed by the international documents – individuals as well as collectivities may be the subjects of rights. The relationships between individuals and the collectives of which they are members are indeed complex, and essentialist interpretations of the collectives are indeed dangerous, but the conclusion that only individuals "exist" does not follow.

37. See e.g. Rawls's *Theory of Justice*, requiring societies to obey the principle of maximin, ensuring that policies will benefit the worst off. See also Dworkin's writings, arguing both for "taking rights seriously" and that equality is a basic tenet of liberalism. For an analysis of Nozick's argument see Scheffler. Samuel Scheffler, "Natural Rights, Equality and the Minimal State," *Canadian J. Phil* VI, 1976.
38. For very sensitive discussions see Wellman and Jacobs. Both are very sympathetic to claims of social justice, and both are rigorous enough to point out the difficulties in establishing rights to welfare or deriving specific conclusions from them. Carl Wellman, *Welfare Rights*, NJ, Rowman and Littlefield, 1982; Lesley A. Jacobs, *Rights and Deprivation*, Oxford, 1993.
39. See Nozick, at pp. 30–35. The structure is similar, though not identical, with Dworkin's trumps and Raz's exclusionary reasons.
40. It is not determinative when equality is seen as a human right. Some may argue that in particular societies, the commitment to equality does require, or prohibit, certain arrangements. Decisions of international courts are quite interesting in this regard, seeking to give "equality" a significance that transcends the arrangements of particular societies. The ambiguity of the implications of liberty or equality create interesting institutional questions in municipal systems. I believe that they would call for a policy of judicial deference, for the reasons clarified by, among others, O. W. Holmes. Such deference may be progressive when the court is asked to invalidate progressive arrangements, such as affirmative action, or conservative when the court is asked to declare that such measures are required by the constitution.
41. For a systematic treatment of such claims see the chapter of Tatsuo Inoue in this volume.
42. See A. Sen, "Freedom and Needs," *New Republic* 31, 1994, and his recent *Democracy and Development*, 1999. I rejected the argument that the protection of CP rights could, in itself, guarantee the satisfaction of SE concerns. Yet it may be true that CP rights can make an effective contribution to an adequate protection of SE rights.
43. On this point see the analysis of Professor Pierre de Senarclens in this volume.
44. While rights of due process may be temporarily suspended during emergencies, the right not to be tortured or the right to life cannot be suspended.
45. ICESCR, Article 2(3).
46. The insistence on including SE rights as rights of equal status in the UDHR was the result of the demand of the USSR and its block of nations. While it was agreed to do that in the declaratory document, there was no willingness to incorporate the same mechanism at the conventions stage.
47. The recent legislation incorporating the European convention into English law is an interesting exercise in constitutional development. But even this Human Rights Act stops short of giving the courts the power to overrule legislation.
48. I do not deal here at all with the urgent normative questions raised by Henry Shue's paper, concerning the nature and scope of the duties that states and individuals in the developed world may owe to the needy of the undeveloped world. My comments are concerned with the impact of globalization on "old" background conditions of social systems. However, my general attitude to rights talk does suggest that its extension in the way suggested by Shue may raise serious problems. I would therefore prefer a direct discussion of moral duties, and their scope, to their derivation from the language of rights and strong entitlements.
49. But see Nozick's explanation, pp. 274–275, suggesting that the majorities usually do not have an interest in supporting the weak.
50. See Eyal Benvenisti, "Exit and Voice in the Age of Globalization," *Michigan Law Review* 98, 1999, p. 167.

51. For example, national solidarity was supported, to some extent, by nation states and cultural ties. And the life of poor people was made richer and meaningful by memberships in religious and cultural communities of support. Globalization, with waves of migrant workers, often disrupts these frameworks. The job markets created in undeveloped countries create great disparities of wealth, while breaking up traditional structures. The predicament of unskilled people in the developed world creates desperation and unrest, and breaks traditional family structure. These processes in turn create a large underclass, which is alienated and dependent on public welfare. The ancient and persistent problems of tensions between rich and poor thus become complicated with ethnic, religious, and social issues. Poor people may have less of a supporting community, which would have helped them cope better with poverty and its implications. Attempts by states and international forces to address these problems, whether as rights or in other ways, should be sensitive to these complexities.

2

The incorporation of civic and social rights in domestic law

Claire Archbold[1]

It is not surprising that the second half of the twentieth century has been described as the Age of Rights. In his book of that title, Henkin argues that the modern human rights movement has sought to achieve "the internationalisation of human rights, the transformation of the idea of constitutional rights in a few countries to a universal conception and a staple of international politics and law" (1990: 13–14). The effect of this transformation when the international standards are incorporated into national law is interesting. Do the standards survive intact, or, as they are adopted and integrated into national law, do they become less universal? Does national incorporation mean that standards are flexible enough not to be monolithic, or so flexible as to become something other than universal? This chapter considers two examples which indicate that international norms can become part of national law, fitted to local circumstances, without losing their essential character.

Human rights – the moral and/or legal claims arising from the inherent dignity of human beings (Honderich 1995) – were part and parcel of a Lockean view of constitutionalism, and their potential political effects were perhaps most notably demonstrated in revolutionary France and America at the end of the eighteenth century. At that time, rights were seen as liberties of the individual which had to be ringfenced against invasion by the state. They were negatively phrased and absolute. In the twentieth century, this liberal idea of rights has developed and evolved as circumstances have changed, and commentators now refer to a roughly chronological development of three generations of rights. First generation rights are those civil and political liberties recognizable to the eighteenth century constitutional drafters. Second generation rights are social and economic rights, such as the rights to basic nutrition, shelter, education, and health care. Third generation rights are a mixed bag, consisting of more recently developed individual rights, such as the right to a healthful environment, as well as minority and group rights. Although human rights are often described as indivisible, indicating that the effective guarantee of any right requires the respect for all of them, the diverse nature, and occasionally competing demands of each generation of rights, can seem to give rise to tensions.

The question of how rights are to be made effective within nation states requires that they be incorporated into national law and practice. Human rights consciousness and enforcement "trickle down" from international to national levels in several ways. At the broadest level, the language of human rights is used when the community of nations attempts to put pressure on nations which have little regard for the rights of their citizens. Within nation states, the language of rights is used by non-governmental organizations and human rights monitors, as well as by politicians, as a motor for social or political change. In more concrete terms, national governments sign human rights treaties, and several United Nations treaties[2] require them to make periodic reports on the extent to which the rights in question are secured for their citizens. Other treaties, such as the European Convention on Human Rights, have their own judicial institutions, and can be effective in indicating areas in which human rights protection could be better. But a human rights culture will only really be created in a particular society if human rights are incorporated into its national law. This may be by "ordinary" legislation, or, in the common law world in particular, by judicial application of internationally recognized human rights norms in national courts. But the most effective way to secure human rights for national citizens is by enacting them as entrenched legislation, which has a special status and cannot be easily changed, such as a Bill of Rights or constitution.

In the Vienna Declaration of 1993, the United Nations stated that civil and political, social and economic, group and individual rights are unified and indivisible. However, when it comes to incorporation and implementation of human rights at nation state level, this statement is less self-evident. Human rights norms are not incorporated into national law without some element of selection and modification resulting from national political and social circumstances. This process may be most evident in the debate surrounding enactment of an entrenched national Bill of Rights. Canada and South Africa, discussed below, both provide examples of this process. Both are states which have chosen to entrench particular human rights norms in their national law as part of a process of constitutional transition. However, selection and modification do not mean that human rights norms are entirely mutable when enacted at a national level. The selections made in both jurisdictions have indicated the points of tension in those societies. Further, engagement with international human rights discourse can in its turn modify national political and constitutional discourses in terms of international human rights thinking, and this is also evident from the Canadian and South African examples.

While one cannot draw general conclusions from such a small number of examples, Canada and South Africa do provide illustrations of many interesting issues, and it is hoped that this chapter will provide a springboard for thinking about the wider issues explored throughout this volume.

The road to incorporation

A nation envisioning itself – Canadian experiences[3]

A constitution may be seen as "a set of fundamental laws, customs and conventions which provide the framework within which government is exercised in a state" (Pepin-Robarts 1979: 29). But this definition skates over the surface of the deep difference even within Western thought between the Lockean view, predominant in countries such as the US, of the constitution as a social compact by which the people establish the institutions of government and assert the limitations on it (Henkin and Rosenthal 1990: 385), and the Burkean view, whose heritage is most evident in the United Kingdom, of the constitution as an organic assemblage and accretion of laws, institutions and customs of government. Canada has a Burkean constitutional heritage, arising from its origins within the British Empire, but since independence was first mooted, the process of enacting an autochthonous constitution, a social contract between the people of Canada, Canadian constitutionalism has been incorporating increasing elements of Lockean thinking.

The Canadian Charter of Rights and Freedoms[4] of 1982, the Bill of Rights under discussion, did not emerge from a vacuum, but is part of a long, and as yet incomplete process of constitution making. Unusually, Canada did not hasten to independence from Britain, because the main linguistic communities in the territory, the French-speaking community which formed the majority in Quebec, and the mainly English-speaking community which formed a majority in the rest of Canada, could not agree on the balances of power within an independent constitution. The Dominion of Canada was founded by the British North America Act of 1867, and has a highly decentralized federal system of government, which, possibly together with its size and the dispersed nature of much of its population, has meant that traditionally provincial loyalties are stronger than loyalty to any sense of "Canada" as a whole. After the Balfour Declaration of 1926, by which the British government expressed its intention that Commonwealth countries should become autonomous and self-governing, the Canadian provincial governments met, and it became clear that Canada would not be able to agree a means of amending a national constitution. The Statute of Westminster granted Canada self-governing autonomy in other regards, but provided that the Canadian Constitution would continue to be amended in London.

Creating a satisfactory balance of power, in particular around the issue of constitutional amendment, between the English-speaking and French-speaking communities, has been at the heart of constitutional negotiations attempting to conclude the patriation process for the rest of the century. Formulas for constitutional amendment were negotiated amongst the provincial premiers at Charlottetown in 1964, at Victoria in 1971, and in the negotiations which rumbled on throughout the 1970s, but were unacceptable to some of the provinces, particularly to Quebec, which became increasingly nationalist and separatist as its so-called Quiet Revolution gathered force from 1965.

The constitutional debate in Canada, from the British North America Act onwards, may be characterized as a process of accommodation between the political elites of the French and English-speaking communities, typical of consociational democracies. This background made it more difficult for other minorities, such as Native Canadians, to make their voices heard in a Bill of Rights debate. Negotiations between top-level representatives of the provincial and federal governments had no input from ordinary citizens for much of the century, although they were broadcast on television from 1968.

The explicit human rights discourse included in the debate, most notably by Pierre Trudeau after 1965, was not a "tool" which instantly solved the country's problems. Equally, the focus of attention in Canada was on those human rights which were at the site of the constitutional problems – group rights; in particular the linguistic and cultural rights of the people of Quebec, and their right to self-determination (although the latter aspiration could be seen as being sought for a province, and not for a people). This was the problem which meant that the groups could not agree the technical mechanisms of constitutional government. On one hand, Trudeau's attempt to raise support for the idea of individual human rights held equally by all Canadians as a "fundamental Canadian value" was a way of trying to shift the debate away from this impasse, reflecting the idea that "universal" rights are uncontentious. On the other hand, individual rights have become associated with one side of the constitutional disagreement in Canada, but even in this context without necessarily losing their substantive conceptual power. The ongoing history of how human rights have been "personalized" to the Canadian discourse illustrates both how national experience acts to modify expressions of universal human rights and how human rights discourse soaks into the fabric of national constitutional debate, facilitating the constitutional conversation. It may be argued that part of the value of human rights in this situation lies in this facilitation and process of osmosis, rather than in its influence on the formal legal outcome of the constitutional conversation.

Individual human rights made their first significant appearance in national debate in the 1958 elections, when a Canadian Bill of Rights was an electoral platform of the Prime Minister John Diefenbaker. When enacted in 1960, it was a first step towards a constitutional declaration of rights. Macklem et al. (1994: 107) suggest that the Bill of Rights had a number of shaping influences; notably the Universal Declaration of Human Rights, the liberal interpretations of the US Supreme Court in the 1950s, fear of expanding government, a sense that the Cold War was, at its heart, a struggle for individual rights, and finally, unease at certain denials of civil liberties which had taken place in Canada during World War II and in the post-War period.

Despite good intentions, however, the Bill of Rights was a limited document, particularly because it was narrowly interpreted by the courts.[5] Its influence is in sharp contrast to that of the Canadian Charter of 1982, which in its substance and in the manner of its incorporation, was to have a significant influence on the shape of the wider Canadian constitutional debate. The Charter project was close to the heart of Pierre Trudeau, premier of Canada for most of the period 1968 to 1984, a Quebecer by birth, whose vision of Canada's political future was based not on Quebec nationalism, but on the equal enjoyment of liberal-democratic rights and bilingual language rights by all Canadians, defined and maintained by federal institutions. Trudeau's multicultural federalism was not only the response of a lawyer with a strong commitment to the idea of human rights, but an attempt at nation-building. A new vision of Canada as a multicultural, federal society of individual rights holders, equal before and equally supported by the law, would effectively nullify Quebecois claims to be given special treatment because of their language and cultural heritage – francophone Canadians would have the same rights as all other Canadians of English and non-English descent. Trudeau's personal political vision shaped the incorporation of human rights into Canadian law; and his personal contribution to the Charter process cannot be overestimated.

The customary mechanism for constitutional amendment in Canada was agreement by all the provincial governments, and this agreement was impossible to attain at the end of the 1970s. In 1980, Trudeau attempted to break the constitutional logjam by appealing over the heads of the politicians to the people of Canada. The Charter of Rights was a cornerstone of "the people's package," which he announced on national television. Human rights had come to the fore in Canada in the 1970s. Canada acceded to the ICCPR in 1976, and most provinces enacted human rights legislation in the 1970s. The package proposed by Trudeau would allow full patriation together with a few constitutional changes, including a formula for constitutional amendment, a national Charter of Rights and a declaration of the principle of fiscal equalization between the richer and poorer provinces in Canada. Equalization, which was a commitment to promote equal opportunities for the well-being of all Canadians, was a policy of national social welfare, and it is interesting that something so closely akin to economic rights was part of the "people's package," albeit not expressed in rights language.

To build legitimacy for the package, Trudeau set up a special parliamentary committee in the fall and winter of 1980–1981, which marked a new departure in Canadian constitution making. This is arguably the point at which the Canadian human rights debate became multi- rather than bi-cultural. The Committee mainly heard evidence from interest groups, rather than officials, experts or individuals. Russell characterizes the wide spectrum of interests represented: "native peoples, the multicultural community, women, religions, business, labour, the disabled, gays and lesbians, trees and a number of civil liberties organizations" (1993: 114). The concrete changes in the Charter which these groups achieved, in particular in relation to the Charter's equality provisions,[6] internationally regarded as among the most influential elements of the Charter, are considered in the next section. The process also created a new public expectation about popular participation in constitution making, and produced a new set of players in the constitutional process – interest groups (deJong 1985). The inclusion of these new players in the Canadian constitution-making process illustrates how the rights element of the "people's package" changed the nature of the Canadian constitutional conversation and facilitated the development of a new social space, a new language, and new identities in the mainstream "national" consciousness.

Trudeau was only required by the letter of Canadian law to have the approval of the federal Parliament, and not the unanimous accord of all the provinces, before sending the "people's package" to London for implementation. However, the provinces challenged the legitimacy of Trudeau's referral of the "people's package" to London for enactment, and although the Supreme Court (Supreme Court Reference on Constitutional Amendment, 1982) held that in strict law Trudeau did not require the consent of the provincial legislatures, constitutional convention required "a substantial degree" of provincial consent. A first ministers' constitutional conference followed, at which the compromises included the "notwithstanding" clause in the Charter of Rights, and "substantial agreement" was reached, with all provinces except Quebec consenting. However, before the accord went to London, two more amendments were forced, both by public pressure. The first was the absolute guarantee of sex equality in section 28, and the second was the recognition of Native Canadian land rights.

The passage of the United Kingdom Canada Act 1982 gave Canada full independence from Britain, and added the Charter of Rights and Freedoms to the existing constitution (contained in the British North America Act and subsequent enactments of the UK Parliament), as well as recognizing the "existing" rights of Canada's aboriginal people. However, it did not create a completely new constitution, which would still have to be agreed by the provincial premiers. The next round of constitutional negotiations were hastened by discontent in Quebec at the passage of the Canada Act without their consent. However, the field of players in the debate had now widened and the claims of aboriginal Canadians were also a factor in the next round of constitutional negotiations. Native Canadian claims had been given a great boost by the wider public consultation processes of the "people's package," although it was the Supreme Court's recognition of Native Canadian land claims in the *Calder* case of 1973 which brought aboriginal rights into the constitutional debate. After that case, the Trudeau government had entered into land claim negotiations with them, and the strengthening of their political organizations over the next 20 years has been likened to another Quiet Revolution (Russell 1993: 95).

The next round in negotiations culminated in the Meech Lake Accord of 1987. At this point, while individual enjoyment of equal rights was the value which won support of most English-speaking Canadians, for French-speakers, the prime constitutional value was still maintaining and developing their distinct identity. Canadians had tasted a more democratic form of constitution-building, and Meech Lake, a return to the closed-door elite accommodations of the past, was bitterly attacked by the interest groups which had been successful in the 1982 process. Nor did Meech satisfy interests in Quebec, and perhaps the strongest opposition to Meech was among the aboriginal peoples of Manitoba and the population of Newfoundland, which, like other maritime and western provinces, felt outnumbered and unrepresented in the agreement.

After Meech Lake, any constitutional accord would have to satisfy four aspirations; Quebec nationalism, aboriginal self-government, regional alienation on the part of "outer Canada," and Canadian nationalism – a range of sentiments ranging from social democrats seeking Canada-wide standards of social policy and a strong collectivist central government, Charter Canadians in the middle, and on the right the business community seeking a more efficient and competitive nation (Russell 1993: 156). Furthermore, Canada had lost its enthusiasm for top-down negotiations, and a democratic and participative process was called for. Alongside a Citizens' Forum, a parliamentary committee (the Beaudoin-Edwards Committee) considered the problem of constitutional amendment at federal level, while a separate consultation process went forward in Quebec. Other provincial bodies for considering constitutional matters ranged from an executive task force in Alberta and a legislative committee in Ontario and Prince Edward Island to a committee of citizens from outside the legislature in Saskatchewan and Nova Scotia. A parallel process was set up for consultation among the four streams of aboriginal peoples in Canada.

The Federal Government's proposals for constitutional reform in Shaping Canada's Future Together (1991) would have added a "Canada clause," containing a statement of national identity, to the Constitution, amended the Charter to recognize Quebec as a distinct society, guaranteed property rights and amended the notwithstanding clause so that a 60 per cent majority would be necessary to pass non-compatible legislation. These proposals were the subject of a series of conferences which culminated in the Beaudoin-Dobbie Report and became the basis of the Charlottetown Accord. It urged a stronger economic union between provinces, and a social charter, including a commitment to maintaining standards across the country in fields including comprehensive and universal health care, adequate social services, high quality education, the protection of collective bargaining rights, and the integrity of the environment. These social and economic rights were not expressed as court-enforceable rights, but because of the positive nature of the obligations involved, were stated as policy objectives, subject to a soft political model of enforcement using an intergovernmental agency to assess and report on performance to provincial and federal governments.

The Charlottetown Accord of 1992 which resulted from this process was thus the product of multilayered consultation and multilateral negotiations involving the provincial governments but also representatives of

Yukon, the North West Territories and the four main Native Canadian organizations. Quebec did not participate, but waited on the sidelines for the "best offer" from the rest of Canada before deciding whether to have a sovereignty referendum.

The Canada clause in the Charlottetown Accord was an interpretative section of "fundamental constitutional characteristics." The characteristics selected summarize the difficulties of reconciling individual and group rights in Canada; of envisioning the citizen as an equal holder of civil and political rights before the law, or as an individual in context, with equal rights to exercise his or her linguistic and cultural preferences (Russell 1993: 203). The characteristics were:

1. Parliamentary democracy and Canadian federalism;
2. Rights of Aboriginal peoples;
3. Quebec's distinct society;
4. Linguistic duality;
5. Racial and ethnic equality;
6. Respect for individual and collective human rights and freedoms of all people;
7. Equality of women and men;
8. The equality of provinces, while recognizing their diverse characteristics.

Despite some misgivings at the selection of some interest groups for special constitutional status, without mentioning others, however, the Canada clause is a testament to the extent to which engagement in a human rights discourse has broadened the constitution-making debate in Canada beyond its "two nations" core. The Charlottetown Accord was put to a national vote, and was defeated in a referendum on 26 October 1992. Inside Quebec, it was seen as giving insufficient weight to the Quebec vision of the state defined in terms of two founding nations; in the rest of Canada, it was seen as giving too much to Quebec at the expense of English-speaking Canada (Russell 1993: 229). The human rights focus which resulted in the Canadian Charter and which was so deeply ingrained in later negotiations did not provide a "quick fix" to the tensions causing constitutional disagreement in Canadian society. Furthermore, the range of rights included in the Charter may be seen to be largely limited to first generation (civic and political) and linguistic/cultural rights. Although international human rights norms may be seen as a unified and indivisible whole, individual societies prioritize those rights which are most relevant to the points of tension in their culture and circumstances.

However, the achievements of the Charter story may be seen as twofold. First, the Charter consultations were the first to include a broad base of non-parliamentary Canadians, and were the occasion for many more voices to enter the constitutional dialogue, expressing and under-

standing their claims in human rights terms. Second, despite the unfinished nature of Canadian constitution making, the courts have used
the Charter to develop a strongly rights and equality-based jurisprudence
which is seen in many cases by other jurisdictions as a model of the way
in which human rights may be ingrafted to national jurisprudence. Both
the process and the substance of the Charter, therefore have contributed
to the support it has gained from, and the affection with which it is seen
by, the majority of Canadians. The process of interacting with human
rights norms itself can modify the political life of the society and begin to
remake it in line with those norms.

Rebuilding a nation – South African experiences

Canada might be seen as an affluent nation with a mature democracy
stating in its Charter rights which were already fairly well protected in
law. Despite the controversies and difficulties which have meant that to
date Canada has been unable to develop an autochthonous constitution,
in world terms it could be argued that the institutions of the Canadian
state operate successfully to protect most of the rights of most of the
people for most of the time. Chan and Ghai (1994) characterize the
drafting of a Bill of Rights in such a society as akin to fine-tuning its
constitution for optimum performance. This chapter has argued that in
Canada it has gone a little beyond that, both broadening the groups who
participate in the constitutional conversation and helping to create (for at
least some Canadians) a focus for national identity. Chan and Ghai suggest that in a less affluent country, or one without a tradition of democracy, the role of a Bill of Rights must go beyond even this. It must create
a human rights consciousness, lay a basis of fair administration and accountability, strengthen the separation of powers, enhance the role of the
judiciary, and mobilize public opinion around themes of justice and fair-
ness. Furthermore, they make the trenchant point that progressive doctrines do not change the reality of poverty, and without widely available
(and often expensive) enforcement mechanisms, "universal rights" can
remain the prerogative of the wealthy and influential.

   The next jurisdiction under consideration faced many of these difficulties, although it was also heavily influenced by the Canadian experience (Cachalia et al. 1994). The development of the Fundamental Rights
chapter of the South African Constitution[7] is one of the most important
recent examples of how, and why, human rights might be incorporated
into national law. There is no need to reiterate the injustices and denial
of rights to whole communities perpetrated under the apartheid system in
South Africa under white minority rule. Even such basic first-generation
rights as that to participate in public life were denied to the vast majority

of the population. Transforming the country into a "rainbow nation" of equal citizens, educating them as to their rights, and creating a common sense of identity was an extensive and difficult task.

The Transitional Constitution

It is perhaps surprising that the incorporation of fundamental rights was one of the less controversial issues in the process of negotiating a new constitution. The language of rights could have become a site of contention when in 1983 the Botha government proposed to introduce a "Bill of Rights" which would declare both individual and "group" rights. This was a blatant attempt to dress apartheid in rights language and was not pursued after being roundly criticized by the South African Law Commission and dismissed by the National Party. At that stage too, in Dugard's view (1994) ANC thinking was less concerned with rights than with national liberation.

However, in the late 1980s he suggested that both principal players in South Africa began to explore the role human rights might play in the transition process. In 1985, the governing National Party enacted a declaration of rights for Namibia as part of its evolution to independence. In 1986, the government asked the South African Law Commission to investigate the role of courts in protecting group and individual rights and to consider the desirability of instituting a Bill of Rights. Its report, proposing the adoption of a Bill of Rights to protect individual civil and political rights, was published in 1989, the same year as the ANC's Constitutional Guidelines for a Democratic South Africa. Human rights were by this stage clearly part of the agenda of constitutional change.

After a series of stalled negotiations in the early 1990s, discussions about a transitional constitution were commenced by the the Negotiating Council of the Multi-Party Negotiating Process (MPNP) in Kempton Park in early 1993. Each political grouping had two representatives, one of whom, by prescription, had to be a woman. Given the difficulty of drafting a Bill of Rights, the Council appointed a number of committees to advise it, including the Technical Committee on Fundamental Rights during the Transition, which had five members, all with expertise in human rights.

Chapter Three of the Transitional Constitution is not a full Bill of Rights. One of the most important preliminary debates was whether the MPNP should attempt a full list of rights, or only those indispensable to the political process of transition. Du Plessis and Corder (1994) state that the majority of parties in the Negotiating Council, including the ANC and National Party, were minimalists, who saw the MPNP as an insufficiently representative and therefore not a legitimate political forum for taking such a significant decision. Pragmatically, Du Plessis and Corder suggest that the parties may have "hoped that the Technical Committee would come up with an acceptable political compromise disguised as 'objective' expert advice, and this is more or less what happened." (1994: 90). The transitional document by and large does not include second and third generation rights, but concentrates on those basic to the functioning of a democratic system of government. Those few second and third generation rights which are included have restricted protection, but the MPNP was the forum in which some of the major themes of debate about the constitution were developed. It was also the site of interesting cross-party alliances, notably between the female delegates. As a foundation for the further growth of the new style of government, Du Plessis and Corder suggest that the final list of rights was "from a jurisprudential point of view ... neither fatally anorectic nor satisfactorily comprehensive" (1994: 90).

A Bill of Rights for South Africa

The development of the Bill of Rights in the South African Constitution was an essentially political process, and is shot through with the same themes as the wider process of constitutional negotiation. The choice of fundamental rights can be seen to itself be the site of a struggle for political power, as well as of deep ideological differences. In the negotiations, Du Plessis (1994) differentiates between the ideological stance on human rights taken by the libertarian parties (essentially those representing the establishment) and that taken by the liberationist parties (largely those representing the previously disenfranchised majority). He suggests that both shared a "basic commitment to liberal-democratic values, but with a marked difference in emphasis" (1994: 92). In a country still characterized by an acute maldistribution of material means and opportunity, the ideology of the two groups tended to reflect the sections of society they represented and to be divided along have/have-not lines. The ensuing struggle for power can be seen in some of the particular rights which various parties espoused. The importance they assumed in negotiations can be seen as a measure of the power of the parties espousing them. While establishment parties were particularly concerned to include rights to economic activity, and to protect the employer in relation to labour rights, the ANC placed a heavy emphasis on social and economic rights.

While pragmatic desires to obtain or retain power are inevitably intermingled with ideology, Du Plessis and Corder (1994: 23–39) suggest that the tensions inherent in the MPNP go beyond pragmatic politics, into the realm of ideology. They identify three tensions in the negotiations. The first is the perennial tension between libertarianism and egalitarianism in human rights, which give pre-eminence to, respectively, individual autonomy and equality as the core value for a Bill of Rights. In the South African context, mainstream egalitarianism did not dispense with tried liberal values, but saw a Bill of Rights as having a role in achieving socio-economic equilibrium, giving effect to second and third generation rights.

Second, Du Plessis and Corder note the tension between both egalitarian (liberationist) and libertarian delegates to the MPNP and the traditional leaders who stressed the communitarian orientation of traditional African culture, and were sceptical of the need for an expression of individual rights in that culture. The tension was particularly apparent around the issues of gender equality and African customary law.

The third tension which Du Plessis and Corder identify is that between male and female negotiators. The "prescribed" inclusion of women in the process resulted in cross-party alliances on some issues, such as customary law and children's rights. The strengthening of the section 30[8] guarantee of children's rights may be seen as a direct achievement of the female delegates, but they were not acting on the basis of an express, coherent feminist "shopping list," and their other main contribution to the process was to take issue with the traditional leaders on the subject of customary law. The wider issues arising from this tension will therefore be dealt with alongside the second one.

Social and economic rights

Politically protected economic injustice has been so closely bound up in the history of South Africa that it is unsurprising that the South African negotiations moved quickly beyond the traditional scope of civic and political rights. There was strong interest, on both sides, in using a Bill of Rights to promote varying visions of social and economic justice. Dugard (1994: 133) stated that:

South Africa, as it seeks to draft a Bill of Rights in the 1990s has little choice in this matter. Social and economic rights must find their place in the constitutional compact, if it is to have any legitimacy. A Bill of Rights must address the legacy of 40 years of apartheid.

In sharp contrast to the largely negative obligations placed on the state by first generation rights,[9] second and third generation rights can place a positive obligation on the state, and can even arguably require action by private individuals. The distinction between old and new might be seen as the distinction between freedom from and freedom to, with second and third generation rights reflecting an acknowledgment of the state's responsibility to promote the welfare of its subjects (Du Plessis and Corder 1994: 24). Opponents of second and third generation rights argue that social and economic rights are so dependent on external factors, such as the availability of resources, that except in the richest countries they are little more than a "wish list," and are certainly not rights which are enforceable and justiciable in court. Supporters (Chan and Gai 1994) retort that a failure to safeguard and develop meaningful social and economic rights will render even the most basic civil and political rights illusory outside of affluent countries and sectors of the population. For many in the debate, this argument about the extent and unity of human rights goes beyond questions of enforceability, involving questions of deep political belief about the role of government and the market. It can easily be seen why the debate was so central to the South African constitution-making process.

The positions which would be taken up were articulated as early as 1989. The South African Law Commission, in its Report of that year espoused a fairly establishment position, stating that only free market principles would create a successfully functioning economic system, and arguing for the inclusion in any Bill of Rights of a right to engage in economic enterprise. The ANC in its 1989 Constitutional Guidelines for a Democratic South Africa declared that the state should ensure that the entire economy serves the interests and well-being of all sections of the population, and envisaged a strong centrally planned economy.

As Albie Sachs (in Dugard 1994: 131) points out, the historical situation also makes property rights particularly significant for South Africans. He said:

... any entrenchment of property rights has to take account of the fact that a reality has been constructed in terms of which 85 per cent of the land and probably 95 per cent of productive capacity is in the hands of the white minority. What is required is a constitutional duty to rectify these percentages, not one to preserve them.

While social and economic rights are an accepted part of international law, many nations fight shy of incorporating them in national law as rights, not only because they impose positive obligations on the state, and are dependent on the availability of resources, but also because traditional Western legal thinking perceives disputes around social and economic rights as unsuitable for judicial decision making, resource allocation being far outside the normal function of the judiciary. For example, in the Charlottetown Accord in Canada, the social and economic rights are treated as entrenched policy objectives, to be enforced by a system of reporting and monitoring, rather than as individual rights enforceable in court. However, social and economic rights are not necessarily uniformly hard to enforce in traditional legal fora. Furthermore, the role of the court in determining resource-based issues in areas such as health or education is already seen, to some extent, in the control of administrative action exercised, for example, in the judicial review jurisdiction in the common law world. In addition, the existence of highly developed economic indicators in many fields allows courts at least to test the reasonableness of public authority decision making on resource allocation issues.

Concerns at justiciability and enforcement were behind the South African Law Commission's proposal that only those second generation rights which could be protected in the same negative way as first generation rights be included in a Bill of Rights. However, Etienne Mureinik (quoted in Dugard 1994: 135) argues that courts do have potentially wider review powers in relation to social and economic rights, in that they can review government action which is lacking in sincerity and rationality. Further, there is an emerging consensus that these rights should be in a Bill of Rights. And importantly, a written constitution must correspond to the way the nation is truly constituted – otherwise the protection of rights is nothing more than words on paper.

Group rights and customary law

The second of Du Plessis and Corder's tensions is that between customary law and individual rights. This comprises two issues. The first is the apparent conflict between group rights and individual rights, the second is whether the whole idea of individual rights is a Western construct, which it is imperialist to impose on other cultures.

Perhaps the two most significant are the right of peoples to self-determination[10] and the rights of minority groups. Although some group rights are classified as third generation rights, others, because of their relatively long historical pedigree may be seen to go back to a period before the development of modern human rights thinking. For example, balancing the linguistic and representational rights of English and French-speaking Canadians was one of the main features of the British North America Act of 1867, which also dealt with group rights of "Indians" and Métis. The treaties forming the new states of Eastern Europe after World War I also contained quite extensive provision for protection of minorities in certain limited spheres. In the modern age, the cultural and linguistic rights of minorities and aboriginal peoples are a recognized feature of international human rights law.[11]

Collective rights could be seen as challenging the equality basis of much of human rights law, being predicated not on a right to sameness of treatment or status, but on claims for recognition and protection of a group's differences – its "distinct group survival" – especially where the group is under threat. Kallen considers the link between individual and group (collective) rights and sees the two sides as part of a unitary whole, because:

... fundamental human rights derive from the distinctive attributes shared by all members of humankind as a single species. Individual human rights represent the principle of biological unity, the oneness of all human beings as members of the same biological species. Collective human rights represent the principle of cultural diversity, the differentness of the unique ethnocultures developed by the various ethnic groups which, collectively, comprise the human species. Together, individual and collective human rights represent the twin global principles of human unity and cultural diversity. (1995: 7)

The concerns of African traditional leaders in the MPNP that their group rights should be preserved were focused around African customary law. They argued that it, along with their authority, should be preserved intact, despite the fact that certain aspects of the law, especially relating to women, would not pass the equality test in section 8 of the Interim Constitution. The problem of traditional law pitted a cross-party coalition of women delegates against the traditional leaders. Ultimately the compromise which was determined was the inclusion of a right "to participate in the cultural life of one's choice" (Interim Constitution section 31), while not exempting customary law from the equality provisions of the constitution. This pragmatic compromise seems far from Kallen's vision of the unity of group and individual rights and possibly reflects the differing negotiating power of the various participants.

The question which is raised is whether a legal system should permit cultural violations of allegedly universal human rights. Bennett (1994: 2) suggests that African governments have been ambiguous about human rights, and comments that:

... they had every reason to be on their guard, for the human rights movement has become western imperialism in a new guise, a criterion used to determine diplomatic and economic relations with developing nations.

He contrasts the functions of customary and Western systems of law, in particular in the absence of fixed rules and emphasis on tradition in customary law, as compared to the "constant momentum of purposeful change" (1995: 3) of the latter. He suggests that customary law conceives of the individual in community, and might rather be seen to support his or her human dignity than "human rights."

The problems which arise when human rights thinking is challenged as a foreign, Western way of perceiving the world, are not confined to Africa. In an Asian context, Gong Xiang Rui (1993) describes the Chinese view:

In China, it is the state that comes first, the collective second, and the individual the last. If any conflict should occur, the collective benefit (such as that of the family, the school and the union) should be sacrificed for the state's interest, similarly, the individual's personal interest should give way to the interest of the collectives and the state ... On the other hand, the Western theorists adopt an opposite idea: individual – collective – state. (1993: 492–493)

Xiang, like Little and Reed (1989), suggests that the subordination of the individual in Chinese legal thought is not a modern innovation, but has roots deep within the Confucian vision of society and the individual's role within it.

The South African negotiations illustrate that an off-the-peg adoption of international standards of universal human rights is not a realistic way of solving the specific problems of specific societies. As politicians and citizens discuss and negotiate the human rights to be included in their constitution, they inevitably prioritize them, selecting those which seem most relevant to their situation. However, this process is a necessary one, especially in a young democracy, because it is the very process of encountering and discussing the rights which allows human rights thinking to take root in national political life.

Agreeing the final constitution

It will already be evident that the final South African Constitution of 1996 was the product of much thought and argument. There was no significant debate on the constitutionalization of participatory political rights, citizens' rights, language and cultural rights, or on the extensive list of due process rights, indicating a broadly based commitment to a core of liberal and democratic values. Contentious issues at the stage of the Kempton Park negotiations were dealt with by a six-person Ad Hoc Committee, mainly consisting of members of parties in the Negotiating Council who expressed strong views on the various issues. After the transitional constitution came into being, the Constitutional Assembly continued the process of negotiation. However, as in Canada, it was recognized that the legitimacy of the constitution depended on the participation of citizens far beyond the political "professionals" in the constitution-making process. The Preamble to the final document states that:

... the process of drafting this text involved many South Africans in the largest public participation programme ever carried out in South Africa. After nearly two years of intensive consultations, political parties represented in the Constitutional Assembly negotiated the formulations contained in this text, which are an integration of ideas from ordinary citizens, civil society and political parties represented in and outside the Constitutional Assembly.... The text therefore represents the collective wisdom of the South African people and has been arrived at by general agreement.

Once the Constitutional Assembly had been elected, and had begun negotiations, a process of wide public participation commenced, by way of public meetings, sectoral hearings, workshops, a telephone hotline and an internet site. Two million submissions were received, which are maintained on an internet database.[12] The public consultation programme documents, like the constitution itself, are drafted in very clear plain English; a newsletter kept citizens informed of the progress of controversies, and of the main arguments on both sides, in measured and neutral language. The thought put into the wide range of consultation media, and the sheer volume of responses received, are clear indicators of the extent to which the making of the South African Constitution was a national "conversation" about how South Africans were to govern themselves. In the case of South Africa, perhaps even more than in Canada, this conversation was not just about the mechanisms of government, but about what it meant to be South African. Human rights norms provide a language in which those values to which a country aspires can be set out and debated, as well as a framework for negotiating and accommodating difference. To this extent, a Bill of Rights is important not only for its substantive protections, but for its myth-making potential. One function of a constitution is as a statement of how a country imagines itself, and the widest possible participation in that process is to be welcomed.

National and international law

The history of how the Canadian Charter and the Fundamental Rights chapter of the South African Constitution came into national law is inevitably a political one, and the documentation inevitably focuses on the role of national players, especially the politicians whose negotiations were the public story of the incorporation of human rights standards in national law. However, such a version of the story inevitably gives a false picture, and fails to explain why the national politicians in each case arrived at something so closely resembling international human rights standards. In both cases, the domestic politicians were bargaining in full knowledge of the international standards. However, the "official" version of the story does not indicate the extent to which the international community, international academic experts and human rights NGOs provided information, advice, and assistance at all stages of the process. On one level, politicians incorporate human rights which are relevant to problems in their country, and may argue strongly for rights which protect the section of society which they represent. While they are influenced by pragmatic considerations, they are also influenced by their knowledge of the available international standards, and by the sophisticated jurisprudence of international courts. The awareness that other countries and international organizations are watching them is a further encouragement to frame debate within accepted international parameters. They will be influenced also by the shape and success of other nations' earlier attempts at incorporation – Canadian human rights expertise has been acknowledged in both South Africa and Northern Ireland. While watching a nation engaged in incorporating human rights, especially in the context of constitutional reform, one focus of attention is perhaps the extent to which the process is democratic at a national level – the extent of popular consultation and influence. However, the less obvious element of the picture is the variety of, often hidden, international influences on the process, and it is important to bear this in mind.

The rights incorporated

Having discussed how the Canadian and South African Bills of Rights came into being, the next question is which substantive rights they contain. Each document is compared, in the Appendix table, with the range of rights set forth in the ICCPR, the ICESCR and one of the other most significant regional treaties, the ECHR.

The Canadian Charter

In relation to the Canadian Charter, it can be seen that social and economic rights are not guaranteed. The fundamental freedoms (s. 2), democratic rights (ss. 3–5), mobility rights (s. 6) and legal rights (ss. 7–14) set out in the Charter are squarely civil and political. Existing aboriginal rights are guaranteed by s. 35, and English and French are recognized and protected as the two official languages of Canada. Rights of the local linguistic minority (English or French) to be educated in their own language (s. 23) are protected, and it is stated that the Charter does not abrogate from any privileges enjoyed by languages other than English and

French (s. 22). Culture is therefore largely addressed through the, for Canadians, contentious issue of language. The provisions illustrate that the defining constitutional disagreements in Canada centred around this very issue, and that a fine line had to be trodden between Trudeau's vision of a multicultural Canada and the desire of French-speaking Canadians for special recognition by the English-speaking majority. The way in which linguistic and cultural rights are dealt with in the Charter illustrate that even among democrats human rights are not necessarily neutral and "above the fray." They do not provide a panacea, but can assume massive sectional political significance which requires careful negotiation and compromise.

Perhaps one of the best known aspects of the Charter outside of Canada, and that which gives it its distinctive flavour, is its provisions relating to equality. Section 15 provides that:

Every individual is equal before and under the law and has the right to the equal protection and equal benefit of the law without discrimination and, in particular, without discrimination based on race, national or ethnic origin, colour, religion, sex, age or mental or physical disability.

Affirmative action is permitted by s. 15(2). Further clarification occurs in s. 25, which preserves existing aboriginal rights, s. 27, which requires the Charter to be interpreted "in a manner consistent with the preservation and enhancement of the multicultural heritage of Canadians," and s. 28, the only absolute guarantee in the Charter, which provides that "Notwithstanding anything in this Charter, the rights and freedoms referred to in it are guaranteed equally to male and female persons."

It has been argued that the broad guarantee of equality rights, and the absence of property rights ensure that the Charter cannot be used in socially or economically regressive ways, but Petter (1986) sees the Charter as an essentially libertarian document, limiting the ways in which government can interfere in the individual's life. He suggests that many of the rights are amorphous unless and until they are infused with political content, in particular the section 15 equality right, which does not give a guarantee of social equality, but merely inhibits government from bringing about or perpetuating inequality.

However, it must be said that the courts have not adopted the restrictive style of interpretation which so inhibited the earlier Canadian Bill of Rights. For example, in the recent case of *Vriend* v. *Alberta*,[13] the Supreme Court was prepared to read a prohibition of discrimination on the grounds of sexual orientation into the Alberta Individual's Rights Protection Act.[14]

For many in Canada, the Charter has had the effect which Trudeau envisaged. Wilcox (1993) suggests that Canadians have adopted the Charter as an important statement of what it means to be Canadian, and envision Canada as a nation of multicultural individual rights bearers, equal before the law. Russell, however, argues that (1993: 147) this vision of identity is limited to a centrist, English-speaking Canadian audience, and that, for example, many Quebecois would understand their identity in terms of the rights of the Quebecois people to express their group identity by means of language and self-determination. While there is not disagreement as to whether or not human rights are a good thing, individual and group rights have been sucked into the discourse of division in Canadian society. Despite this, as discussed earlier, both the process of Charter incorporation significantly extended the list of protagonists in the Canadian democratic process, and the courts' interpretations of the Charter rights have profoundly influenced Canadian jurisprudence. Although human rights have not proved a panacea for Canada's specific ills, human rights thinking may be seen to be entering the nation's bloodstream by a process of osmosis.

The South African Constitutional Bill of Rights

Chapter Two of the South African Constitution of 1996 begins with a statement of principle that the Bill of Rights is a cornerstone of South African democracy, enshrining rights and affirming the democratic values of human dignity, equality and freedom (s. 7). The state is obliged to respect, promote and fulfil the rights, and all organs of state are bound by the Bill, as are natural and juristic persons in some circumstances (s. 8). The Bill then sets out the principles of equality and non-discrimination (s. 9), and of human dignity (s. 10), before stating the main first generation rights; life (s. 11), freedom and security of the person (s. 12), a prohibition on slavery (s. 13), right to privacy (s. 14), freedom of religion and opinion (s. 15), freedom of expression, assembly (etc.), and association (ss. 16–18), political and citizenship rights (ss. 19–20), and mobility rights (s. 21). The Bill of Rights then deals with labour relations (ss. 22–23), environment (s. 24) and property (s. 25), before declaring the rights to adequate housing, health care, food, water, social security, and education (ss. 26–27, 29). The special rights of children are set out in some detail (s. 28), and the linguistic, cultural, and religious rights of individuals and groups are expressed (ss. 30, 31). Access to information and just administrative action (ss. 32, 33) are set out, before a detailed outline of the right of access to a court, and rights of arrested, detained and accused persons (ss. 34, 35). There is a general limitation clause (s. 36) and provisions for the creation of a State of Emergency (s. 37).

The equality provision (s. 9) was in itself uncontroversial in relation to equality before and equal protection of the law, and the list of general and specific grounds for non-discrimination. The bone of contention at the Kempton Park negotiations was the prospect of affirmative action. Libertarians wanted such actions to be subject to a test of reasonableness, but the Negotiating Council decided that reasonableness was inherent in the requirement that affirmative action measures be "designed" to protect or advance persons. The requirement of design indicated a need for a rational scheme which would have to advance a particular purpose. The fact that the rights impose duties on individuals in certain circumstances (s. 8) is intended in particular to put an end to private discrimination, and this horizontal enforceability of the Bill of Rights is an important example of this way of extending human rights protection outside the realm of state action.

Of the debates and controversies surrounding various clauses of the Bill of Rights, perhaps the most interesting for this project are those around the labour rights and social and economic rights which have already been touched on. The "right freely to engage in economic activity" which was the subject of debate in the MPNP has disappeared from the final draft, and is replaced by the right of individuals to "choose their trade, occupation or profession freely" (s. 22). Likewise, the drafting of s. 27, the right to collective bargaining and to join a union still reflects a history of controversy. At the time of the transitional constitution, there were worries from unions that the right to freedom of association would have an adverse effect on closed-shop agreements, and a threat from Congress of South African Trade Unions (COSATU) at a late stage to strike if a proposal to entrench the employer's right to lock out workers was carried through.

As already indicated, the property clause gave rise to particular difficulties, as it had to both give some element of reassurance to property owners, and to provide justice to those previously dispossessed of land. At the transitional stage, the parties soon reached agreement that the right to acquire, hold, and dispose of rights in property should be entrenched, and that the constitution should also allow for expropriation by the state in return for proper compensation. This is the basis of s. 25 of the final constitution, which also includes a strategy for restitution of rights in land to persons who have been dispossessed as a result of racially discriminatory policies. Safeguards are included in the form of a requirement that property be expropriated only by law and by the statement of a list of factors for just and equitable compensation on expropriation.

The rights to housing, health care, food, water and social security are subject to a limitation, namely that the state "must take reasonable legislative and other measures, within its available resources, to achieve the progressive realisation of the right." Children's rights are not subject to any specific limitation, but nor is there a specific requirement that the government take steps to protect them. Kader Asmal expressed the dilemma well in the Constitutional Assembly, saying:

Our people did not give their lives in exchange for the mere freedom to walk the streets relatively unharassed, nor to suffer continued deprivation while the architects of the old rules lived in splendour ... we have won the debate on whether economic and social rights should or should not be included in the Constitution ... what we need to do is work out how far the new and relevant rights should go ... is it practical or ethical that a child's right to nutrition should be secured while the mother and father starve?

The process of accommodation between communities in South Africa was carried out in the light of international human rights standards. The tensions which arose pinpoint with accuracy the sites of injustice and disagreement between communities, and the course of negotiation by which the constitution was reached illustrate clearly the way in which a society selects and modifies international human rights norms in the light of its own circumstances. The process might be seen as the personalization of human rights standards. The inequalities in South African society include much economic injustice. Thus, the constitution makers had to squarely face the question of whether civic and political rights are purely illusory unless backed up by social and economic rights. The issue of property rights also required the constitution makers to consider the extent to which human rights can regulate distributive justice. But despite the compromise and negotiation which characterized the creation of the South African Constitution's chapter on Fundamental Rights, the process of its development, as well as the substance of the wide statement of rights which it guarantees, illustrates the extent to which the "rainbow nation" of the new South Africa defines itself in international human rights terms, and the deep level at which the national constitutional debate and institutions have been infused with human rights thinking.

Bringing rights home?

Of course incorporation without more is insufficient to make guarantees of human rights real to citizens. Effective enforcement of human rights is a huge subject, and detailed consideration would go far beyond the scope of this chapter. For present purposes, what is more important than the fine detail is Hill's statement that:

... declarations and statutes proclaiming human dignity and human rights are not enough. There must also be (1) effective enforcement; (2) public education; and (3) strong administration, if people are to be accorded equal opportunity in fact as well as in theory. (1969: 401)

Enforcement does occur at the international level; through courts such as the Inter-American Court of Human Rights, or the European Court of Human Rights, through the requirement in certain treaties to file reports to bodies such as the UN Human Rights Committee, and through the channels of international diplomacy. However, this enforcement is at best slow, and at worst does little to practically improve the human rights of the affected individual. To make human rights real to the majority of people in a nation, adequate enforcement mechanisms at national level are perhaps more important than the list of rights protected on paper. In their 1994 paper, Chan and Ghai doubt whether a Bill of Rights document will protect the rights of any but the affluent who can resort to privately funded litigation, without creative and imaginative enforcement and education measures (see also Asante 1969). Three aspects are particularly worthy of note.

Strong court-based enforcement of human rights

The Canadian example illustrates how a Bill of Rights can become a strong part of national identity, and how, even in a mature democracy, provisions such as the equality clauses can reshape jurisprudence in a number of areas. Even where problems relating to group rights have remained unsolved, the Supreme Court's strong enforcement and intepretation of the Canadian Charter has created a distinctive jurisprudence, particularly around equality issues, which has been instrumental in the way in which Canadians identify with "their" Charter. In the South African context, given the history of exclusion and systematic denial of rights, the symbolic significance of the constitution and of a diverse Constitutional Court interpreting it cannot be underestimated. The constitution is a focal point for defining the new South Africa and the inclusion of social and economic rights in it provides a concrete task for the Constitutional Court in relation to the real inequalities which remain in the society.

A human rights commission

Human rights commissions are an increasing feature of national human rights protection, and are recommended both by the UN "Paris Principles"[15] and by the Council of Europe.[16] The Paris Principles are the yardstick by which such bodies are measured, and they suggest that a national human rights institution's mandate, composition, and role should be established by the state's constitution or by statute. Its mandate should be "as broad as possible and its responsibilities include the right, acting on its own initiative or by request to submit opinions, proposals, reports, and recommendations to Parliament, government, and other competent authorities on any human rights issue, including any violation of human rights, and to publicise its opinion" (Spencer and Bynoe 1998: 46).

Canada has Human Rights Commissions,[17] at federal and provincial levels. Their mandate is generally limited to advice on areas such as public sector employment. Although they may have some influence on good administrative practices and raising public awareness of human rights, their role is limited when analysed in terms of the Paris Principles. By contrast, South Africa's new human rights institutions conform closely to the international standards. In addition to a Human Rights Commission, South Africa has a Commission for Gender Equality, as well as a Commission on the Restitution of Land Rights. Bringing us back to Hill's formulation, above, the South African Human Rights Commission[18] meets the second and third criteria. It monitors public administration and encourages the development of a human rights culture in the public sector, while supporting and educating the public as to their rights. This enforcement mechanism is a specific means to further the conversation about rights that was ignited by the consultation preceding the enactment of the constitution itself. It is thus thoroughly consistent with the broader project of constitutionalizing human rights through grassroots connections in the new South Africa.

Rights and the constitutional conversation

At the beginning of this chapter, incorporation of an entrenched Bill of Rights was identified as only one of several ways in which human rights could be implemented in a society, albeit perhaps the strongest mechanism for so doing. The focus on incorporation in two countries, South Africa and Canada, illustrated the processes by which the national context causes those drafting the bill to select and modify those international norms which will be included, and by which the international norms in their turn can profoundly affect national law and even the processes of political democracy. The form and content of a Bill of Rights must reflect the political and social climate of the nation for which it is written. While part of the appeal of human rights is their universality, and the promise which they hold out of government under law, there can be fundamental differences of opinion as to what values human rights are protecting, particularly as to whether primacy should be given to liberty or equality, and the views about human rights of competing communities in relation to sites of conflict within a society may also vary dramatically. While incorporation of social and economic rights as rights was vital to the legitimacy of the South African Constitution, the sites of debate in Canada were around cultural identity (which was also an important issue in South Africa), and social justice was less hotly contested. Human rights do not provide a panacea for national difficulties, and the international norms cannot be crudely transplanted into national law on a "one size fits all" basis. It is not fatal to the project of incorporation that a nation should prioritize those rights which seem most relevant to its situation.

The versions of human rights which may reach national law are not, therefore, infinitely mutable, nor is it hopeless to expect the international norms to be incorporated in a recognizable form. The national debate in both Canada and South Africa was fully informed by knowledge of the international instruments, of the jurisprudence of the international enforcement mechanisms, and of the way in which other jurisdictions had incorporated or interpreted the international norms. Furthermore, even though the substantive rights incorporated may be limited, as in Canada, the way in which courts and public authorities react to them can strengthen the human rights consciousness in a society, so that further steps toward broadening the range of rights acknowledged become easier, and a culture of rights develops.

In a post-modern age, particularly in a divided society made up of individuals and groups with sharply different, and even competing interests and needs, a Bill of Rights provides a further important function. Human rights offer a set of ground rules for society; Dworkin's antidote to the utilitarian demands of majoritarianism (Dworkin 1977). Even though it may be an imperfect compromise, the document's significance is that it is agreed. The nation-building power of a widely agreed Bill of Rights was acknowledged both in South Africa and in Canada, and will be tested in other jurisdictions in transition such as Northern Ireland.

While it may be argued that this function is myth-making, it is important not to underestimate the power of myth, nor the importance, particularly in a divided society, of creating a set of values with which as many communities and interest groups as possible can identify. Human rights can shape the process of agreement itself, and can provide a language and a framework which facilitate the constitutional conversation between groups with widely divergent interests and views. Particularly in a society in transition, the sophisticated framework and tools of analysis provided by international human rights norms and jurisprudence provide a syntax from beyond each side's partisan perspective, which can allow the parties to imagine new ways of relating. It may not be overstating the case to say that it is a function of human rights discourse to allow the parties, in the words of the Northern Irish poet, Seamus Heaney ("Voices from Lemnos" 1998: 330), to:

"... hope for a great sea-change
On the far side of revenge.
Believe that a farther shore
Is reachable from here.
Believe in miracles
And cures, and healing wells."

Appendix: Comparative table of rights

Right	ICCPR	ICESCR	ECHR	Canada	South Africa
Equality/non-discrimination	Art. 2	Art. 2.2 (non-discrimination), Art. 3, gender	Art. 14	ss. 15, 27, 28	s. 1, s. 9
Right to life	Art. 6	–	Art. 2	s. 7	s. 11
No torture etc.	Art. 7	–	Art. 3	s. 12	s. 12
No slavery/servitude	Art. 8	–	Art. 4		s. 13
Liberty/security of person	Art. 9	–	Art. 5	s. 7	s. 12 + bodily integrity
Rights of prisoners etc	Art. 10	–	Arts. 5, 6	ss. 9, 10, 11	s. 35
No imprisonment for breach of contract	Art. 11	–	Prot. 4(1)	–	–
Liberty of movement	Art. 12	–	Prot. 4(2)	s. 6	s. 21
Restriction on expulsion	Art. 13	–	Prot. 4(4)	s. 6	s. 20
Equality before courts, fair and public hearing	Art. 14	–	Arts. 5, 6	ss. 13, 14 (wider due process), s. 15	Right to just administration, s. 33; access to courts, s. 34
Rights in criminal process	Art. 14	–	Arts. 5, 6	ss. 10, 11	s. 35

Appendix: Comparative table of rights (cont.)

Right	ICCPR	ICESCR	ECHR	Canada	South Africa
No retrospective criminal offences	Art. 15	–	Art. 7	–	–
Recognition as person by law	Art. 16	–	–	–	–
Protection of privacy, family, home, correspondence, honour and reputation	Art. 17	–	Arts. 8, 10(2)	s. 8	s. 14
Freedom of thought, conscience and religion	Art. 18	–	Art. 9	s. 2	s. 15
Freedom of opinion and expression	Art. 19	–	Art. 10	s. 2	s. 16; access to information, s. 32
Right of peaceful assembly	Art. 21	–	Art. 11	s. 2	s. 17
Freedom of association	Art. 22	–	Art. 11	s. 2	s. 18
Rights in marriage and family	Art. 23	Art. 10, protection for families, etc.	Art. 12, Prot. 7(5)	–	–
Rights of children	Art. 24	Art. 10, special protection	–	–	s. 28
Right to participate in public life	Art. 25	–	Prot. 1(3)	s. 3	Equal citizenship, s. 3; political participation; s. 19; deprivation of citizenship, s. 20
Equality before and equal protection of law	Art. 26	–	Art. 6(1) (implicit)	s. 15	s. 9

Appendix: Comparative table of rights (cont.)

Right	ICCPR	ICESCR	ECHR	Canada	South Africa
Rights of minorities	Art. 27	Art. 1, self determination		Linguistic rights, ss. 16–22, ss. 25, 27	s. 6 (langs), language and culture of choice; ss. 30, 31, (group rights)
Right to education	–	Arts. 13, 14	Prot. 1(2) (not to be denied)	s. 23 (language)	s. 29
Right to property	–	–	Prot. 1(1)	–	s. 25
Right to work/ just conditions of work	–	Arts. 6, 7	–	–	Freedom of trade, occupation and profession, s. 22
Right to form, join etc. trade union	–	Art. 8	–	–	s. 23
Right to social security		Art. 9	–	–	s. 27
Right to health	–	Art. 12	–	–	Access to health care, s. 27
Right to participate in cultural life	–	Art. 15	–	–	s. 30
Miscellaneous	–	–	–	–	Respect for dignity, s. 10; environment not harmful to health, s. 24.

Notes

1. I am indebted to all those whose discussion has contributed to this chapter. I would like to thank the other members of the Working Group and those who attended the meeting at Princeton in October 1999. I would especially like to thank Professor Fionnuala Ni Aolain of the University of Ulster for her thoughtful and detailed comments and her help in bringing the project to fruition.

2. For example, the Convention on the Elimination of All Forms of Discrimination Against Women, the Convention on the Rights of the Child, as well as the International Covenant on Civil and Political Rights and the International Covenant on Economic, Social and Cultural Rights.

3. This section draws heavily on the excellent historical chronology and political analysis provided by Peter Russell, in *Constitutional Odyssey – Can Canadians become a Sovereign People?* Toronto, University of Toronto Press, 1993.

4. Schedule 1 of the Canada Act 1982, an Act of the United Kingdom Parliament.

5. Despite decisions such as *R* v. *Drybones* [1970] SCR 282, 9 DLR, 3D, 473, the courts' narrow interpretation of the rights may be seen in cases such as *Canada* v. *Lavell* [1974] SCR 1349, 38 DLR, 3D, 481, and *Bliss* v. *Attorney General Canada* [1979] 1 SCR 183, 93 DLR, 3d, 417.

6. Charter sections 15, 25, 27 and 28.

7. A copy of the constitution can be found at www.polity.org.za/bills/consnew.html.

8. Section 30 of the Interim Constitution became s. 28 of the Final Constitution.

9. Although recent developments suggest a trend towards implying some positive element into certain first generation rights. For example, in *A* v. *United Kingdom*, ECHR 100/1997/884/1096, 23 September 1998 and *Osman* v. *United Kingdom*, ECHR 87/1997/871/1083, 28 October 1998, the European Court of Human Rights recently moved towards a possible finding that the UK was in breach of its obligations to protect the rights to life and freedom from torture of individuals within its jurisdiction, ECHR Arts. 2, 3, when state agents failed to intervene effectively to protect their lives from threats posed by other private individuals. In *A*, the applicant was a boy who had been subjected to severe beatings with a cane by his stepfather. In *Osman*, the applicant was a boy whose father and friend were killed, and himself seriously injured by a schoolteacher who became dangerously fixated on him and engaged in an ultimately murderous stalking campaign.

10. Common Article 1(1) of the International Covenant on Civil and Political Rights, hereafter ICCPR, and the International Covenant on Economic Social and Cultural Rights, hereafter ICESCR, in 1966.

11. Particularly following the 1992 UN Declaration on the Rights of Persons Belonging to National or Ethnic, Religious and Linguistic Minorities, UN General Assembly Resolution 47/135 of 18 December 1992.

12. www.constitution.org.za/.

13. Judgment of Supreme Court of Canada, 87/997/871/1083, 2 April 1998; see Childs, 1998.

14. Revised Statutes of Alberta 1980, c. 1–2. The Act has since been renamed the Human Rights, Citizenship and Multiculturalism Act.

15. General Assembly Resolution 48/134 of 20 December 1993.

16. Recommendation No. R97, 14 of the Committee of Ministers to Member States on the Establishment of Independent National Human Rights Institutions.

17. The Canadian Human Rights Commission website is at www.chrc.ca.

18. The South African Human Rights Commission website is at www.sahrc.org.za.

REFERENCES

Asante, S. K. B., "Nation Building and Human Rights in Emergent African Nations," 2 *Cornell Int Law J* 2, 1969, p. 72.

Bennett, T. W., *Human Rights and African Customary Law under the South African Constitution*. Kenwyn, Juta and Co. Ltd, 1995.

Cachalia, Azhar et al., *Fundamental Rights in the New Constitution*, University of Witwatersrand Centre for Applied Legal Studies/Juta and Co. Ltd, 1994.

Chan, Johannes, and Yash Gai (eds.), *The Hong Kong Bill of Rights: A Comparative Approach*, Hong Kong, Butterworths, 1998.

Childs, Mary, "Constitutional Review and Underinclusive Legislation," [1998] *Public Law* 647.

De Jong, Katherine, "Sexual Equality: Interpreting Section 28," in Bayefsky and Eberts, eds., *Equality Rights and the Canadian Charter of Rights and Freedoms*, Toronto, Carswell, pp. 493–528.

Dugard, John, "Human Rights and the Rule of Law in Postapartheid South Africa," in Robert Licht and Bertus de Villiers, eds., *South Africa's Crisis of Constitutional Democracy – Can the US Constitution Help?* Washington, AEI Press, 1994.

Du Plessis, Lourens, "A Background to Drafting the Chapter on Fundamental Rights," in Bertus de Villiers, ed., *Birth of A Constitution*, Kenwyn, Juta and Co. 1994, pp. 89–100.

Du Plessis, Lourens and Hugh Corder, *Understanding South Africa's Transitional Bill of Rights*, Kenwyn, Juta and Co. Ltd, 1994.

Dworkin, Ronald, *Taking Rights Seriously*, London, Duckworth, 1977.

Gong Xiang Rui, "Constitutional Protection of Human Rights: The Chinese View under the Notion of 'One Country, Two Systems'," in Johannes Chan and Yash Gai (eds), *The Hong Kong Bill of Rights: A Comparative Approach*, Hong Kong, Butterworths, 1993.

Heaney, Seamus, *Opened Ground – Poems 1966–1996*, London, Faber and Faber, 1998.

Henkin, Louis, *The Age of Rights*, New York, Columbia University Press, 1990.

Henkin, Louis and Rosenthal, Albert, *Constitutionalism and Rights: The Influence of the United States Constitution Abroad*, New York, Columbia University Press, 1990.

Honderich, T. (ed.), *The Oxford Companion to Philosophy*, Oxford, Oxford University Press, 1995.

Kallen, Evelyn, *Ethnicity and Human Rights in Canada*, 2nd edn, Toronto, Oxford University Press, 1995.

Little, R. and Reed, W., *The Confucian Renaissance*, Sydney, Federation Press, 1989.

Macklem, P. et al., *Canadian Constitutional Law (Vol II)*, Toronto, Emond Montgomery Publications Ltd, n.d.

Pepin-Robarts Task Force on Canadian Unity, *Coming to Terms: The Words of the Debate*, Ottawa, Supply and Services Canada, 1979.

Petter, Andrew, "The Politics of the Charter," 8 *SCL Rev* 8, 1986, p. 473.

Russell, P., *Constitutional Odyssey – Can Canadians become a Sovereign People?* Toronto, University of Toronto Press, 1993.

Spencer, Sarah and Bynoe, Ian, *A Human Rights Commission – the Options for Britain and Ireland*, London, Institute for Public Policy Research, 1998.

Wilcox, Murray, *An Australian Charter of Rights?* North Ryde, NSW, The Law Book Company Ltd., 1993.

Part 2

The practice of human rights at the regional level

3

Comparative practice on human rights: North-South

James Mouangue Kobila

This chapter focuses on the comparison between human rights practices in developed countries with a liberal tradition (North America and Western Europe) and those of southern countries (Latin America, Africa, South Asia and the Pacific). The special relevance of this comparison amounts to the fact that it is made half a century after the adoption of the Universal Declaration of Human Rights (UDHR) on 10 December 1948, and some ten years after the chain reactions and extensive social changes brought about by the wave of democratization which broke on to the southern region in the early 1990s, following the collapse of communism.

The chapter will mainly focus on the following pilot rights: the right to equality, the right to education and health, the right to political participation, freedom of expression, and freedom of press. These rights will be considered according to two major axes: first, the comparison of human rights practices in the North and the South and second, their evolution. The chapter will conclude with putting forward concrete suggestions designed to enhance the universalization of human rights practices, especially in the South.

Basic differences of human rights practices in the North and South

There are striking differences in human rights practices in the North and South, independently of the existence of regional mechanisms for the protection of human rights. This is what we intend to examine in this section. We will try to do so by looking into two layers of human rights practices. First, we will touch upon the variety of practices displayed by human rights institutions on both sides of the North-South divide. Second, we will identify the differences of human rights practices in the North and South when regional human rights institutions are hardly at work.

Heterogeneity of practices by similar institutions in the North and South

The regional level is generally regarded as the determinant realm for the appreciation of human rights practices and the implementation of international instruments on human rights.[1] In this context, regional commissions for human rights are a convenient entry point to assess human rights practices in the North and South. We will then use regional jurisdictions on human rights to further the comparison between North and South.

Regional commissions for human rights

Regional commissions, as understood in this chapter, operate in three regions: in Europe, the Americas and Africa. Since human rights commissions constitute the first or only stage for the plaintiff or victim of a human rights violation, as well as the inevitable passage of bringing a case before other regional institutions, they make up the cornerstone of regional systems for the protection of human rights. The comparison of regional human rights commissions in the North and South leads one to focus on the conditions in which they were established and how they functioned. We will see that, in spite a number of similarities, differences dominate both when it comes to the establishment and the functioning of regional commissions for human rights.

The establishment of regional commissions for human rights – The European Commission for Human Rights was created through Article 25 of the European Convention on Human Rights (4 November 1950) and adopted within the European Council. Similarly, the African Commission for Human and Peoples' Rights was instituted by the African Charter for Human and Peoples' Rights in June 1981.[2] By contrast, the Inter-American system does not follow the "European" model as regards the establishment of the Human Rights Commission. The Inter-American Commission has indeed not originally been based on an international instrument for the protection of human rights of a constraining nature.

Unlike the European system, the Inter-American system was set up before the commission as well as before the Inter-American Convention for Human Rights. Whereas the Inter-American Convention was adopted in 1969, the Inter-American Commission for Human Rights was created in 1959, and became operational in 1960. Its mission was to supervise the states' implementation of commitments (as regards human rights) included in the 1948 Organization of American States (OAS) charter by this organization and in the Declaration of Human Rights and Duties adopted by the OAS at Bogota in the same year.[3]

Furthermore, it must be stressed that in contrast to Europe, where the process which led to the adoption of an instrument for the creation of a human rights commission only lasted two years (between Winston Churchill's appeal for a European charter for human rights at the European Congress in 1948, and the adoption of the Convention for the Protection of Human Rights and Basic Liberties in 1950), there was to be a longer duration of the same process in the Americas and Africa. It took 12 years in the case of the Inter-American system (between the Inter-American Declaration for Human Rights and Duties, prepared by the Inter-American judicial committee in 1947 and the creation of the commission in 1959).[4] It took 20 years in the case of Africa, between the African conference on the rule of law which was held in Lagos in 1961, where a non-governmental organization, the International Commission of Jurists, invited all African states to study the possibility of adopting a regional convention for human rights, up until the adoption of the African Charter on Human and Peoples' Rights in 1981.[5]

The rhythm at which and the manner in which regional instruments on human rights were adopted therefore shows a big difference between the North and South. This difference in rhythm seems like the logical consequence of two determining factors; the almost bicentenarian anteriority of the French and American revolutions from the outset of the preoccupation for human rights in the North, compared with the South, where the preoccupation for human rights dates back some decades at the very most[6] on the one hand, and the degree of difficulty[7] in accepting human rights in the South, on the other.

Composition and principles of functioning of regional commissions for human rights – As regards the composition and functioning of regional commissions for human rights, many similarities can be observed between the North and the South. For instance in both cases, members of human rights commissions are at least formally independent and thus do not act in their capacity as state delegates. Also, a state member can call upon the commission to rule against another state member. In addition, an individual is authorized to bring a case before each of the commissions considered. Each of them gives a ruling on the admissibility of a claim and can undertake enquiries and resolve differences brought before it. The commissions may also prepare reports on the states, receive communications from non-governmental organizations[8] or individuals, solicit information from governments and make recommendations. Their competence covers all areas under consideration. Finally, their role is mainly to promote an amicable or conciliatory settlement.

So, as we can see, similarities are noticeable. Yet the differences dominate. In this respect, the African Charter for Human and Peoples' Rights stresses for instance the negotiation dimension, including the period before the matter is referred to the commission. Furthermore, the African Commission has been granted other powers that the European Commission does not have. These deal more particularly with the promotion of human rights in general (Article 45.1a and c), the pre-legislative power as regards human rights (Article 45.1b), the examination of reports by member states[9] and the supplemental powers entrusted to it by the Organization of African Unity (OAU) heads of state and government by way of a council (Article 45.4).[10] These special rights are also explained by the non-existence ab initio of an African court for human rights in the African regional system. The court was indeed judged as "premature" at the time when the commission was established.[11] This being said, the main weakness of the African Commission lies in the fact that (contrary to its Inter-American equivalent), it may only publish its report after authorization from the conference of OAU heads of state and government.[12]

Incidentally, one of the apparent weaknesses of the African Commission for Human and Peoples' Rights rests in the fact that, according to the letter of the African charter, it does not treat individual cases. The only ones concerned are "series of serious or massive violations of human and peoples' rights" (Article 58). This conventional restriction regarding cases concretely referred to the commission seems to have a specific counterpart: its automatic access saves the condition for a preliminary declaration of the member state's acceptance against which a communication is directed, as in the case of European and Inter-American Commissions.[13] However, astonishing as it may appear, the African Commission has concretely developed a "case law" contra legem on this point. Contrary to what has often been written,[14] the African Commission agrees to treat claims pertaining to individual cases.[15] On the same note, it must be pointed out that the African Commission found a way to conduct inquiries and to obtain all the necessary collaboration in treating these cases from interested party states.[16] Joseph Essombé-Edimo thus

notes that no temper outburst has been observed, nor has any state receiving recommendations attempted to block a report.[17]

At the time when the African Commission was being set up, links
between the regional and the national levels were however closed owing
to a lack of trust from widespread one-party state regimes in Africa.[18]
African states were to adopt the same distrustful attitude with regard to
NGOs committed to defending human rights. These NGOs enjoy neither
a good reputation, nor a good reception on the part of the governors.[19]
Nevertheless, states now tend to be more welcoming of the commission.[20] This change in the states' attitude seems to spring from the commission's missions dispatched on the field, like the 1996 mission in Mauritania,[21] after which the Mauritanian government clearly indicated its
intention to cooperate with the commission with a view to improving the
human rights situation in the country.[22]

Obviously, good relations with the regional institutions for the protection of human rights are more constant and more concordant with states
respecting human rights. The latter generally give valuable assistance to
regional instruments, which do the same in turn, within the dynamics of a
"virtuous circle" in favour of human rights.

This is especially the case in the North, where there tends to be be a
somewhat constructive interplay between the regional and the national
levels. To be sure, although at the begining the rights leverage to be
promoted and protected in the North was restricted, it was progressively
extended through the "supplementary law making" technique,[23] doubled
by a system of commitment with a variable content. This system allows in
particular member states of the Council of Europe to adjust their obligations.[24] This option has the double advantage of taking into account the
level of development of each state and seeing that the states totally respect commitments subscribed "à la carte" so to speak, on the basis of a
stage-by-stage process.

From this perspective, in Europe, only a handful of civil and political
rights have been taken into account at the beginning of the process in the
European Convention for Human Rights of 4 November 1950.[25] Subsequently, up to 10 optional protocols have been adopted with the object
of extending the range of rights to protect and improve respect for them.
The European social charter which comprises economic and social rights
was not to be adopted until 18 October 1961.[26] In the Inter-American
system (the closest to the North process within the South), economic,
social, and cultural rights have also been put aside to begin with, as much
with regard to the Inter-American declaration as to its convention. A
distinct convention on economic, social, and cultural rights was only to
be adopted in 1988.

By contrast, the African Charter, adopted after the first European and Inter-American instruments, was immediately to include two categories of rights: civil and political rights and economic social and cultural rights.[27] Would it be because the African Charter is essentially the work of jurists assembled within the International Commission of Jurists?[28] Such normative boldness was however not followed by concrete implementation. Indeed, the African Charter is the least applied instrument, despite the audacity of the Banjul commissioners. As Minkoa She points out:

The OAU does not involve itself enough in the promotion and protection of human rights on the territory of member states. This relative indifference can be compared with the active role of the Council of Europe with regard to its members and central and eastern European states knocking at its door. It must be said that the panafrican organisation's charter is unduly favoured on the principles of state sovereignty and non-intervention, to the detriment of principles for democracy, primacy of law and respect for human rights.

The European Commission of Human Rights' effectiveness mainly results from the possibility of individual claims based on the respective state's facultative declaration (provided for in Article 25 of the convention). From experience, the impact of individual standing thus formalized has proved to be infinitely more determinant for the protection of human rights than state standing. In this respect, Michael Reisman argues that individual standing has proved to be important, because 1,000 times more individual cases than interstate claims had been filed as of 1993. The cumbersome role of the commission and the court has even been talked about, for direct access to the Commission of Human Rights granted to individuals has been widely used by citizens of member states.

As Frédéric Sudre points out, in a period of 11 years ending in 1992, 1,827 claims came from France, 1,328 from Germany, 1,074 from Italy, 1,639 from the United Kingdom and 416 from Spain.[29] In consideration of the fact that ratio of reports to friendly settlement among admissible claims was 4:1 in 1991,[30] the determining role of the European Commission in the protection of human rights within the European space will be agreed. Frédéric Sudre writes that individual claims propel all contentious issues and powerfully contribute to spreading the ECHR within state domestic law.[31]

Compared with the European context, it is therefore clear that the functioning of the African arrangement for the protection of human and peoples' rights is far from having reached its level of optimal efficiency,

especially since it is fair to argue that human rights violations are certainly greater on the African continent than they are in Western Europe.
For instance, up until 1996, only 17 member states out of 51 had already
provided the commission at least once with the biennal report on legislative measures taken with a view to making an impact on the African
Charter's arrangements.[32] To date, the commission has not registered
any communication by a member state of alleged violations against another member state. This shows how much an institution entitled to
make coercive decisions is indispensable for an efficient protection of
human rights at the regional level.

Regional jurisdictions in charge of human rights

Two types of jurisdictions deal with human rights in the North and
South: regional courts for human rights and international penal courts.

Jurisdictions with a general competence: regional courts for human rights
– Two regional courts for human rights are in operation, one in the
North and the other in the South: the European Court of Human Rights
and the Inter-American Court of Human Rights. The protocol of the
African Charter for Human and Peoples' Rights creating an African
court in charge of human and peoples' rights was only adopted in Addis-
Ababa in December 1997, and has not yet come into force.[33] Con-
sequently, our comparison will be restricted to European and Inter-
American courts. The latter drew much of its inspiration from the
former.

Initially, direct individual standing was not accepted by any of the two
courts under consideration. Any case used to be brought before the court
either by the commission after reported failure of an attempted friendly
settlement, or by a member state other than the one implicated. The decision to submit a case to court pertained to the discretionary power of
each Commission for Human Rights. The plaintiff was then indirectly
represented before the court by the commission. And in any event, the
commission was obliged to participate in hearings relating to all the cases
it brought before the court. The commission literally had the role of
public prosecutor.

This schema is somewhat modified as regards the European court,
through protocols 9–11 of 11 May 1994. According to the new Article 34
of the ECHR, direct recourse to the court applies henceforth to any
physical person, any NGO, any group of private individuals claiming to
be victim of a violation of one of the convention's arrangements.[34] If the
court considers the convention to have been violated, it will order for the

restoration of the victim's rights and will possibly prescribe the payment of equitable damages to the victim whose rights have been ignored. For instance, in March 1999, a decision by the European Court for Human Rights ordered France to pay US$80,000 to Ahmed Semouni, arbitrarily detained for four days and beaten by five policemen.

There are additional differences between the European and Inter-American courts. For instance, contrary to the European court, the Inter-American court has a preventive consultative role in addition to settling litigations. This is particularly the case as regards the compatibility of a law with the Inter-American Convention for Human Rights and Duties or with any other relevant text relating to human rights in the affected region. Furthermore, matters referred to the Inter-American court still require the commission's preliminary intervention. Moreover, the status of the court contains no provision stating that a dispute as to whether the Inter-American court had jurisdiction shall be settled by decision of the court.[35] Another point distinguishing the two courts considered here is that the Inter-American Convention does not provide measures to ensure that the court's decisions are respected.[36]

The European court also appears to be different from the American court as regards its efficiency. In 1992, France was compelled to make amends in the region of US$198,300 to victims of human rights violations and US$96,300 to victims for procedure costs.[37] More generally, certain decisions on the non-conformity of national law with the European Convention in cases of general interest have led national authorities to resolve the problem by amending the national law – so that progressively, the ECHR is leading to the Europeanization of the legal systems of European states, as Frédéric Sudre shows in the French case.[38]

The efficiency of the European jurisdictional system for the protection of human rights is moreover usefully completed through the action of the European Union law courts. The European Union's judge has thus effectively realized and sanctioned a system of "droit mixte"[39] (mixed law) elaborated through the integration of norms coming from laws of member states (constitutional traditions common to member states) and diverse international instruments (particularly the European Commission for the Protection of Human Rights and Basic Liberties). These possibilities are ruled out in the Inter-American system.

Ad hoc courts: the international penal court for the former Yugoslavia and the international penal court for Rwanda – The last decade of the twentieth century has witnessed the establishment of two special international courts, one in the North and the other in the South, to ensure the sanction of atrocities constituting large-scale international crimes in the former Yugoslavia and Rwanda (massive killings, systematic rapes, ethnic cleansing).

The international penal court for the former Yugoslavia was created (following upon a French initiative) by the Security Council on 22 February 1993 to judge those presumed reponsible for serious international human rights violations committed under the jurisdiction of the former Yugoslavia since 1991 (Resolution 808(1993)). These crimes were committed during hostilities between Serbs on the one hand, Croatians and Bosnian Muslims on the other, following Croatia's and Slovenia's unilateral declaration of independence on 25 June 1991. This was the starting point for Yugoslavia's dissolution. It was mainly this situation that made Bosnia-Herzegovina the theatre for ethnic armed confrontations.

Basing itself on Chapter VII of the Charter,[40] the Security Council adopted the international penal court statute through Resolution 827 of 25 May 1993. The court has the power to judge persons suspected of having violated or given the order to seriously violate the 1949 Geneva conventions, war laws, and customs and the order to commit genocide or crimes against humanity.

The constitution of the international penal court for Rwanda followed in 1994, after similar violations of humanitarian international law between the Hutus and the Tutsis from 6 April to 15 July 1994 (Resolution 955(1994) of 8 November 1994). The organization and functioning of this court, while being traced from the international penal court based in the Hague with which it shares the same court of appeal, differs from it in many respects.

Because of the specificity of the Rwandan conflict, the Rwandan government was able to intervene in the elaboration of the Rwandan special court statute, and its ratione loci competence was extended to neighbouring countries where atrocities were committed in refugee camps.[41]

Contrary to an accepted idea, the establishment of this penal court for Rwanda did not give rise to any controversies between Africa and the United Nations. Divergences came up between Rwanda alone and the United Nations, on the court's headquarters, its composition, its competence, the sentence to be passed and the place of detention.[42] The Rwandan government's objections illustrate its desire to control the court's functioning. The Rwandan government thus requested that the court's headquarters be fixed in Rwanda (the place of massacre), that a Rwandan sat as a judge there, that the court's ratione temporis competence date back to October 1990, that the maximum sentence should be the death penalty and that the detention place for those condemned to prison sentences should be Rwanda. With the double concern of avoiding the risk of a vengeful partial justice[43] and ensuring the primacy of international norms as regards the administration of justice, the United Nations did not give entire satisfaction to any of these demands to begin with. The court's headquarters were fixed in Arusha, Tanzania. Not one Rwandan figures among its judges, the jurisdictional ratione temporis competence (dies a quo) was maintained at 1 January 1994, the only sentences retained by the statute are those of imprisonment[44] and the place of detention is not exclusive to Rwanda.[45] At the time, Rwanda, a non-permanent member of the Security Council, had voted against the resolution creating the special court.

Subsequently, the persistence of profound divergences between Rwanda and the United Nations had plunged this court into a crisis, and problems of cooperation between the latter and the Rwandan authorities were worsened by the weak impact of the achievements of the court's first deputy public prosecutor. The fact is that up until mid-1997, the court only imprisoned nine persons, without any bill of indictment for five of them. Six months after, there were 23, each of them having a precise bill of indictment. By 24 October 1998, the number of charges rose to 33.[46] The court made its first two decisions in the second half of 1998.[47] To establish the court's credibility, the United Nations had to compromise, by accepting the idea that some of the court hearings could be held in Rwanda.

From the start, the court's creation was greeted by Africans as an element of awareness of the value and importance of human life[48] against the usual impunity of African rulers.[49] For his part, Mutoy Mubiala stresses the undeniable pedagogic value and the dissuasive effect of the penal court for Rwanda, whose decisions unfortunately do not enjoy the same media attention as the court for the former Yugoslavia.

The small number of sentences which characterizes both courts is no doubt, at least partly, linked to what appears as the most serious gap in the statutes of the two courts – the question of judgment in absentia.[50]

Differences of human rights practices in Northern and Southern regions where regional institutions operate little or do not exist

The North American region can be compared to the South, understood here as Asia and the Pacific, where a regional mechanism for the protection of human rights still does not exist.[51] Yet, because in North America human rights practices can rely on constitutional democracies, which are more or less lacking in the South, the lack of influential regional mechanisms in the two regions is felt differently.

The North American region

The starting hypothesis here is that despite the fact that North American countries (United States and Canada) are parties to the Inter-American system for human rights, human rights practices in this part of the Northern hemisphere rely neither on the Inter-American Convention, nor on regional institutions and mechanisms preceded by this convention. In North America, the protection of human rights is rather dependent upon legal authorities and institutions created by the constitutions and parliaments. This approach is corroborated by John Quigley when, having pointed out the weak impact of the national courts' growing tendency to apply international norms for human rights to the United States, he emphasizes: "When US government agencies take adverse action against an individual, and the individual asserts a treaty-based norm in response, both federal and state courts often avoid applying that norm."[52] With regard to decisions made by international justice, the same attitude is observed in the United States. For instance, in two cases relating to the Vienna Convention on Consular Relations (*Paraguay* v. *United States of America* and *Germany* v. *United States of America*), two people sentenced to death for homicide were executed in the United States, despite rulings from the International Court of Justice requesting the United States to take measures to prevent the planned executions while awaiting a final decision.[53]

As for Canada, to be sure, it displays greater consideration than the United States as regards the application of international norms on human rights. However, together with the United States, Canada is subject to the essentially domestic nature of the causes of its human rights practices.

The South Asia and Pacific region

The South Asia and Pacific region does not usually have a tradition for respecting human rights, including India, the largest world democracy where serious discrimination is for instance noted against widows,[54] and for religious motives. Attacks on equal rights are very frequent in the region, particularly in China, North Korea, Pakistan, and Afghanistan.[55] In China especially, regular discrimination is on the increase against baby girls.[56] And yet, women's rights have generally and freely been recognized as human rights by states of the region.[57] This paradox is explained by the fact that many countries here are still under the spell of the one-party state regime.[58] Moreover, the extreme diversity of the region's societies makes them unsuitable for the relative standardization carried by the human rights concept.

Consequently, if the decade that has just ended bore witness to the extension of ratifications of human rights instruments and the emergence of national institutions aiming to promote respect for human rights in the South Asia and Pacific region,[59] the gap between the theory and the principles on the one hand, and the ground reality on the other hand, remains widespread in this region, particularly in the domain of civil and political rights.

In spite of the resolutions of the UNCHR each year (and for almost 15 years) requesting states to reach agreements with a view to the establishment of a human rights mechanism in the Asia and Pacific region, progress has been very slow.

As a result, there are great differences in the North and South concerning human rights practices, be they civil and political or social and economical, both as regards becoming actual law and as in respect for them from a practical viewpoint. Generally, both civil and political rights and social and economic rights have a high level of application in the North but are very poorly respected in the South. Just to give a few figures, in the North, about 10 per cent of the people are undernourished, whilst this proportion reaches and sometimes exceeds the 50 per cent mark in the South.

In the South, in spite of liberal proclamations on solidarity principles and the emphasis laid on social and economic rights, the conjuncture resulting from the general ignorance of civil and political rights and the surrounding underdevelopment, is hardly favourable to the respect for social and economic rights, whose implementation requires considerable material resources.[60]

The evolution of human rights in the North and South: significance of changes and problems of universality

The human rights situation is not static. The human rights discourse and human rights practices are the product of history, and part of history. The way human rights have been inspired by American and French revolutions, the way they have been incorporated over time in the constitutions of democratic nations and in international law, the way the normative and political pressure they have come to represent has contributed to more domestic and international changes, are a testimony of this state of affairs. It is therefore fitting to assess the evolution human rights have gone through in recent years in the North and South and the tendency towards the reinforcement of the universality of human rights norms.

Evolution of the practice of civil and political rights and economic and social rights

Historically, since the end of World War II, in the North, the determinant pressure for the ratification of human rights has come from within states. By contrast, in the South, the determining pressure for human rights came from the outside. In the North and South, the divisibility of human rights has been observed from a legal viewpoint giving priority to civil and political rights in the North and to social and economic rights in the South. Except that once again, willy-nilly, in practice, civil and political rights are generally respected in the North and the social and economic situation has reached a very high standard there, whereas in the South, violations of civil and political rights and ignorance of social and economic rights continue to be massive and worrying. Violations of the second category of rights are all the more out of tune in the South as countries in this hemisphere are those which have pushed for the adoption of these rights and have always given preference to social and economic rights owing to their cultural particularisms. In this respect, we should note a greater coherence in the attitude of countries from the North which have preferred civil and political rights from the beginning, and rather satisfactorily ensure respect for them.

In recent years, progress can be noted both in the North and in the South. In the North, progress has been particularly remarkable within the European Union with the current reinforcement of the Union, especially with the adoption and amendment of the Treaty of Maastricht which explicitly states that no state candidate can be admitted into the Union if it does not respect basic rights.[61] Improvement of human rights practices in the North also results from the current extension of the European Union to former countries of the Eastern Bloc. In North America, particularly in the United States, four important treaties on human rights have been ratified over the past 15 years.[62]

In the South, the human rights situation remains very problematic. Indeed, although widely recognized, social and economic rights, which require resources in order to be implemented, are rarely respected for what they are.[63] In a similar way, civil and political rights are generally not respected in the South, especially when it concerns rights to political participation, that is, the right to free participation in the management of public affairs and the right of equal access to public office.[64] Yet, progress has also been made in the South. At the national level, there are fewer and fewer countries detaining political prisoners. At the regional institutional level, Chidi Anselm Odinkalu and Camilla Christensen make the following point:

A comparison of the decisions (of the African commission for human and peoples' rights) over the years shows that while room remains for considerable improvement, the quality of the commission's reasoning and decision making has continued to evolve positively. In the past two years, the decisions of the Commission have been both more substantive and elaborate on the issues of law and fact that are raised in and considered by communications.[65]

In certain countries of the South like Ghana, Malawi, Mali, Benin, Namibia, or South Africa, to which can be added Nigeria and Niger, the human rights situation has progressed so much that, particularly with regard to civil and political rights, these countries can be compared to countries of the North.[66] This progress results from the end of apartheid in South Africa and current democratization processes in Africa and South America over a decade, as well as from the speeding up of the ratification of human rights conventions in South Asia and the Pacific, often prolonged by the incorporation of international norms on human rights in constitutions.

Nevertheless, with the list of declared rights thus lengthened,[67] the gap between declared rights and those respected remains unchanged especially with regard to economic and social rights. A lot needs to be done as far as inhuman, cruel, or degrading treatments are concerned, and with regard to political participation, freedom of expression and of the press where a rather gloomy picture still remains in the South. Ouguergouz attributes this state of affairs regarding Africa to "the catastrophic economic situation of almost all the continent's states,"[68] particularly as regards the right to work, housing, food, medical aid, the right to health and life,[69] the right to education and to decent living conditions.

The universality of human rights: a long-term objective

There are three stages in the universality of human rights: the universalism of conception, the universalism of formulation, the universalism of control and the reality of human rights.[70] The universality of human rights is established on three traditonal supports of international legislation: non-conventional concerted enactments like the Universal Declaration of Human Rights, international conventions like the two treaties of 1966 and international case law (i.e. the famous obiter dictum of the International Court of Justice in the case of *Barcelona Traction, Light and Power Company Ltd.*, according to which states are under an obligation erga omnes to respect basic human rights, an obligation existing vis-à-vis states as a whole).[71]

In 1993, it was declared at the World Conference on Human Rights, organized by the United Nations:

All human rights are universal, indivisible, interdependent and interrelated. The international community must treat human rights globally, in a fair and equal manner, on the same footing, and with the same emphasis.

If state representatives who met in Vienna have emphasized the universal nature of human rights, this is certainly because the universality of human rights is far from being a tangible reality at the present time. According to Pierre de Senarclens, the universality of human rights only exists today because people, movements, and governments are fighting in its defence in Africa, Asia, America, and Europe.[72] This statement illustrates the universal vocation of human rights, whose objective is to transform theoretical thought recorded in the international instruments into an organic impulse and show everything proclaimed by the conventions in daily living.[73] The universal respect for human rights is indeed an objective worthy of being pursued particularly on account of its positive effects on the dignity and freedom of mankind (universally protected value) and on development.[74] But in spite of these considerations, universality remains problematic.[75]

In the South, the principles proclaimed in the instruments on human rights often clash with the harsh realities of generalized national practices deeply rooted in culture. These practices are often based on principles that are a challenge to specific rights. Certain "beautés acides" (venomous beauties) from Southern cultures result from a privileged relation with divinities conditioning traditional structures. Their impact takes place within national contexts which tend to cater to two objectives difficult to reconcile: the simultaneous reinforcement of the nation state's provisions on the one hand, and an exuberant practice of traditional rites contrary to international textual statements on human rights on the other. The telescoping of these two tendencies is on the increase.

In this perspective, one must acknowledge that the human rights philosophy often collides head on with the cultural support which the societies of the South rely on.[76] African animist societies convey their own conception of man. Here, the individual is assimilated by the group. Fatsah Ouguergouz writes that the traditional African society is strongly impregnated with community feeling.[77] The individual can only situate himself when in relation with the group. Kéba Mbaye goes further to say that the individual and his rights are swathed in protection assured to all, by the family and by other communities.[78] Then we have what one author calls the principle of the supremacy of genealogical reasoning.[79]

This is a principle at the root of absolute respect for and priority to the elders, especially with regard to succession and representation, the subordinate status of women and altruistic values. In this respect, Fatsah Ouguergouz emphasizes the African states' aversion for any form of legal or arbitral resolution of their differences and their correlative predilection for non-jurisdictional and non-institutionalized methods of peacefully settling disputes.[80] From this viewpoint, adopting the protocol to the African Charter relating to the creation of an African court for human and peoples' rights, is at the same time a regression in African particularisms and an advancement towards the universalization of human rights.

In Arab-Muslim societies of the South, the Western human rights' civilization carried by the progress in legal culture is often broken, as in Egypt, on the reefs of national law and order established on the principles of Islam,[81] or even based on the heritage of Islamic law.[82] Consequently, numerous contradictions between Arab-Muslim norms and international texts on human rights exist and are as much cases of "non-applicability" of universal rules. In this manner, women are victims of discrimination since, under Islam, they can only accede to certain public offices such as that of a magistrate. As regards succession, the Koranic rule, that the male share is equal to that of two girls, is strictly applied. The same goes for spouses: the man inherits twice the amount from his deceased wife than she would have inherited were her husband to die. Restrictions are also made as regards marriage: Islam banning it between Muslims and non-Muslims.[83]

In a similar way, David Annoussamy reports that in India where legal dynamics are nevertheless very favourable to human rights, "the high court's decision declaring that a divorced Muslim woman had a right to food allowance had been rendered invalid by a later law, which was interposed after pressure from reactionary Muslims. The High Court itself has just taken a step back by declaring that the law, be it in the form of a modern or traditional legislative text, will escape the rule of conformity with basic rights if it related to personal status."[84]

The Hindu-Confucian civilizations have some points in common with the African and Arab-Muslim animist or traditional civilizations, with values often opposite to Euro-Christian culture – the matrix of the human rights philosophy. These societies are however particularly restive when it comes to the ritualization of human rights registered in universal instruments. As Harriet Samuels argues about the main features of the dominant civilization in the South Asia and Pacific region:

The phrase "Asian values" is taken to mean an emphasis on the community and societal harmony over the individual, a sense of loyalty and duty towards one's family, self reliance, thrift, a general tolerance of benign authoritarianism, a stress on education, respect for the elders and respect for the accumulation of wealth.[85]

It is in this context that some argue that it is still premature to discuss specific arrangements relating to the setting up of a formal human rights mechanism in the South Asia and Pacific region such as those existing in Europe, America, or Africa.[86] This leads to revisiting what human rights mean for this region, a preoccupation which appears much more than in Africa.

Indeed, if those who conceived and wrote the African Charter were bent on adopting an instrument reflecting the African specificity,[87] the chosen option pertained more to the appropriation than to the adaptation of the human rights culture inspired by the West. It is in this context that the African Charter makes a reference to the general International Law for Human Rights (Article 60)[88] and does not accept particularisms and other "African practices" except when they are in compliance with international norms relating to human and peoples' rights (Article 61). This appropriation option has straight away settled the question of the conceptual universality of human rights in Africa where difficulties arise essentially at the level of effective application of human rights and governments' respect for them.[89]

As for Central and South America, it is a singular case. This southern region, which is exposed to the double influence of the European "maximalist"[90] regional model and the North American model based on internal arrangements, was the first to open up to human rights' precepts. This in itself could have been used as a way to enhance the discourse and practice of human rights. Unfortunately, the fact that Central and South America has been crippled by social and economic problems, and by authoritarian regimes, has prevented any influence from human rights practitioners. What happened is rather the opposite. The legacy of colonialism and of neo-colonialism, while making room for a formal universality of human rights – to which most Latin American constitutions pay tribute – has gone some way to prevent human rights from becoming part of daily reality.

In the end, the difficulties encountered in the stimulation or acceleration of social changes show us that a relative homogeneity of human rights practices in the North and South can not be a short-term objective, where uniformity could be a risk.[91] Universality will have to find its way through diversity.[92] There cannot be any mechanical transposition in the South. The universalization of human rights cannot be dissociated from the complex historical process spreading Western Christian civilization to other regions.[93] And it will take some time to be realized in the midst of the recognition of diversity, especially in Africa and in South Asia and the Pacific.

In several regions of the South, particularisms have been set up as obstacles, either to slow down or to prevent respect for human rights."[94] The fact is that particularisms are able to justify the progression of human rights implementation, but certainly not their negation.

In our view, the balance between universalism and particularism is not desirable. The solution for the conflict between them must be taken from the one existing in several of the national rights in the South, between traditional customary law and the law produced by the nation state. In the conflict between the international standard of human rights and practices common to certain regions, the former will have to prevail sooner or later,[95] according to the principle of priority of international law over domestic law. This principle has found an interesting and relevant application with the statute of the international penal court for Rwanda in which Article 8, paragraph 2 states that the international court for Rwanda has the priority over national jurisdictions of all states. At any stage of the procedure, it can officially ask national jurisdictions not to proceed with cases in their favour.[96]

The process can oscillate between a positive and regressive evolution; but finally the particularisms will have to be disregarded. The universality of human rights is the objective of the present process. No fate condemns the people from the southern regions to human rights violations – synonymous with contempt for their dignity. However, if we want to maintain the assertion that human rights are without bounds, we have to keep in mind that they can only be realized to the extent permitted by the social system.[97]

Some practical elements on problems encountered in the implementation of human rights in the South

In the end, the obstacles to respect for human rights in the South are the following:
- Bad governance and embezzlement of public funds
- Non-existence of law and order in the states confronted with civil war or in states where civil peace is strongly disturbed[99]
- General lack of legitimate governments and nationally autonomous democratic systems based on the protection of human rights
- Underdevelopment and poverty
- The debt burden

- Difficult access to and/or the corruption of the judicial system[100]
- The ineffectiveness of the law in southern countries[101]
- The fact that developed countries do not always fulfil their obligations concerning aid to underdeveloped countries
- The existence of cultural models clashing with the rule of law and universal norms for human rights
- The African tendency to conciliation and resignation[102]
- Lack or rarity of judicial or administrative punishments for instigators of violations
- Poor legislation on human rights which is, if not incomplete, at least inoperative on account of the systematic reference to application texts whose adoption is itself adjourned sine die, or the uncertainty of human rights on account of their incorporation in the constitutions' preambles
- The political context characterized by electoral fraud and the "consensus du sommet" ("consensus at the top")[103] able to lead to parliamentary majorities so wide that controlling the application of human rights, starting with the control of law constitutionality, becomes paralysed
- Lack of financial resources for national and regional human rights institutions, as in the case of the African Commission for Human and Peoples' Rights
- Lax selection of policemen and the absence of or poor provisions for human rights in their training programme
- Total lack of education on human rights within the greatest part of the population
- The continual illegality of private radios and/or televisions and the relative control of governments over the media.

As a result, a number of suggestions can be made to try to surmount these obstacles to enhance respect for human rights in the South. In this context, it is particularly important to:

- Speed up the establishment of democratic institutions and the rule of law in the southern states[104]
- Lead massive campaigns to explain human rights in the South
- Look for and determine areas where rapid progress can be accomplished
- Set up free legal procedures relating to human rights as is often the case regarding elections
- Work towards increasing aid for development and making it more effective
- Reinforce national and international mechanisms for the protection of human rights

- Select policemen after checking up on their moral conduct, and systematically training them in human rights
- Begin to educate populations on human rights as early as primary school
- Combat corruption in the judicial system justice and police forces (vectors of negative social values)
- Punish those embezzling public funds
- Strengthen the freedom of the media by adopting laws allowing for the creation of private radio and television stations within the southern states
- Channel the action of human rights organizations on to specific rights through specialization
- Promote the universal ratification of international instruments on human rights and arrange for their complete incorporation in the state's domestic law
- Speed up the establishment of a regional mechanism for human rights in the South Asia and Pacific region
- Promote the culture of human rights in radio and television programmes
- Increase the struggle against traditional practices challenging human rights

What these obstacles and the suggested ways to overcome them show is that in the South social and economic problems are intertwined with civil and political rights. The lack of respect for these two types of right goes together. As such, this situation is a telling illustration of the lack of overall social integration, of the socialization of a significant number of countries of the South.

Ultimately, it is from the ability to take seriously suggestions regarding the respect and implementation of civil and political rights, and social and economic rights, and to follow the policy prescriptions they contain, that the improvement of the human rights situation in the South largely depends.

Notes

1. See Jacques-Ivan Morin, *L'émergence de l'état de droit en tant que principe du droit international*, RCADI, t. 254, 1995. See also Jacques-Yvan Morin and Emmanuel Decaux, eds., "Conclusions générales, universalité, effectivité, droit à la paix," in *Série les droits fondamentaux*, 14 video tapes with a 26-minute duration, director, Fouquet, Thierry, production, Aupelf/Uref-U Media Production, University of Nantes, 1996, No. 14.

2. The African Charter for Human and Peoples' Rights, adopted by the 18th Assembly for Heads of State and Government in Nairobi-Kenya in 1981, came into effect in 1986. Out of the 53 members of the OAU, including the democratic Sarawi Arab "republic," 51 had ratified it in 1996. See the 2nd annual report of the African Commission for Human and Peoples' Rights, 1996/1997, adopted by the 32nd ordinary conference for OAU heads of state and government, Banjul, p. 1.

3. See Michael Reisman, "Establishment of a Regional Human Rights Arrangement in the Asian and Pacific Region" in Fourth Workshop on Regional Human Rights Arrangements in the Asian and Pacific Region, Report, Kathmandu, 26–28 February 1996, United Nations, New York and Geneva, *World Compaign for Human Rights*, pp. 25–27.

4. This duration may be extended to 21 years, if one includes the period between the adoption of the Inter-American Convention in 1969 and its coming into force in 1978.

5. See Kéba Mbaye, *Les droits de l'homme en Afrique*, Pedone, International Commission of Jurists, Paris, 1992, p. 148. See also Reisman above, pp. 31–40. In Africa's case, the duration of the process may be extended to 25 years, if we include the period between the adoption of the African Charter in 1981 and its coming into effect in 1986.

6. In the South itself, a difference in rhythm can also be observed between different regions, because of South America's and Africa's automatic opening to the West, contrary to Islamic-Confucian societies of South Asia and the Pacific.

7. It is relevant to use Mauritania as an illustration where slavery was only officially abolished in 1981, through a decree. See Mbaye, p. 64.

8. At the end of the 1996/1997 evaluation, the number of non-governmental organizations enjoying observer status within the African Commission amounted to 205. See above-mentioned report, p. 5.

9. The Inter-American Commission does not proceed either with the periodic examination of reports from member states. The impact of the African Charter's innovation in this respect is to date weak, both on account of the number of states carrying out this duty, and the quality of reports presented to the commission, see below. Cf. Adolphe Minkoa She, "Droits de l'homme et droit pénal au Cameroun," in *La Vie du droit en Afrique*, Economica, Paris, 1999, p. 96.

10. See Karel Vasak, Report at the Dakaar conference on the African Commission for Human Rights of 19 June 1987, quoted by Mbaye, p. 218.

11. See Mbaye, pp. 26 and 218.

12. In this respect, Minkoa She argues that African states have up until now preferred the prince's authority to the judge's wisdom, p. 97. For a systematic account of the African Charter's weaknesses, see Makau Mutua, "The African Human Rights Court, a Two-Legged Stool?" *Human Rights Quarterly* 21(2), 1999, pp. 343–344.

13. Cf. Minkoa She, p. 97.

14. This can be seen in Erica-Irène A. Daes's study, "Status of the individual and contemporary law, promotion, protection and restoration of human rights at national, regional and international levels," Centre for Human Rights, Study Series 4, United Nations, Geneva, New York, 1992, doc GE. 91–15640, p. 54, para. 488. For a balanced viewpoint on the work of the African Commission, see Fatsah Ouguergouz, *La charte africaine des droits de l'homme et des peuples, une approche juridique des droits de l'homme entre tradition et modernité*, preface by Kéba Mbaye, foreword by Georges Abi-Saab, PUF, Paris, 1993, pp. 347–349, and Minkoa She, p. 97, no. 224. See also John Quigley, who also follows this doctrinal trend, writes, "In Africa, a continent-

wide human rights commission is beginning to play a meaningful role." See John Quigley, "Human rights defenses in US courts," HRQ 20, 1998, p. 555.

15. See cases 39/90. Annette Pagnoulle, acting for *M. Abdoulaye Mazou/Cameroon 97/93*; *K. Modise/Botswana* 103/93; *Alhassan Abubakar/Ghana*; and *Monja Zoana/ Madagascar* 108/93. In these three cases, the African Commission declared that there was an opening in the African Charter and has recommended to all governments implicated to "devise all the legal consequences following from this decision." See the 10th Report of the African Commission for Human and Peoples' Rights, pp. 87–112.

16. Essombé-Edimo, p. 5.

17. Ibid., p. 11.

18. In this respect, Judge Kéba Mbaye argues that African governments display a determined hostility with respect to any organization fighting to preserve human rights, from the moment this fight concerns the territory on which they exert their powers, p. 119.

19. Ibid., p. 119 – conversely, the NGO relations are much better with the Commission, which they have a tight collaboration with, as shown above.

20. Essombé-Edimo, p. 9.

21. This mission's report of 19–27 June 1996 figures in Annex IX of the 10th annual report on activities of the African Commission for Human and Peoples' Rights, pp. 63–79. In the period from 1 June 1996–31 May 1997, the African Commission carried out similar missions; in Senegal from 1–7 June 1996, in Sudan from 1–7 December 1996 and in Nigeria, from 7–14 March 1997. See above, 10th report, pp. 4–5.

22. Ibid.

23. See Reisman, p. 32.

24. See Nguyen Quoc Dinh, *Droit international public*, Paris, 1994, p. 652.

25. Ibid., p. 31.

26. A revised version of this text was adopted in Strasbourg on 3 May 1996.

27. In this respect, Fatsah Ouguergouz speaks about an "audacious juxtaposition," p. xxii.

28. See Mbaye, pp. 147–160.

29. See Frédéric Sudre, "Le contentieux 'français' à Strasbourg, Bilan de onze ans de recours individuals," in *Le droit français et la convention européenne des droits de l'homme 1974–1992*, ed. N. P. Engel Kehl, Strasbourg, 1994. Proceedings of the 1993 Montpellier Conference organized jointly by the Institute of European Law for Human Rights, IDEDH, of the University of Montpellier I and the Human Rights Institute of the Montpellier Bar, Strasbourg-France, pp. 61–99.

30. Reisman, p. 34.

31. Sudre, p. 94.

32. See the 10th Report of the African Commission for Human and Peoples' Rights, pp. 17–20.

33. See Hamid Boukrif, "La cour africaine des droits de l'homme et des peuples, un organe judiciaire au service des droits de l'homme et des peuples en Afrique," *African Journal of International and Comparative Law*, RADIC, 1998, pp. 60–87.

34. Nguyen Quoc Dinh, p. 877.

35. Daes, p. 51, para. 477.

36. Ibid., para. 483.

37. See Sudre, pp. 93–94.

38. Ibid., p. 51.

39. Expression borrowed from Jean Vergès, "La protection des droits fondamentaux dans

la communauté européenne," in *L'effectivité des droits fondamentaux dans les pays de la communauté francophone*, p. 449.

40. The Security Council has indeed considered that serious human rights violations are a threat to international peace and security. See Nguyen Quoc Dinh, p. 686.
41. Cf. Minkoa She, p. 272.
42. See Mutoy Mubiala, "Le tribunal international pour le Rwanda," in *Afrique 2000* 20, 1995, pp. 5–13, esp. pp. 6–7.
43. Ibid., p. 12.
44. The first consequence of this state of affairs is that some of the accused judged by the Rwandan state risk the death penalty, whilst others among whom are former political leaders of the regime which organized and planned the genocide only render themselves liable to life imprisonment if judged by the International Penal Court for Rwanda. The argument of the public prosecutor's deputy, Bernard Muna, who explains that this court generally judges the accused who had placed themselves beyond the reach of the Rwandan national system, does not change this objective evidence. See his interview in *l'Expression* 226, 21 January 1998.
45. Ibid.
46. Cf. Senyéebia Yawo Kakpo, Le Tribunal pénal international pour le Rwanda, TPIR, Organisation et procédure, DESS dissertation, Institut des relations internationales du Cameroun, IRIC, Cameroonian Institute of International Relations, University of Yaounde II, Yaounde, 1998, p. 82.
47. Cases ICTR/97/23/5 and ICTR/96/4/T. The first was made on 4 September 1998 against former Rwandan Prime Minister Jean Kambanda and the second on 2 October 1998 against Jean-Paul Akayeru, former mayor of the Taba Commune.
48. Cf. Kakpo, p. 82.
49. Ibid., p. 14. For his part, Mubiala points out that the international penal court for Rwanda which ensures a balance between the objective of crime punishment and the concern for objectivity will allow for the eradication of cyclic inter-ethnic massacres in Rwanda, p. 12.
50. See Nguyen Quoc Dinh, pp. 55, 684.
51. The development process for a regional mechanism for human rights in South Asia and in the Pacific is underway. A series of seminars have been held there since 1990, including the one in Manila which took place from 7–9 May 1990, the Jakarta seminar from 26–28 February 1993, the Seoul seminar from 18–20 July 1994, the Amman seminar from 5–7 January 1997 and the Teheran seminar from 28 February–2 March 1998. See Commission on Human Rights, report on the 54th session, 16 March–24 April 1998, *Economic and Social Council Official Records*, 1998, supplement no. 3, United Nations, E/1998/23/E/CN04/1998/177, p. 152.
52. See Quigley, p. 557.
53. The first case was brought before the International Court of Justice on 3 April 1998. Angel Francisco Breard was executed as planned in the state of Virginia on 14 April 1998. Paraguay was to withdraw through a letter dated 2 November 1998, after depositing its memoir on the facts of the matter, 9 October 1998. The case was removed from the International Court of Justice's roll on 10 November 1998. CIJ, communiqué no. 98/36 of 11 November 1998. In the second case, Germany referred to the court on 2 March 1999. The prescription indicating conservatory measures was ruled on 3 March 1999, shortly before the execution, which took place on the same day.
54. Cf. United Nations, 1995, *Les femmes dans le monde, des chiffres et des idées*, p. 11.
55. Cf. Arvonne S. Fraser, "Becoming human, the origins and development of women's

human rights," *Human Rights Quarterly* 21(4), 1999, pp. 853–906, where attention is drawn to the case of Afghan women since the Talibans came to power in 1994.

56. Cf. United Nations, *Les femmes dans le monde, des chiffres et des idées*, p. 1.

57. See Clarence J. Dias, "Regional Human Rights in the Asian and Pacific Region, Progress Made and some Options Available," in Fourth Workshop on Regional Human Rights Arrangements in the Asian and Pacific Region, 1998, p. 72, para. 3.

58. China constitutes a case in point. Despite the fact that it signed the 1966 treaty on the two categories of rights referred to here, opposition continues to be treated as a pathological phenomenon in China. Gao, the founder of China's democratic party in 1998, the first opposition party which dared to fill out an acknowledgement claim, was sentenced to eight years in prison after a speedy trial. Already in 1989, he had been taken to a "re-education through work" camp for his excessive sympathy towards the Tiananmen students. In March 1999 however, Beijing amended the constitution, stipulating that the People's Republic respect the rule of law.

59. Briand Burdekin has observed that, "In the brief period since the adoption of the Vienna Declaration and Programme of Action in June 1993, national institutions with charters premised on the implementation of human rights have grown more rapidly in Asian and Pacific countries than in any other region," p. 59, para. 1. So, in 1994, India and Indonesia established new human rights commissions. In this respect, see Briand Burdekin, p. 62, para. 11. On a more general note, statisticians indicate that three countries join the ranks of democracy each year.

60. Ouguergouz, p. 124.

61. See Marcelino Orejia, "La révision institutionnelle de l'Union Européenne," *Académie de droit international*, 29 July 1997, p. 11. See also European Commission, Task Force for the Intergovernmental Conference, news report, 1997, p. 1, where it is mentioned that the treaty formalizes the court's competence to control the application of basic rights by community institutions and extends this control.

62. The 1984 Convention against Torture and other Cruel, Inhuman or Degrading Treatments, the 1948 Convention on the Prevention and Repression of Genocide, the 1966 International Treaty Relating to Civil and Political Rights, and the 1965 International Convention on the Elimination of All Kinds of Racial Discrimination. Cf. Quigley, p. 556.

63. Jean-Marie Breton thus argues that economic and social rights seem more universal and constant. See Jean-Marie Breton, "Débats sur les droits économiques et sociaux," *Le Juge de l'administration et les droits fondamentaux dans l'espace francophone*, in "Droits d'expression et d'inspiration françaises," Cairo Conference Proceedings of December 1997, Bruylant-Idef-Agence de la Francophonie, Romanian Institute for Human Rights, Brussels, p. 560.

64. Article 13 of the African Charter, paras. 1 and 2. The non-respect of these rights in Africa partly results from their enunciation in unsatisfactory terms, cf. Ouguergouz, p. 119, as much as a multiplicity of other factors. Whatever might be the causes of non-awareness of rights to political participation, their frequent violation is attested by Tessy Bakary. This expert today observes a general decline in the importance of electoral processes in Africa, after the formal return to pluralism in the early nineties. According to Bakary, the decline is shown through authoritarian elections. See Tessy Bakary, "La Démocratie en Afrique, l'ère post-électorale?" in *Bulletin du Codesria* 314, Dakaar-Senegal, 1998, pp. 9–11.

65. See Chidi Anselm Odinkalu and Camilla Christensen, "The African Commission on

Human and Peoples' Rights: The Development of its Non-State Communication Procedures," *Human Rights Quarterly* 20, 1998, p. 278.

66. See Makau Mutua, "The African Human Rights Court, A Two-Legged Stool?" *Human Rights Quarterly* 27(2), May 1999, p. 344.

67. Article 65 of the Cameroonian Constitution of 18 January 1996 included all the international instruments on human rights ratified by Cameroon, a total of 30 at 1 January 1998. Cf. Minkoa She, pp. 291–292, and which are referred to in the Preamble, and in the Constitution itself; but four years after, the situation on the field has not evolved much. Cf. James Mouangue Kobila, "Le préambule du texte constitutionnel du 18 janvier 1996, de l'enseigne décorative à l'étalage utilitaire," in *Lex Lata, Bulletin bimensuel d'annonces légales, de chronique juridique et d'affaires*, special issue on the constitutions, 23–24, February–March 1999, pp. 33–38. See also James Mouangue Kobila, "Création des normes, les occasions manquées du nouveau parlementarisme pluraliste au Cameroun," *Solon* [African journal on parliamentary government and democracy] 1(1), note 21, p. 54.

68. Ouguergouz, p. 386.

69. See above.

70. See Mbaye, p. 47.

71. Ibid.

72. See Pierre de Senarclens, "Un idéal commun pour l'humanité," in *Fédération internationale des droits de l'homme: Droits de l'homme et relations Nord-Sud*; preface by Danielle Mitterrand, L'Harmattan, Paris, 1985, p. 138.

73. See Pierre Charles Gérard, "La problématique des droits économiques et sociaux," ibid., p. 56.

74. In Chaillot, 1991, francophone heads of state have stressed the interrelation between the respect for human rights and development in a phrase which deserves to be repeated, "There is no development without freedom, and no freedom without development." See Guillou, p. 13.

75. See Boutros Boutros Ghali, p. 11.

76. In this respect, Kéba Mbaye (p. 40) points out that, and strongly too with regard to Article 9 of the statute of the International Court of Justice, it is a fact that there are "great forms of civilization" representing the main legal systems in the world.

77. See Ouguergouz. On the same note, Frank Moderne writes that "Dans la conception africaine, lato sensu, la référence première est le groupe," [In the African conception, lato sensu, the first reference is the group]. See his contribution in "Débat sur les normes internes," in Etienne Picard, p. 180.

78. Myabe, p. 155.

79. Ebele Wei, "Le paradis tabou, Autopsie d'une culture assassinée," ed. Cerac, Douala-Cameroun, 1999, p. 112.

80. Ouguergouz, p. 387. See also p. 78. This state of affairs is explained through the functioning of the African traditional justice. The objective sought after is not so much to punish but to settle the difference while restoring the harmony of social relations, Pierre François Gonidec, "Les droits africains, évolution et sources," Paris, LGDJ, 1968, p. 195, quoted by Maurice Kamto, see below note 101, p. 58, through the accomplishment of a symbolical gesture of reconciliation, which may consist in sharing a kola nut, drinking from the same cup one after the other or just simply shaking hands. The African legal tradition stands strongly in contrast with the modern justice described by Maurice Kamto as a merciless battle of arguments and means of procedure which has to conclude dramatically, with a winner and a loser who turn their backs on each other when leaving the court-room. Ibid.

81. See Eid Ahmed El-Ghafloul, "Le Juge de l'administration et les normes internes constitutionnelles ou infraconstitutionnelles relatives aux droits fondamentaux en Egypte," in *Le Juge de l'administration et les droits fondamentaux dans l'espace francophone*, above, p. 106.

82. Abdel Hamid, Mohamed Sami, p. 36.

83. Cf. El-Ghafloul, pp. 103–104.

84. David Annoussamy, "Les Droits fondamentaux dans l'Inde," in *Le Juge de l'administration et les droits fondamentaux dans l'espace francophone*, pp. 119–120.

85. Harriet Samuels, "Hong Kong on Women, Asian Values, and the Law," *Human Rights Quarterly*, 1999, p. 712.

86. See Human Rights, Fourth Workshop on Regional Human Rights Arrangements in the Asian and Pacific region, Report, p. 3.

87. Cf. Mbaye, p. 162. See also, Ouguergouz, p. 388, at the end.

88. References to law and "international conventions" are frequent in the African Charter, Art. 12, para. 3; "Les déclarations et conventions internationals" [Declarations and international conventions], Art. 18, para. 3; "Les principes du droit international" [Principles of International Law], Art. 21, para. 3; and "Les moyens reconnus par la communauté internationale" [Resources acknowledged by the international community], Art. 20, para. 2, also have an important place in it.

89. Mbaye, p. 46.

90. Term borrowed from Ouguergouz, p. 78.

91. Cf. Hassam Tabet Rifaat, "De quelques réflexions au sujet des droits économiques et sociaux au Liban", in *Le Juge de l'Administration et les droits fondamentaux dans l'espace francophone*, 1999, p. 526.

92. See Etienne le Roy, 1994, "Les Droits de l'homme entre un universalisme hâtif et le ghetto des particularismes culturels," in Aupelf/Uref, p. 64.

93. See de Senarclens, p. 134.

94. See Alan Ganoo, "Discours d'ouverture au colloque de l'Aupelf-Uref," 1994, p. 34.

95. Cf. Reisman, p. 64.

96. A hierarchical-type relationship between the international penal court for Rwanda and the states is also illustrated in its regulations. States must carry out the court's rulings such as warrants for arrest, search warrants, summons or transfer, and give effect to any other legal decision. Cf. Kakpo, p. 68.

97. See Annoussamy, p. 114.

98. Kenneth I. Cain writes that "between 1990 and 1997 approximately 200,000 Liberian citizens were killed in war." He reports cases of ethnic murders, political assassinations, rape, torture, cannibalism, looting and other violations of civil and political rights in "The Rape of Dinah, Human Rights, Civil War in Liberia, and Evil Triumphant," *Human Rights Quarterly* 21(2), 1999, pp. 267, 307, and pp. 269–289.

99. In Algeria, 60 journalists have been assassinated since 1988.

100. Briand Burdekin points out that "the reality, even in developed countries, is that the courts are inaccessible to a large proportion of the population because of the extremely high costs involved," p. 64.

101. See Maurice Kamto, *Pouvoir et droit en Afrique, Essai sur les fondements du constitutionnalisme dans les Etats d'Afrique noire francophone*, Bibliothèque africaine et malgache, LGDJ, Paris, 1987, pp. 439–447.

102. Fatsah Ouguergouz speaks more of a lack of spirit to file claims and of the Africans' relative inertia, p. 40.

103. Negotiations between political parties in power and the opposition after the elections.

104. The organization of societies in the form of a rule of law has first priority among Irina Moroianu Zlatescu's three conditions for human rights to become a legal reality, next to the existence of a pre-established legal framework and precise legal guarantees. Cf. Irina Moroianu Zlatescu, "Le Libre accès à la justice et les droits de l'homme en Roumanie," in *Le Juge de l'administration et les droits fondamentaux dans l'espace francophone*, p. 718.

4

Human rights and Asian values

Tatsuo Inoue[1]

Some influential political leaders in Asia have been resorting to the so-called "Asian values" for a rationale for defying the international criticism of their governments' violation of civil and political liberties that are the basic components of human rights. They object that such criticism is based on the specifically Western concept of human rights alien to and incompatible with the core values embedded in Asian culture and tradition and that the West's attempt to impose its own concept of human rights on Asia constitutes cultural imperialism. Some intellectuals are also criticizing the current human rights discourses as involving West-centric bias although their arguments are more sophisticated and nuanced.[2]

One of the major factors promoting the Asian values discourse is, certainly, the rapid economic development in several Asian countries that enhanced their self-confidence. Did their recent economic setback deprive the Asian values discourse of its force? I do not think so. The structural conditions that are to sustain the influence of this discourse still obtain and will continue to do so in the foreseeable future.

First, as for economic conditions, we should not confuse the short-term fluctuations and the long-term trend. There is no compelling reason to deny that economic development will continue, even if with less impressive growth rates, in Asia in the long run. Apart from that, the grave impact of the Asian economic setback on the global market involving Euro-

American economies has made the Asian as well as Western people aware that the presence of Asia in the global network of economic interdependency can no longer be belittled.

Second, the fundamental source for the influence of the Asian values discourse lies not in economy but in history and politics. The proponents of Asian values appeal to Asian people's deep-seated "ressentiment" (ambivalent mixture of resentment and inferiority complex) against Western colonialism and hegemony. Economic success gave vent to this psyche. But economic failure can also stir it up. Actually, some Asian political leaders blamed the recent Asian economic crisis upon the wanton speculations of the Western financial capitals, not unsuccessfully propagating the perception that their nations must defend their Asian way of life against the new invasions of the economic forms of Western colonialism.

So I think that the Asian values discourse will remain a focus of controversy in human rights practices for some time. In this chapter I will argue that the attempt to oppose "Asian values" to the "Western" concept of human rights is untenable and dominated by the Westcentrism that those who make this attempt claim to overcome and that Asian societies have their own endogenous reasons to accept and develop the civil and political components of human rights that underlie liberal democracy.

The manipulation of Western normative languages

The Asian values discourse is illegitimately parasitic on Westcentrism in two ways. First, it abuses or manipulates the Western normative languages: the state sovereignty and socio-economic rights to subsistence. Second, this discourse is dominated by the orientalist stereotype of Asia that has been functioning as the epistemic device for rationalizing Western hegemony over Asia. I take up the first and second issues in this and the next sections respectively.

Strangely enough, those proponents of Asian values who adamantly reject civil and political liberties as specifically Western values make no scruple of resorting to the West-originated notion of sovereignty to immunize Asian governments against the criticism of their violation of these rights. Sovereignty, however, cannot be used as a "trump" over human rights because sovereignty depends on human rights for its legitimation in the following three respects.

First, the sovereign state eroded the medieval or feudal system of pluralistic and decentralized power structures that functioned as a safeguard against the tyranny of a monarch or any other centre of power. The human rights doctrine emerged to counterbalance the highly centralized and reinforced power of sovereign states. It is a substitute for the medieval safeguard against tyranny. Accordingly, sovereignty cannot be accepted without being coupled with human rights.[3]

Second, the sovereign state needs human rights not just as a safeguard against its tyrannical potential but also as its raison d'être. It is only part of the story to say that diffused powers in the medieval system checked the tyranny of centralized power. They were themselves the sources of social discrimination and oppression. As is shown by the history of the French Revolution and modern social contract theories, the modern sovereign state emerged and was justified as the liberator of individuals from feudal fetters although it exposed them to new threats of its own. Even in contemporary societies the sovereign state has an important role to play as a powerful protector of human rights against the social tyranny of informal and intermediary powers. Such a formidable and dangerous Leviathan as the sovereign state can be allowed to exist only if its purpose is the effective protection of human rights.[4]

Last, sovereignty and human rights are conceptual twins. The human rights of individuals are projected on to the sovereignty of states. They share the same normative function and justification: protecting weaker agents by giving them a veto over the demands imposed on them by stronger agents. Both of them equalize the normative status of the factually unequal agents. Just as helpless individuals and vulnerable minorities need human rights more desperately than those with power resources in the domestic context, so the weaker states that want to protect themselves against the oppression of superpowers stick to the principle of equal sovereignty more persistently than the latter. Because the principle of equal respect for the powerless constitutes the common justificatory ground for human rights and sovereignty, Asian developing countries that run counter to this principle by denying dissident individuals and minorities civil and political rights in the domestic context will lose moral standing when they resort to the protective function of sovereignty in the international context.[5]

These considerations imply not just that the proponents of Asian values are unjustified in using sovereignty as a trump over human rights, but also that the proponents of human rights, especially those in the developed countries, should appreciate the important role that sovereignty can play in reinforcing the international status of the developing countries effectively and protecting the human rights of their citizens against informal obscurantist social forces.

There is another normative language that the Asian values discourse manipulates to defy civil and political rights: social and economic rights to subsistence. This concept is an integral part of the traditions of social democracy in Europe and welfare-state liberalism in the United States, and so has a wide appeal to Western audiences. The Asian values proponents take advantage of this appeal and claim that the top priority of developing countries is to assure their people of the socio-economic rights to basic means of subsistence and that civil and political rights are luxuries that only the developed countries can afford to enjoy.

This argument can be refuted in two ways. First, as Amartya Sen showed convincingly in reference to the problems of famine in developing countries, civil and political liberties are a prerequisite for implementing socio-economic rights.[6] I will not take up this issue here. I want to emphasize another fallacy involved in the argument. The alleged priority of socio-economic rights over civil and political rights is a topsy-turvy logic. As a matter of fact, civil and political rights are more accessible to developing countries than socio-economic rights, not vice versa.

To implement socio-economic rights adequately, the government has to supply sufficient resources for subsistence to needy individuals. This is possible only if the country in question has already achieved that level of economic development where it has accumulated sufficient social surpluses to swallow the costs of redistribution and labour protection without devastating its economy. That is why in Western countries socio-economic rights came to be recognized and respected later than civil and political ones.

To be sure, even civil and political rights involve some cost, but I do not think it is prohibitive for developing countries. The cost involved in civic education should not be exaggerated because the best school for democracy is the democratic practice itself. As for the cost in terms of economic efficiency, it is often said as a defence of authoritarian developmentalist regimes that democratization incapacitates developing countries from taking off for successful industrialization because democratization would enable people to use political power to redistribute social resources in such a myopic way that adequate accumulation and efficient allocation of capital would be hampered.[7] But, as is exemplified by the development of post-war Japan, the redistributive function of democratization, if not up to the welfare state ideal, can work in such a way that the discontents of those social sections affected badly by rapid industrialization are channelled, thereby helping to form a national consensus on developmentalist policies and maintain political stability.[8] Under an authoritarian regime, on the other hand, the ruling class, unchecked by democratic control, has an incentive to interfere politically in the market economy to promote their private interests and thus thwart efficient resource allocation and spoil productive morale.

So I think that priority of human rights for developing countries should be set the other way around: civil and political rights, first; social and economic rights, second. The realities of Asian developing countries show that their genuine priority lies not in protecting the socio-economic rights of their citizens but in carrying out developmentalist industrial policies that may well conflict with these rights for the time being. I do not reject their developmental aspiration as illegitimate. My point is that the developmental needs may give them a temporary excuse for trading off social and economic rights, but not for trampling on civil and political rights.

Now I must respond to a couple of objections that can be addressed to me here. A Japanese international lawyer, Onuma Yasuaki, recently objected that the Western criteria for assessing and comparing human rights records in various countries give civil and political liberties preference over social and economic rights and thus are unfair to non-Western developing countries that have greater concern for the latter. He does not reject civil and political rights as inapplicable to Asian countries but requires that socio-economic rights should be given the same weight as civil and political rights.[9] My response to his objection is this: the priority of civil and political rights over social and economic rights as assessment criteria is not concerned with their moral weight but with their feasibility or accessibility. Even if we admit that these two sets of human rights have equal moral weight, we can still say that civil and political rights should be given priority in assessing human rights records of developing countries because they have fewer economic obstacles to implement, and so less excuse for failing to implement this set of rights as opposed to socio-economic rights. Actually, it would be unfair to them to demand that they should implement socio-economic rights as adequately as civil and political rights despite their limited resources.

This response may invite the further objection that I wrongly assume that civil-political rights are "negative" rights which simply require abstention or non-interference of the state whereas socio-economic rights are "positive" rights which demand a more active role of the state in regulating economic activities and redistributing wealth. The attempt to undermine the dichotomy of negative and positive rights has now become conspicuous in the current human rights discourse, as exemplified by Ruth Gavison in her contribution to the present volume. It is said that effective implementation of civil and political rights requires the state not just to refrain from intervening in social life but to take positive measures and bear the considerable expenditure for establishing an institutional infrastructure for legal enforcement, judicial remedies, public education and so on, while socio-economic rights involve negative restraint, such as respect for privacy of the welfare recipients, as well as positive aid and service. Those who share this observation may hold me to be misguided in asserting that the economic urgency of developing countries may excuse a temporary trade-off of socio-economic rights but cannot justify them in violating civil-political rights. They may object that my criteria for assessing human rights records are unfair to the developing countries because I am led, by identifying civil-political rights with negative rights, to underestimate the difficulty that they have in bearing the cost of implementing civil-political rights.[10]

This objection, however, is confused, and the grain of truth in it does not affect my point. First, I do not deny that civil-political rights have both negative and positive components. In fact, I emphasized above, as one of the internal connections between human rights and state sovereignty, that the state should play an active role in protecting the civil and political rights of individuals against oppressive and discriminatory practices of intermediary social powers. But this does not imply that the distinction between the negative and positive components of civil-political rights collapses. Civil-political rights impose two distinct kinds of duties on those who control state power: they have a negative duty to abstain from using their political power and resources to violate these rights by their own hands; in addition to this, they have a positive duty to use their power and resources to give their citizens effective protection against private violence and informal social oppression and discrimination practised by other individuals and groups. No matter how much cost is involved for the holders of state power to fulfil their positive duty, it does not excuse them for violating their negative duty. The point to be stressed is that the managers of authoritarian developmentalist regimes cannot justify their own political oppression by the implementation costs of civil and political rights. The critics of the negative and positive rights dichotomy should not blur this crucial point.

To rebut this point of mine, one might say that even the negative component of civil and political rights entails a non-negligible cost. The Chinese Communist Party, for example, has claimed that forbearing from punishing anti-government speeches involves grave costs such as social disorder. But anti-government speeches can bring about social disorder when there is no institutional route for the peaceful power change that democracy can provide. Social disorder is a consequence of the violation, not implementation, of civil and political rights.

It is true that civil-political rights, including free speech, are not "absolute" rights that must be implemented at any cost whatever. No one may indulge in the joy of self-expression by shouting "Fire!" for fun in a crowded movie theatre. Some sort of principled trade off is needed when the implementation of civil and political rights for some people involves the consequence of others' legitimate rights, whether civil-political or socio-economic ones, being violated. But allegations of such harmful consequences are often groundless or dubious, as we have seen about the alleged economic cost of democratization. If they are sound, they constitute a reason not for negating civil and politcal rights but for limiting the way these rights are exercised (e.g. restricting the time, place, and manners of political demonstrations rather than forbidding them). This kind of trade off concerns the internal limits of civil and political rights applicable to both developing and developed countries. It does not mean special excuses for violating civil-political rights only applicable to developing countries. What is more important, people need rights to free speech and political participation just in order to make sure that the costs of the others' rights that they bear are given due consideration in the political decision-making process for the legal regulations that are to accommodate people's competing rights.

Now I turn to my second reply to the objection concerning the implemetation costs of civil-political rights. It is hardly credible that authoritarian developmentalist countries lack resources for decently implementing the positive component of civil-political rights, as far as we take this to mean the state-backed legal enforcement of the immediate requirements of these rights (not inflated by a more extensive interpretation that we will see subsequently). Provision for "law and order" is given a top priority by such countries in their resource allocation. Their regimes can hold oppressive domination over their citizens because they have a very effective (or even too powerful) state apparatus. Those who manage this apparatus can use it to protect their citizens against the social tyranny of informal intermediary powers, instead of using it, as they do, to maintain their own political tyranny. What they lack is not political muscle but the political will to use it properly.

It may be retorted that they lack political muscle to control the intermediary powers and have to let the latter wield social tyranny if their regime is dependent on a coalition of such powers for its survival. This may be true, but it only shows that such a coalition is too weak to be the authoritarian developmentalist regime that it purports to be. Lacking a strong consistent political leadership backed by centralized power, it cannot discipline the intermediary powers so that they will not obstruct capital accumulation and the efficient resource allocation necessary for the rapid growth of the national economy by seeking their own special interests. Latent internal conflict of the coalition forces makes it too unstable even to secure "law and order" persistently. In a word, it lacks the power to carry out its own project that it advances as an excuse for violating civil-political rights. It is politically inadequate to have its moral claims taken seriously.

Third, the range of positive components of civil-political rights can be extended, if you like, in such a way that it covers socio-economic rights.

As a general rule we may say that an adequate implementation of these rights helps to ameliorate social conditions that produce the crimes violating civil rights and helps to ward off the influences of poverty and social discrimination that prevent people from exercising their political rights effectively. This may lead us to say that developing countries cannot fully implement civil-political rights just because they lack sufficient resources for substantiating socio-economic rights. This argument, however, cannot justify the political power holders in defying the two core duties that are shown above, namely, the negative duty to abstain from tyranny and the positive duty to enforce the legal protection of civil-political rights against direct assault on them by informal powers. All it can show is that their limited resources temporarily excuse them for failing to complement and reinforce the formal and legal protection of civil-political rights by adequately implementing the socio-economic rights of their citizens so as to correct the social causes of threats to civil-political rights. This does not refute but simply reiterates my point. It may be true that the implementation of civil-political rights cannot be improved beyond a certain point unless socio-economic rights are adequately implemented. But it would be a deceptive argument to say that the cost involved in going beyond that point justifies the governments of developing countries in failing to reach that point because of their wrongdoing and ineptitude.

Last, it would be wide of the mark to castigate my criteria for assessing human rights records as West-centric in the sense that they favour Western-developed countries. My point that developing countries with their meagre resources have fewer excuses for their failure to implement the core civil-political rights than for their failure to implement socio-economic rights, implies that developed countries with their affluence are less excusable for their failure to implement socio-economic rights more adequately than developing countries. A further implication is that fair assessment of overall human rights records should rank those developed countries with a poor performance in social welfare as low as those developing countries with poor civil-political rights records even if the former's civil-political rights record is passable and the latter's socio-economic rights record is not. For example, the United States, whose social security system is, despite huge spending on it, so inefficient and unfair that "forty million Americans have grossly inadequate medical coverage or none at all"[11] cannot boast that its overall human rights record matches the role of human rights preacher that it wants to play, even if we disregard the demerits of its civil-political rights record vitiated by legacies of slavery, racism, religious bigotry, anti-Communist fanaticism, and so on.

All these considerations show that we have to retain our sensitivity to the asymmetry of civil-political and socio-economic rights in terms of the difficulty of their implementation in order to debunk the deceptions of both the developed and developing countries and to give a fair assessment of their human rights record.

Breaking the spell of Orientalism

Let me turn to the second and more fundamental sense in which the Asian values discourse is dominated by Westcentrism. The proponents of Asian values deny the universal validity of the liberal and democratic components of human rights (i.e. civil and political rights) on the ground that Asia has a unique cultural essence alien to these rights. By doing so, they reproduce the Orientalist stereotype of Asia.

By Orientalism I mean the dichotomous differentiation of Asia (the Orient) and the West (the Occident), which has the following two features: first, Asia as a whole is essentially and monolithically differentiated from the West. It is postulated that the total system of Asian culture, religion, language, art, politics, economy, and history can be explained in terms of the unique essence ascribed to Asia. It is also assumed that the West is privileged to understand this essence and to guide Asia, which lacks the intellectual resources for self-knowledge.

Second, and what is more important, the underlying motive of this essentialist characterization of Asia is the West's desire to establish its own identity as the creator and bearer of modern civilization, or as the promoter of the progress of world history. The West needs Asia as "the Other," as the negative background against which its positive figure is set off. If the West is to represent the glory of modern civilization, Asia must represent the darkness of pre-modernity or counter-modernity. This dual identity construction implies an asymmetry between the West as the civilizing agent and Asia as the object to be civilized that has always supplied a rationale for Western colonialism and hegemony over Asia. If Western hegemony is to be perpetuated, the "Otherness" of Asia must be fixed as its perennial essence.

I do not claim that my characterization of Orientalism is exegetically loyal to Edward Said's use of this notion.[12] Nor do I claim that all the historical exemplifications given by him for this notion are valid. My point is that Orientalism in the above-presented sense even now has a strong hold over Western perceptions of Asian societies (despite – or, in some cases, owing to – the vogue for "post-modern" discourses in some quarters of the intellectual world)[13] and that the Asian values discourse is an accomplice in perpetuating its hold.

The rapid economic development of Asian countries appears to have discredited the classic forms of Orientalism, such as Hegel's notorious thesis of the ahistorical stagnancy of Asian empires in his philosophy of history and Max Weber's once influential claim that modern capitalism is based on Protestant ethics and incompatible with the Confucian and Taoist traditions in Asia.[14] But Asian economic growth still allows or even incites Western observers to believe that Asian developing countries are dominated by the repressive and authoritarian political culture obstructing civil and political liberties and that their "political backwardness" contributes to making their developmentalist economy "the savage capitalism" that indulges in unfair and aggressive international trade practices, disruption of the environment, and domestic exploitation of labour. These presumptions would imply that the West's guidance, interference, and disciplinary power are indispensable for the political modernization of Asian countries.

The Asian values proponents reject the idea that the West should play the role of moral teacher for Asia in liberalization and democratization of Asian politics. But their reason for this rejection is that civil and political rights are not universally valid but peculiar to Western political culture and alien to Asian culture. This reasoning commits them to accept the Orientalist polarization of Asian and Western identities. Although they equalize or even reverse the evaluative connotations of these stereotypes of Asian and Western identities, they accept their epistemic contents.

By reproducing the Orientalist dichotomy, the Asian values discourse conceals and distorts the internal diversity, complexity, and transformative potential of Asian societies and reproduces the Western prejudiced perception that Asian societies are culturally inadequate to develop human rights and democracy on their own. It also helps to reinforce Western self-sanctification, enabling the West to indulge in portraying itself as the historical paradigm of human rights and democracy and wiping off, or repressing at a subconscious level, its stained record of imperialism, slavery, racism, gender discrimination, and so on.

It is ironical and even paradoxical for the Asian values discourse to accept the epistemic device for the Western hegemony that it attempts to overcome. But this is not hard to understand, because it is based on the same psychological mechanism in which some of the victims of racial discrimination are tempted to affirm positively the racial identity imposed on them by the deep-seated social prejudice against them, in order to heal their marred self-respect.[15] Although psychologically understandable, the reverse use of discriminatory stereotypes is dangerous and ultimately self-defeating. Just as those African-Americans who say, "Black is beautiful," tend to castigate as "oreos" other African-Americans who want to dissociate themselves from the racial stereotype and thereby to reinforce the fixed idea of racist essentialism that "Blacks are blacks," so the Asian values proponents tend to denounce as "bananas" those Asians who rebel against authoritarian regimes for the sake of civil and political liberties and thereby reconfirm the Orientalist ascription of essential political backwardness to Asia.

The Orientalist dichotomy traps both Asian and Western people into self-deception and induces them to escape from self-critical examination of their own human rights records. Once we liberate ourselves from this trap, we can see that both of them share the difficulties, dilemmas, failures, and follies that hamper aspirations for human rights. This offers a starting point for sincere and fruitful dialogue.

As a step to such a dialogue, I will briefly examine and dissolve two specific forms of the Orientalist dichotomy of Asia and the West to show that Asian countries like Western ones have internal diversity and conflicts and that they need to develop civil and political components of human rights to accommodate them.

Accommodating religious and cultural tensions

It is a popular practice to characterize Asia and the West as two distinct civilizations in terms of their religious foundations. For example, "the Judeo-Christian West" is often opposed to "the Confucian-Islamic Asia." Samuel Huntington's discussions of "the clash of civilizations" exemplifies the persistence of this mode of thinking.[16] But the religion-based form of Orientalist dichotomy is clearly untenable. I do not just mean that the cleavage between Confucianism and Islam is too deep for them to be spiritually allied or that many other religions such as Buddhism, Hinduism, Christianity, each with its own divergent denominations, and a myriad of indigenous faiths compete for influence in Asia. The most important fact is that religious and cultural diversity is not compartmentalized along national borders but internalized within many Asian countries. They have even deeper and wider internal religio-cultural diversity and conflicts than most Western countries. For example, Singapore, Malaysia, Indonesia, and China whose governments expound Asian values very vocally are all multi-religious, multicultural and even multinational countries with high degrees of actual and potential tension.

To establish a fair and stable political framework for accommodating this tension, they have to institutionalize liberal tolerance by protecting the civil and political rights of religio-cultural minorities. Let me make a few points to defend and clarify this thesis.

First, some Asian political leaders, such as Lee Kuan Yew in Singapore, claim that the authoritarian regime is needed to prevent the conflicts between the competing religious and ethnic groups of their countries, because democratization would allow the ethnic majority to oppress the minorities and cause violent ethnic strife.[17] There is an element of truth in this argument: unrestrained democracy has the danger of inviting the tyranny of the majority. But this can hardly be an argument for autocracy. This does not show that people's right to democratic participation should be denied. It rather shows that not the simple majoritarian democracy but liberal democracy with constitutional constraints on the majoritarian power, such as judicial review for constitutional rights, separation of powers, power-sharing devices of consociational democracy, minorities' self-rule, and so on, is needed to accommodate religious and ethnic tensions. It shows that not just formally equal allocation of the right to political participation but the institutionally reinforced protection of minority rights is necessary to respect the human rights of all the people equally and fairly in the substantial sense of these terms.

Human rights should not be at the mercy of the majority's preference, but neither should they be at the mercy of the autocrat. If their protection is left up to the autocrat's good will, both the majority and minorities become more vulnerable to unpredictable attack upon their human rights. Fair and stable accommodation of religious and ethnic tensions requires the entrenchment of the human rights of all vulnerable people by the constitutional structure that constrains the arbitrary rule of any power holder.

Second, it may be objected that liberal tolerance in the form of constitutional protection of civil and political liberties is not the only way of accommodating religious and cultural tensions and that there are equally adequate or even better alternatives. The Ottoman Empire, for example, had a long-established form of religious tolerance: the millet system where certain non-Muslim minorities such as the Greek Orthodox, Armenian Orthodox, and Jews were allowed to enjoy collective religious self-rule within their communities.[18] In the contemporary context, some multiculturalists with communitarian sympathies reject liberal tolerance as too individualistic to protect the minorities' group-specific rights to collective cultural survival, which may require some constraint on individual autonomy.[19]

But I do not think these alternatives are adequate to capture the complexity of religious and cultural tensions. The millet system was a confederation of theocracies that were not fair to unprivileged minorities and dissident minorities within each minority. Even the privileged minorities were subject to discriminatory restriction on their religious activities.[20] This system should be regarded not as a full-fledged alternative to liberal tolerance but as an inchoate form of the latter that helps to break the Orientalist stereotype of Muslims as "the fanatic and intolerant fundamentalists." The group-differentiated rights to preferential treatment for cultural minorities as defended by radical multiculturalists can be justified in terms of the liberal principle of fair opportunity if these measures are meant to offset the disadvantages of minorities in cultural competition.[21] But the anti-liberal multiculturalists fail to see that minority cultures will be fossilized rather than vitalized if the dissident individuals within the minority communities are denied the rights to challenge and transform the dominant interpretation and practices of their cultures.

Last, I should add that there are often political obstacles and crises to be overcome before minority rights are implemented, as we have recently seen in East Timor. But this is not peculiar to Asia. We cannot say, for example, that things are and have been much easier and far less bloody in Northern Ireland. This implies two things. On the one hand, Asian governments should not manipulate the political difficulty of implementing minority rights and leave them violated. On the other hand, Western countries should be more self-critical of their own stained record in dealing with religious and ethnic conflicts and more sensitive to the difficulty of the task that Asian countries must undertake to resolve these conflicts in a fair and stable way.

Accommodating individualist-communitarian tensions

The dichotomy of "the individualistic West" versus "communitarian Asia" is another familiar orientalist formula. It may appear more plausible than the religion-based dichotomy, and it still has an irresistible appeal even to sophisticated intellectuals. But it is also hard to maintain. The tension between individualism and communitarianism runs not between the West and Asia but through both of them. The conflict between individual initiatives and communal cohesion or solidarity is a fundamental and universal problem that all societies, Asian or Western, have had to address.

"Civil society" in the West involves both the individualist and communitarian aspects. For example, the United States that has been a stronghold of "rugged individualism" has another face. As de Tocqueville vividly described in the last century, American democracy depended for its vitality on a variety of intermediary communities as a seedbed of civic virtue.[22] This point is re-emphasized as a general condition of civil society by contemporary communitarians and republicans.[23] The tension between liberal concern for individual autonomy and communitarian-republican concern for the sense of public responsibility cultivated in communal life constitutes the main thread of Western political history. The liberal-democratic regime has developed and is yet to be further developed to accommodate this tension.

The same tension penetrates Asia. Here we should emphasize the individualist streams that counterbalance the stereotype of "the communitarian Asia." Each of the complicated religious traditions in Asia has its own internal conflict arising from the individualistic and reformist movements, comparable to that in Christian traditions, such as the liberal component of the neo-Confucian movement with its emphasis on individual development through critical learning; transcendental individualism in Buddhist tradition centred on the self-reliant search for the true self identified with dharma; Sufism as an Islamic Protestantism seeking for the direct communion of individuals with the Deity in defiance of the ulama as authoritative interpreters of the divine texts who lost independence from the Caliph's political power, and so on.[24]

From a socio-economic point of view, the model of the peasant community that has determined the stereotype of "the communitarian Asia" oversimplifies Asian social structure even as a historical prototype. Asian countries have a variety of historical actors of different social layers, such as merchants, artisans, enfeoffed warriors (like samurai in feudal Japan), gentry, learned courtiers, monks, and so on, whose conditions of life had a tendency to cultivate a sense of individuality in the forms of meritocratic competitiveness, contractual mutuality, artistic self-expression, critical disobedience based on the sense of honour, autonomy of moral or religious conscience, and so on. Moreover, social transformations caused by rapid economic development have generated new sources for individualist tendencies.

The individualist streams and tendencies in Asia that I have exemplified above certainly form part of the cultural resources for developing civil and political liberties. But I have to emphasize that communitarian legacies and aspirations of Asian societies, which compete with individualistic tendencies, also enable and require them to develop some or other form of liberal democracy that protects both the political rights to participate in collective self-governance and personal rights to individual autonomy. We have seen that liberal democracy is not exclusively based on individualism but engaged in a project of accommodating the individualist-communitarian tensions in Western countries. The same holds in Asia in the following respects.

First, the communitarian aspect of Asian societies is, or can be rendered, conducive to democracy just as democratic vitality depends on communitarian resources in the Western context. For example, as is shown by W. Theodore de Bary, the doctrines and practices of the community compact (xiangyue) and the community school (shexue) in neo-Confucian traditions offer the historical models for intermediary community as a seedbed of civic virtue and institutional means for democratic control of political power in China.[25] The view that Asian communitarian traditions are authoritarian by nature while Western communitarianism is democratic is another piece of Orientalist dichotomy.[26]

Second, Asian countries need democracy to foster the communitarian virtues that they are seeking for. Authoritarian capitalist regimes in Asia, such as Singapore, are now suffering from the gap between the official communitarian ideology and the individualist reality, because their capitalist economy propels self-interested pursuits while their authoritarian politics deprives people of the experience of participating in communal affairs. Participation in democratic self-governance fosters civic virtue: an active concern and sense of responsibility for the larger community's public affairs.[27]

Third, the liberal components of human rights, which have the structure of individual rights as veto over the pursuit of the collective goal of a given community, are not antithetical to communal virtues sought for in the contemporary Asian context. On the contrary, these rights are necessary to cultivate an inclusive and well-balanced sensitivity to the competing communal responsibilities because they enable individuals to reserve moral energy for such a pluralistically extended communal responsibility by refusing to dedicate themselves totally to one specific communal sphere.[28]

Last, it is wrong to reject the liberal concept of individual rights as inappropriate for Asia on the ground that the Western confrontational legal culture associated with this concept is incompatible with the Asian consensual mode of conflict resolution. The judicial implementation of individual rights is not incompatible with, but rather prerequisite to, a genuinely consensual mode of conflict resolution fit for the communitarian ideal emphasized in Asia, because without effective access to judicial remedies the alleged "consensual" conflict resolution would easily turn into coercion and exploitation of those in a weaker bargaining position.[29]

To sum up: both the individualist and communitarian tendencies competing in Asian countries give them cultural resources and endogenous need for developing both the liberal and democratic components of human rights.

Conclusion

These arguments lead to the conclusion that the proper way in which Asian voices can contribute to the development of human rights practices is to break the spell of Orientalism that entraps both the Asian and Western people into the cage of deceptively polarized self-identities, and to show that it is a valid and unfinished task both for Asia and the West to reconceptualize and implement liberal and democratic components of human rights in such a way that religio-cultural tensions and individual-ist-communitarian tensions are accommodated on a principled and fair basis. The awareness of the shared tasks, difficulties, and failures forms the ground upon which Asia and the West can hold sincere dialogues on human rights that are mutually *self*-critical as well as critical and mutu-ally encouraging as well as enlightening.

Notes

1. This is a condensed and revised version of an earlier paper "Liberal Democracy and Asian Orientalism," in J. R. Bauer and D. A. Bell, eds., *The East Asian Challenge for Human Rights*, Cambridge University Press, 1999, pp. 27–59. While recapitulating the main threads of my argument in the earlier paper, I amplified my argument for the asymmetry of civil-political and socio-economic rights as criteria for assessing human rights records by responding to some major objections to my standpoint about this issue. I also updated the introductory remarks and revised exemplification, notation, and references. In this paper the names of Japanese and some other Asian individuals are shown in the original order, surnames come before given names.
2. For a recent admirable example, see Daniel A. Bell, *East Meets West, Human Rights and Democracy in East Asia*, Princeton University Press, 2000. The author reminds us of the importance of a sound but easily neglected maxim for cross-cultural understand-ing that we should know specific facts about the social predicament and resources of each country before making evaluative judgments and reform proposals about its politi-cal system.
3. I agree with Onuma Yasuaki on this point. My reservation is that this is not the whole story but just one aspect of multifarious connections between human rights and sover-eignty. See Onuma Yasuaki, "In Quest of Intercivilizational Human Rights: 'Universal' vs. 'Relative' Human Rights Viewed from an Asian Perspective," *Occasional Paper No. 2*, The Asian Foundation's Center for Asian Pacific Affairs, 1996, pp. 8f.
4. Higuchi Yoichi has brought to our attention an active role of the state as an enlightened liberator of individuals in modern constitutional history and the necessity of such a role of the state for contemporary Japan, where intermediary communities are left virtually free to violate individual rights by their informal social powers. See Higuchi Yoichi, *Kindai Kokuminkokka no Kenpo Kozo* [The Constitutional Structure of the Modern Nation State], The University of Tokyo Press, 1994; and *Kenpo to Kokka* [The Consti-tution and the State], Tokyo, Iwanami Shoten, 1999. John Haley also points out the fact that the strength of community control in contemporary Japan is interlocked with the weakness of the state and individuals. See John O. Haley, *Authority Without Power, Law and the Japanese Paradox*, Oxford University Press, 1991. I have given my own analysis of the tyranny of intermediary communities in contemporary Japan in Inoue Tatsuo, "The Poverty of Rights-Blind Communality, Looking Through the Window of Japan," *Brigham Young University Law Review* 2, 1993, pp. 517–551; and "Jiyu no Chitsujo" [The Order of Liberty], in Inoue Tatsuo, ed., *Jiyu, Kenryoku, Yutopia* [Free-dom, Power and Utopia], Tokyo, Iwanami Shoten, 1998, pp. 42–62.
5. I have developed this perception of sovereignty to defend a communitarian-anarchist conception of global order of equally vulnerable and mutually dependent sovereign

states as opposed to the current hegemonic order in Inoue, "Jiyu no Chitsujo," pp. 63–68.

6. See Amartya Sen, *Poverty and Famines, An Essay on Entitlement and Deprivation*, Oxford University Press, 1981; J. Drèze and A. Sen, *Hunger and Public Action*, Oxford University Press, 1989.

7. See Jon Elster, "The Necessity and Impossibility of Simultaneous Economic and Political Reform," in D. Greenberg et al., eds., *Constitutionalism and Democracy, Transitions in the Contemporary World*, Oxford University Press, 1993, pp. 267–274.

8. See Kyogoku Junichi, *The Political Dynamics of Japan*, trans. Ike Nobutaka, University of Tokyo Press, 1987, pp. 96–132.

9. See Onuma Yasuaki, *Jinken, Kokka, Bunmei, Fuhenshugiteki Jinkenkan kara Bunsaiteki Jinkenkan he* [Human Rights, State and Civilization, from a Universalistic to an Intercivilizational Conception of Human Rights], Tokyo, Chikuma Shobo, 1998, chs. 5–7.

10. For a criticism of differentiation of civil-political and socio-economic rights in terms of financial cost to the government, see Shin Hebong, "Jinkenjoyaku jono Kokka no Gimu, Joyaku Jisshi niokeru Jinken Nibunron no Saiko" [The Duties of the States in Human Rights Treaties, the Dichotomy of Human Rights in Treaty Implementation Reconsidered], Part 1, in *Kokusaiho Gaiiko Zasshi* [*Journal of International Law and Diplomâcy*] 96(1), 1997, pp. 8–13.

11. Ronald Dworkin, *Sovereign Virtue, the Theory and Practice of Equality*, Harvard University Press, 2000, p. 307.

12. See Edward W. Said, *Orientalism*, New York, Georges Borchardt Inc., 1978.

13. In an earlier paper I have shown that Orientalist mentalities are now reproduced by a variety of "post-philosophical" contextualist tendencies that are now in vogue in the Western intellectual world. See Inoue, "Liberal Democracy and Asian Orientalism," pp. 47–49.

14. See Georg W. F. Hegel, *Lectures on the Philosophy of World History*, trans. H. B. Nisbet, Cambridge University Press, 1975; Max Weber, *The Religion of China*, trans. Hans H. Gerth, Free Press, 1951.

15. For a penetrating analysis of this paradoxical psychology, see K. A. Appiah, "Identity, Authenticity, Survival," in A. Gutmann, ed., *Multiculturalism, Examining the Politics of Recognition*, Princeton University Press, 1994, pp. 149–163.

16. See Samuel Huntington, *The Clash of Civilizations and the Remaking of World Order*, New York, Simon & Schuster, 1997.

17. Lee claims that if a democracy unchecked by his authoritarian regime had been established in Singapore where 75 per cent of the population is Chinese, it would have led to the adoption of Chinese, rather than English, as the official language and to disastrous consequences of riots and disintegration. See Lee's statement quoted in Will Kymlicka, "Multiculturalism, Diversity in the Accommodation of Diversity," Part 1 of his serial lectures "The Future of the Nation-State," given at Tokyo University and Doshisha University in 1998 as the 5th Kobe Lecture sponsored by the Japan Association of Legal Philosophy and IVR Japan, in the Proceedings of the 5th Kobe Lecture, p. 56.

18. See W. Kymlicka, *Multicultural Citizenship*, Oxford University Press, 1995, pp. 156–158, 162–165, 183–184.

19. See Charles Taylor, "The Politics of Recognition," in Gutmann, ed., pp. 25–73.

20. See Kymlicka, p. 157.

21. Kymlicka has elaborately shown the possibility and necessity of integrating the preferential treatment of cultural minorities with the liberal concern for equality and autonomy. See Kymlicka above, and *Liberalism, Community and Culture*, Oxford University Press, 1989.

22. See Alexis de Tocqueville, *Democracy in America*, trans. G. Lawrence, New York, Anchor Press, 1969.
23. For a recent notable example, see Michael Sandel, *Democracy's Discontent: America in Search of a Public Philosophy*, Harvard University Press, 1996.
24. See Inoue, "Liberal Democracy and Asian Orientalism," pp. 50–53.
25. See W. Theodore de Bary, *Asian Values and Human Rights: A Confucian Communitarian Perspective*, Harvard University Press, 1998, esp. pp. 41–89.
26. I have criticized the sanctification of New England communities as historical origins of American democracy to give a more balanced and fairer comparison of the limits and potentialities of the Western and Asian communities in Inoue, "Liberal Democracy and Asian Orientalism," p. 55. Some Western political philosophers with communitarian sympathy show sensitivity to democratic potentialities of traditional Asian communities. See Bell, pp. 279–336; Charles Taylor, "Conditions of an Unforced Consensus on Human Rights," in Bauer and Bell, eds., pp. 122–144.
27. See D. A. Bell, "Democracy in Confucian Societies, the Challenge of Justification," in D. A. Bell et al., eds., *Towards Illiberal Democracy in Pacific Asia*, New York, St. Martin's Press, 1995, p. 39.
28. See Inoue, "The Poverty of Rights-Blind Communality, Looking Through the Window of Japan," pp. 545–551.
29. Accordingly, the currently fashionable term ADR, Alternative Dispute Resolution, is a misnomer as far as it implies an idea that non-adjudicative modes of conflict resolution can and should replace judicial protection of individual rights because of the former's superiority in efficiency. ADR cannot be an alternative to judicial remedies because its legitimacy depends on the effective accessibility of the latter.

Part 3

Human rights at the international level: Implementation and distributive justice

5

The politics of human rights

Pierre de Senarclens

The World Conference on Human Rights in Vienna (June 1993) will certainly be remembered for the virulence of its polemics on the perennial issue of universality. This debate is far from new within the United Nations since it started with the very conceptualization of the Universal Declaration of Human Rights (UDHR). In 1947 several scholars consulted by UNESCO expressed doubts about the idea of proclaiming universal human rights. Today the main arguments for or against universality are not very different from those expressed in the past in spite of the fact that most states are part of the United Nations and that by the very act of joining the organization they have committed themselves to the principles enshrined in the Charter. However, the opinions of experts and of government representatives are still very divergent on this issue, especially on the institutional structures and the socio-economic and political conditions necessary for the protection of human rights.

Human rights discourse has become irrepressible all over the world and few states would publicly justify their denial of a democratic form of government. Nevertheless it is doubtful that the Human Rights Commission and the General Assembly of today would underwrite the Universal Declaration as it was proclaimed in 1948. The opposition would not only come from authoritarian governments. Several Western countries would be reluctant to support the social and economic rights defined in the Declaration, in particular the right to work or protection against unemployment. Conservative ideology is so dominant today that many states have become hesitant to protect obligations that might hamper free exchange of goods and services or alter the sacrosanct principles of competition and productivity. Moreover globalization tends to erode state sovereignty and governments' capacity to deliver the public goods which are necessary for the implementation of human rights. Before tackling this last issue, I intend to clarify some common misunderstandings about the universality of human rights.

Historical background

The debate on universality bears a clear resemblance to the discussion on natural law. Are there some abstract norms to which any rational individual could adhere to all over the world? Philosophers and anthropologists have been struggling with this issue for ages and I doubt whether the recurrent dispute within the United Nations adds anything new to this debate. Although some common norms might exist in every society, such as the prohibition of incest and of killing, human rights cannot be universal unless they are understood to comprise a very limited definition of human dignity. Human rights should not be conceived as abstract principles and ideals of individual liberty and justice. They entail by definition a system of rights and obligations which necessitates a political order founded on democratic institutions and social welfare. Effective universality would require a world society ruled by a common government capable of implementing human rights as a set of positive laws to be valid everywhere. Fortunately there is nothing of this sort and therefore states will continue to hold ultimate responsibility for the promotion and defence of human rights. They will necessarily have their own institutions, legal arrangements, and social policies for the protection of these norms.

The intellectual origins of human rights are diverse and complex. They can be traced back to all values, norms, and institutions which tend to protect human dignity and which are therefore inherent in most civilizations. However, human rights have a political, institutional, and socioeconomic history and should not be confused with a catalogue of moral values or ethical ideals uprooted from the conditions of their emergence and development. They have their origin in the humanism of the European Renaissance. It expanded as a philosophical conception of man and society during the eighteenth-century Enlightenment. In other words, it sprang from the circumstances which contributed to the development of the capitalist market and the nation state, in particular scientific and technological progress, the process of urbanization and secularization, growing individualism and egalitarianism.

Contemporary human rights, as defined in the Universal Declaration, arose from World War II and resistance to totalitarian regimes of fascist or communist inspiration. The concept first emerged within the United Nations as a set of guiding principles and norms defining the nature of political legitimacy and social welfare. It was indeed proclaimed by the General Assembly as the "common standard of achievement for all peoples and all nations." It expressed a liberal Weltanschaung on man and society. It provided a coherent doctrinal framework for a model of society reflecting the pre-eminence of the individual, but this conception was enriched by a new conception of citizenship based on the ideas of distributive justice and social protection. The Declaration recognizes that the full realization of individual rights requires specific socio-economic conditions. As a matter of fact the protection of the most basic individual rights necessitates an adequate standard of living and access to basic essentials for sustaining human existence, such as food, shelter, clothing, health care.[1] The Declaration asserts not only a democratic, institutional and juridical model protecting individual liberty and freedom; it also proposes a policy framework. Articles 22 to 27 of the Declaration define a comprehensive set of socio-economic and cultural rights. Article 22 states, for example, that: "Everyone, as a member of society, has the right to social security and is entitled to realization, through national effort and international cooperation and in accordance with the organization and resources of each State, of the economic, social and cultural rights indispensable for his dignity and the free development of his personality."

In the perspective of the Declaration, the state must provide the right to work, to free choice of employment, and protection against unemployment. For everyone who works, it must implement "the right to just and favourable remuneration ensuring for himself and his family an existence worthy of human dignity." It must also make sure that everyone has the right to rest and leisure and provide all the necessary components for their personal fulfilment and well-being. Education is also an essential part of human rights. The Declaration therefore gives not only content and finality to the rule of law, which is the bedrock of democracy, but it also provides a precise outline of the aims of the welfare state. As a matter of fact, this universalism expresses the dominant social democratic ideology of Western nations after World War II. It can indeed be interpreted as an attempt to give universal validity to the ideal of the welfare state.

There is no blueprint for establishing the institutional and socio-economic conditions necessary for the full realization of human rights, but unquestionably states remain the ultimate guardians of the security and welfare of individuals. States are indeed the principal authorities for political and social integration and no other source of authority actually exists to arbitrate or mitigate their internal conflicts, control market dynamics, carry out redistribution of wealth by means of tax systems, ensure protection of vulnerable groups, establish and maintain the appropriate infrastructures for production, exchange and the distribution of goods and services, as well as prevent environmental damage. The rule of law protected by democratic institutions and a fair and efficient judicial system is a prerequisite for the protection of human rights. But so is economic and social welfare whose realization depends as much on governments' public policies and socio-economic development as on legal instruments. States should not only protect civil and political rights, but also ensure fair distributive justice among social groups, granting special attention to the most vulnerable individuals and to sociological minorities. They are also responsible for developing social infrastructures such as education, vocational training, health and social security. They must create the material conditions such as transport and communication which promote economic and social well-being without degrading the environment. It has been admitted that states violate their core obligation under the Covenant on Economic, Social and Cultural Rights when a significant number of their individuals are deprived of essential foodstuffs, essential primary health care, basic shelter and housing, or the most elementary forms of education.[2] One can agree with Jack Donnelly when he writes: "All actual liberal democratic welfare states fall short of realising all human rights even for their own nationals. Nonetheless, only such states are systematically committed to the full range of internationally recognised human rights. Only in such states do robust markets and democracies operate within systematic limits set by human rights."[3]

Human rights discourses

Within the United Nations, human rights has always consisted of different overlapping discourses and concomitant practices. The first discourse is essentially ideological and defines principles of political legitimacy. The second expresses juridical norms. The third is of a political nature and includes deliberation on the strategies for implementation of human rights. I will try first to analyse the evolution of these different aspects of human rights, focusing on the major contemporary challenges of human rights implementation.

Human rights as an ideology

The catalogue of human rights as defined by the Universal Declaration and international covenants being very extensive, governments tend to promote a specific national discourse on these rights which reinforce their own political interests. In the 1960s, for example, third world and socialist governments used human rights, especially people's rights, as a propaganda tool to legitimize their state power and development objectives. This practice has not disappeared with the disintegration of the Soviet Empire. Several Asian governments have tried to restrict the universality of fundamental human rights by insisting on specific communitarian values which are supposed to be part of their civilization and traditions. This discourse, which came to the fore during the Vienna Conference in 1993, has sometimes been a propaganda tool to legitimize authoritarian and corrupt regimes.

On the other hand, human rights are often viewed by Western governments and public opinions as a set of principles and ideals mostly related to civil and political liberties. They envisage these norms as a decalogue of moral injunctions or ethical principles related to justice and liberty instead of reflecting on their legal, institutional, and political dimensions. In particular there is a lack of interest in the institutional mechanisms, which are necessary for their protection, such as legislative and juridical procedures. Issues related to the socio-economic conditions that facilitate their implementation are often ignored. During the Cold War, the American government used human rights as a propaganda instrument in world affairs. In so doing it promoted a conception of liberty restricted to the most basic individual, political, and civil freedom and was even selective in the promotion of these norms. The Carter administration, for example, which made civil and political rights a factor in its relations with Latin American countries, was selective since it did not aim at offending governments in Asia, Africa, or the Middle East, which were often responsible for significant or sometimes mass violations of these rights. While refraining from ratifying some fundamental human rights treaties, the United States has continued to promote a very ideological view of human rights. As Reed Broody wrote recently: "The US does not actually argue that the international bill of human rights is not of universal relevance. Rather, and more perniciously, it just consistently behaves as if human rights law does not apply to the United States." As an illustration of this bad record, Broody reminds us that, "the United States is the only country in the world, apart from Somalia, that has not ratified the Convention on the Rights of the Child. It is one of the few countries that has not ratified the Convention on the Elimination of All

Forms of Discrimination against Women. It has also refused to ratify the Covenant on Economic, Social and Cultural Rights or the American Convention on Human Rights."[4] President Clinton's last State of the Union address reminded the Congress that more than 40 million Americans are without health insurance. This also means that their life expectancy is shorter. According to the Center on Budget and Policy Priorities, 1 per cent of the American population has as much income at its disposal, after tax, in 1999 as the 100 million Americans in the lowest income bracket which make up 38 per cent of the population. This social gap has more than doubled since 1977.[5] Although economic growth led recently to a significant reduction in poverty, the poverty rate for children is still at nearly 20 per cent, higher than in most Western industrialized countries.

In the meantime, the US government, as well as most private foundations and corporate donors, are ready to finance human rights programmes in Africa, Asia, or Latin America, but they still refuse to give a penny to monitor torture or degrading treatment of US prison inmates. According to the New York-based organization Human Rights Watch there are currently more than 20,000 prisoners in the United States, housed in special super-maximum security units who live in inhuman conditions. They spend "their waking and sleeping hours locked in small, sometimes windowless, cells sealed with solid steel doors." They are subjected to all kinds of pointless suffering and humiliation. They often stay in these prisons for an indefinite period that may continue for years. Some inmates develop clinical symptoms associated with psychosis.[6] For the political establishment as well as public opinion, human rights violations are supposed to happen outside the United States.

In a similar perspective, French governments, especially under President Mitterrand, have often used human rights rhetoric or humanitarian principles as an instrument for enhancing their foreign policy objectives, while promoting interests and strategies in Africa which are far from congenial to the respect of these norms. As a matter of fact, most OECD countries have increasingly blurred human rights with humanitarian ideals, the defence of the free market and abstract appeals in favour of the defence of good governance, while steadily reducing their economic assistance to developing countries, which is necessary for the promotion and implementation of these rights. NGOs active in the field of human rights have contributed to this vision. Generally from the Western world, they have committed themselves to the realization of specific individual rights, in particular freedom of opinion and expression, the prohibition of torture or slavery, but they have often failed to address the root cause of the violation of these rights and abstained from actively participating in the realization of economic, social, and cultural rights. Of course they are not unconcerned by the fact that every year more than 20 million people die of hunger, that some 800 million people suffer from chronic hunger, but they tend to consider this phenomenon as an issue which is solely development-related.

Human rights as law

The Universal Declaration of Human Rights was not intended to impose legal obligations, but since its adoption by the General Assembly in 1948, most states have endorsed its main provision as jus cogens. The development of legal instruments and procedural mechanisms inspired by the Universal Declaration has been particularly significant in the last decades. The United Nations has promulgated different human rights treaties which are in force. Among these the Covenant on Civil and Political Rights, the Covenant on Economic, Social and Cultural Rights (1966), the Convention on the Elimination of All Forms of Discrimination against Women, the Convention against Torture and Other Cruel, Inhuman or Degrading Treatment or Punishment (1984) and the Convention on the Suppression and Punishment of the Crime of Apartheid. The two covenants protecting civil and political rights, as well as economic, social, and cultural rights which came into force in 1976 have in particular given stronger legal force and precision to the principle and norms of the Universal Declaration. Some 150 states have adhered to these two covenants. The Convention on the Rights of the Child was adopted by the General Assembly in its Resolution 44/25 of 20 November 1989, and came into force on 2 September 1992. Nearly every state, with the exception of Somalia and the United States has ratified it. Within the International Labour Organisation (ILO) several conventions protecting social rights have also been enacted, dealing in particular with freedom of association and collective bargaining, abolition of forced labour, equal remuneration and non-discrimination in employment. For example the questions of child labour, dangerous work, or forced labour have been addressed by a series of conventions within the framework of the ILO. Human rights are also protected at the regional level, the most sophisticated mechanisms in this respect being founded on the European Convention on Human Rights (1950), the European Convention against Torture and the American Convention on Human Rights (1969).

A complex institutional structure consisting of a network of bodies, organs, and complaint procedures has been developed within the United Nations as well as regional organizations to monitor and enforce these rights. On the whole the supervisory mechanisms have been weak at the international level, except within Europe. Most of them are of a non-judicial character. UN organs and bodies receive and comment on periodic reports from state parties on the general human rights situation of their country or on more specific issues such as torture, violence against women, or the protection of children. The aim of the reporting procedure is to help governments bring their laws and practice into conformity with their treaty obligations. Unfortunately, states usually do not submit their reports on time and most of these reports aim at throwing a rosy light on their national reality. This nevertheless gives NGOs an opportunity to react and provide additional critical information. These organs or bodies issue reports, recommendations, and opinions that are legally non-binding. Some of them can also carry out fact-finding missions. The Human Rights Committee was empowered in an Optional Protocol of the Covenant on Civil and Political Rights to receive and consider complaints from individuals alleging violation of the convention by states which had accepted the right of petition, but this complaint procedure has not been widely accepted. Unfortunately, the supervisory mechanism of the Committee on the Rights of the Child does not provide for the possibility of individual communications.

The creation of an International Criminal Court, decided on 17 July 1998, by the diplomatic conference convened in Rome under the aegis of the UN is probably a major breakthrough in the promotion and protection of human rights. The idea of international responsibility of individuals is certainly not a new one, as it was accepted during World War II and implemented at the Nuremberg and Tokyo trials. However, more recent history has highlighted the importance of fighting impunity at the international level. The International Criminal Court, which is due to become operational as soon as 60 states have ratified its convention, is therefore a significant step forward in international protection of human rights and humanitarian law. The court will be capacitated to judge perpetrators of genocide, crimes against humanity, war crimes, and aggression. It will take on this responsibility each time the courts of law of any state are unable to carry out their duties. The International Court will therefore obstruct the law of impunity. This juridical procedure will not only be activated by states and the Security Council, but also by the prosecutor of the future court who will act on his or her own authority.

Nevertheless, numerous obstacles of a political nature are bound to interfere with the implementation of this mechanism. It has been admitted, thanks to the pressure of the French and US governments, that states could ratify the convention while reserving the rights of their nationals not to be prosecuted by the tribunal during the first seven years of the treaty. In addition, this reserve can be extended for another seven years. More generally, the prosecutor will probably hesitate before prosecuting for the most "common" crimes that are almost standard in many states. Nationals of powerful states or countries enjoying strong external protection will obviously be in a better position to avoid prosecution, especially if the United States refuses to support the setting-up of this new court. In any case, it is not even certain whether the United Nations will demonstrate its political will or mobilize the means necessary to prosecute for the crimes listed in the court's statutes, above all if the process of restoring order has implied long and painstaking negotiations between the protagonists.

There is a wide gap between legal obligations and state practice and the ratification of legal instruments and procedure does not always indicate the willingness or capacity of governments to respect their obligations. There are many states that ratify all possible human rights instruments without having the slightest intention or capacity to implement them. In many developing countries there is an enormous rift between the legal and institutional world and practical day-to-day political and social reality. The number of ratifications of international treaties in the field of human rights is therefore not a good indication of real progress in the protection of human dignity. In addition, more and more states have become incapable of implementing their obligations here. A chronic problem has arisen as states neglect their obligation to send in their reports or they accumulate delays in providing them. In many countries governments claim, rightly or wrongly, that they are not in control of paramilitary groups responsible for torture and disappearances. On top of this they appear unable to subdue liberation movements, terrorist groups, or Mafia-type organizations which kidnap, torture, and kill. Civil disorders of this type which have plagued countries like Colombia for decades have become extremely widespread in the 1990s. Moreover, weak states cannot control the activities of transnational corporations, which are sometimes directly responsible for widespread violation of social, economic, and cultural rights. Consequently, progress in the realization of human rights depends less on the growing number of states ratifying conventions to protect these rights than on the crucial political choices to be made at national and international levels to guarantee the conditions necessary for individual security and social well-being.

Human rights as politics

Although they might be weakly implemented and sanctioned, international human rights obligations are nowadays a powerful source of legitimization. As a set of norms formally accepted by most states, they can signal the foundations of political order and good socio-economic policies. There has been an impressive increase in the number of NGOs and grass-roots movements which draw their legitimacy and inspiration world-wide from these international obligations. Thanks to the United

Nations, human rights have become part of the political process of most countries and can also inspire a wide variety of political movements and NGOs all over the world. The UN Conference on Human Rights in 1993 admitted for example that international laws and mechanisms, which had been established to promote and protect human rights, had not so far responded adequately to the concerns of women. The Declaration and Programme of Action adopted in Vienna therefore gave a new visibility to the issue of women. In December 1993, the UN General Assembly adopted the Declaration on the Elimination of Violence against Women. Some months later the Commission on Human Rights appointed a Special Rapporteur on violence against women, its causes and consequences. On 12 March 1999, the Commission on the Status of Women adopted an Optional Protocol to the Women's Convention of 1979 which will strengthen the possibility of using this instrument to end discrimination, including violence, against women.

Paraphrasing Clemenceau, one could say that human rights are such an important issue that they cannot be left to jurists and lawyers alone. Human rights are also a policy issue and William F. Felice has rightly stressed that "we must move beyond human rights law and legal positivism to the realm of international political economy."[7] The legal approach considers human realities without taking into account politics and social organization. This perspective can have dubious consequences. The issue of child labour is a good case in point. From a legal point of view, it is legitimate to apply the international standards of several ILO conventions that prohibit work under the age of 18. But for many children the choice does not lie simply between remunerated economic activity and education, but between work in the informal sector, without any protection, or even prostitution and crimes. Just as development thinking was considered for too long the exclusive domain of financial institutions and economists, human rights has tended to remain the preserve of legal experts or of NGO militants and diplomats gravitating around Geneva-based UN bodies. These people are often ill-versed and not particularly interested in the definition of the strategies that are necessary to establish the conditions required for the protection and development of human dignity. The sectorialization of the UN system along functionalist lines has also hindered reflection on the broader aspects of human rights implementation.

In spite of this dominant legal bias, one of the most contentious issues within the United Nations has been the debate concerning the respective importance of civil and political rights versus socio-economic and cultural rights. The protection of human dignity obviously requires certain basic socio-economic conditions. The United Nations has constantly stressed the indivisibility and interdependence of these rights. This was of course reiterated in the context of the deliberations on the "right to development." The World Conference on Human Rights in 1993 reaffirmed the right to development as a universal and inalienable right and an integral part of fundamental human rights. It stated that while development facilitates the enjoyment of all human rights, the lack of development may not be invoked to justify the curtailment of internationally recognized human rights. The Human Rights Commission has recently underlined that "extreme poverty and exclusion from society constitute a violation of human dignity and that urgent national and international action is therefore required to eliminate them." It has requested states to foster participation by the poorest people in the decision-making process in the societies in which they live. It has admitted that the "existence of widespread absolute poverty inhibits the full and effective enjoyment of human rights and renders democracy and popular participation fragile." There is no freedom of expression and democracy without instruction. It is also true that the implementation of civil and political rights, such as the rights to political participation, freedom of expression and of assembly are also necessary to overcome misery and exclusion since their realization is an essential contribution to the prevention of misrule and injustice which hamper or even prevent socio-economic development. Developing countries are usually unable to provide the economic and social infrastructures that are necessary for the protection of democracy. Experts from the UN Sub-Commission on the Promotion and Protection of Human Rights have also adopted three resolutions in 2001 calling into question the impact of key aspects of the globalization process on human rights. Reacting to claims made by the IMF during the discussion that it is not bound by international human rights standards, the Sub-Commission, in a resolution on Globalization and its Impact on the Full Enjoyment of All Human Rights, reaffirmed the importance and relevance of human rights in international trade, investment, and finance. It urged all governments and international economic policy forums, including WTO, to take human rights fully into account. The Sub-Commission also expressed concern about the human rights implications of liberalization of international trade in agricultural products, especially on the right to food for members of vulnerable communities. In a second resolution applying a human rights perspective to the WTO's General Agreement on Trade in Services (GATS) for the first time, the Sub-Commission called for a report on this matter from the High Commissioner for Human Rights. It also recommended that the WTO include consideration of the human rights implications of the GATS on the provision of basic services, such as affordable and accessible health and education services. The Sub-Commission also addressed the negative impact of the WTO's Agreement on Trade-Related Aspects of Intellectual Property Rights

(TRIPS) on human rights. It signalled continuing concern that the scope and meaning of several provisions of the TRIPS Agreement need to be clarified in order to ensure that states' obligations under this agreement do not contradict their binding human rights obligations. The protection of indigenous peoples' traditional knowledge, food security, access to medicine, technology transfer and development and preventing "bio-piracy" are but some of the crucial human rights issues raised by the implementation of the WTO TRIPS Agreement.[8]

Although representatives of Western governments are still reluctant to define as rights those obligations of a political or moral nature whose holders are difficult to identify, there is less disagreement nowadays within the United Nations on the definition of these norms than on the strategy to follow in order to implement them. This question cannot be resolved on an abstract normative level. It is a sensitive and conflictual problem involving the very essence of politics. It is one thing to proclaim that the right to work or the right to development should be considered as universal human rights, it is quite another to define and realize concretely the policy which will ensure the implementation of these norms.

The contentious impact of globalization

It is in the context of this reflection on human rights as politics that one should examine the impact of globalization on the implementation of these norms. The acceleration of globalization in the 1980s coincided with an extensive process of democratization in Latin America. It has most probably contributed to the disintegration of the Soviet Empire. Trade liberalization, the expansion of direct foreign investment, and the rapidly changing production system have encouraged economic growth and per capita income in many parts of the developing world, especially in East Asia and Latin America.

However, the notion of globalization has turned out to be partly illusory, since the yawning socio-economic gap between different regions of the world prevails, just as it does within developing countries, although the geography of these rifts has changed in the last decades. The majority of the world population still lives off subsistence economy and hardly benefits from the distribution of goods, services, capital, and technology. Globalization has broadened the gulf between those who can integrate into the world market and those who have to stay on the sidelines of modern production and exchange systems. It has been associated within many developing countries with the worsening social conditions of the poor whose income, health, and housing are deteriorating. In its 1997 Report on World Trade and Development, UNCTAD stressed that globalization goes hand in hand with increasing inequalities between North and South. The report affirmed that: "In almost every country which has liberalised its trade, salary inequality has increased, most often in a context of a shrinkage of work on offer for low-qualified workers with ensuing drops in their wages, sometimes plummeting 20 to 30 per cent in some Latin American countries."[9]

Economic growth is increasingly linked to improvement of productivity, but the flow of private investment to poor countries is irregular, sparse, and very selective. Investors demand preconditions – economic, social, cultural, and political – which are, by definition, sorely lacking in these countries. Most poor countries, especially sub-Saharan African countries, with no industry, no producers for their raw materials, which are less in demand now, abandoned by investors and traders, faced with low-output agriculture, environmental damage, an upsurge of lethal epidemics and a very high birthrate cannot escape from an economic and social slump. Globalization has also facilitated erratic movements of capital which bear no relation to production or trade. The deregulation of financial markets, which are dominated by a small number of private institutions, has increased the vulnerability of developing countries to speculative movements of short-term capital. Monetary and financial crises in Mexico, or more recently in the new industrial countries of Asia and Latin America, have engendered social crises of great magnitude, condemning millions of people to lower living standards and misery. According to UN estimates the proportion of poor people in Indonesia has risen from 11 per cent in 1997 to 40 per cent of the population today, affecting tens of millions. Korea, Thailand, and Malaysia have also been badly hit by the crisis, which has had a negative social backlash in many other emerging countries.[10] UNDP affirms that nearly 1.3 billion people have no access to drinking water and "live" on one dollar a day: 840 million people suffer from malnutrition and the gulf between rich and poor is on the increase. The World Bank provides comparable figures with an estimate of 3 billion people living on less than two dollars a day.

As we have seen, the promotion of universal human rights requires the establishment of political conditions which favour a fair distribution of growth among social groups and the full realization of socio-economic rights at the national as well as the international level. Increasing disparities in the distribution of income both within and between societies places stress and poses an important challenge to the whole human rights system. The violence faced by street children, trafficking in women, as well as abuses by the state, or with the acquiescence of the state, against minorities are examples of these realities. Globalization has weakened state capacity to maintain the type of socio-economic regulation and distributive justice that are necessary for the full realization of human

rights. It tends to undermine national specificities regarding social welfare, protection of the environment, and cultural identity. The enormous
expansion of transnational corporations, coupled with the liberalization
of goods and services and the deregulation of financial markets, has coincided nearly everywhere with new social polarization. States compete
to attract foreign investments and this means fiscal restraints and austerity measures in order to defend the value of their currency and to balance their budget. This policy erodes states' welfare function and limits
their capacity to help vulnerable people. The increasingly disturbing
phenomenon of social exclusion characterized by the growing number
of homeless, jobless youngsters and long-term unemployed and people
living in extreme poverty on the outskirts of big cities has accompanied
the upsurge of globalization within OECD countries. This process has
several other negative consequences such as the increase in the number
of prison inmates, especially in the United States.

Matters are made worse for poor countries by the fact that most of
their social security systems are fragile, basic, or quasi non-existent. Poverty considerably hinders the state's capacity to deliver public goods that
create the conditions for the realization of human rights. Adam Prze-
worski has confirmed empirically what intuitively appears self-evident:
that there is a strong positive correlation between economic development
and democracy.[11] James Wolfensohn, President of the World Bank
Group, has recently strongly emphasized good governance as a way to
promote development. "A country must have an educated and well-
organised government. This requires capacity building, an open legislative and transparent regulatory system, properly trained and remunerated officials and an absolute commitment to clean government ...
Without the protection of human and property rights, and a comprehensive framework of laws, no equitable government is possible."[12] In the
1990s, the Inter-American Development Bank also put a great deal of
emphasis on judicial and institutional reform as a way to economic and
social progress. It is true that many Sub-Saharan African, Central or
Southern Asian states have generally continued to rely on centralized
and highly personalized forms of government which are corrupt and
show little respect for fundamental human rights. Unfortunately, there is
also a strong positive correlation between corruption, lack of judicial independence, inaccessibility of the courts, unsatisfactory separation of
powers, lack of transparency, and accountability of official institutions
and poverty.[13] The area governed by tyrannical regimes with methods
which include systematic torture and forced disappearances, corresponds
broadly to the world's poorest regions, where any efforts to construct a
state fail dismally or turn out to be plagued with enormous obstacles.

One should recognize that democratic countries contribute little to the world-wide alleviation of poverty and therefore to the promotion of human rights on a universal basis. Most of them do not really care about the consequences of trade or financial policy for poor countries. Moreover the weakening of the welfare state in OECD countries has also coincided with the erosion of development policies concerning poor regions of the world as well as with the return to charity-related activities. Rich countries are counting on direct foreign investments and trade liberalization to promote economic growth everywhere. They therefore tend to endow the market with social regulation functions as if, according to the theory of comparative advantages, the progression of the goods and services trade was eventually going to reduce areas of poverty and thus ease peripheral political and social conflicts. In the long run, the free functioning of the market is supposed to produce wealth and well-being.

Some of the poor countries are torn apart by conflictual violence and civil wars with an increasingly strong ethnic dimension. By definition civil war entails the destruction of the most basic institutional conditions necessary to the protection of human rights. We usually associate civil wars and repressive regimes with internal phenomena but as a matter of fact they are generally influenced by international politics, even when they appear to have a strong endogenous origin. Indeed, these wars reveal not only the collapse of state integration structures, but also the failure of international cooperation mechanisms. In the 1990s civil wars broke out in countries going through severe social crises, heavily indebted with international financial institutions, private banks, and Western governments. Events in Yugoslavia are proof of this. In the months preceding the crisis and outbreak of war, the IMF demanded that, in return for new loans, the Yugoslav authorities set up a programme of budgetary austerity measures and economic liberalization, which led to recession and an increase in unemployment, while demanding that the different member states of the Federation carry out economic and political reforms that they could not accept. Civil wars and genocides in Africa have stricken countries undergoing profound socio-economic crises, partly determined by international constraints such as the degradation of their terms of trade and the diminution of economic assistance. At the same time, in the 1990s, OECD countries noticeably reduced the size of their development assistance of which a significant steadily increasing chunk is concentrated on humanitarian operations.

The failures of international institutions

International organizations are mandated to support cooperation regimes in the socio-economic or political domains that states cannot manage independently. Their expansion is wrongly associated with the erosion of national sovereignty, whereas their mission should be to support a state's capacity to fulfil its main functions in terms of security and welfare. As a matter of fact, the divide between the states' level of development also reflects a difference in the nature and solidity of their regional or international cooperation mechanisms whose intergovernmental institutions are an important instrument. OECD countries have reached a high degree of socio-economic and political integration among themselves. This is even more so within the European Union. However, international society as a whole is characterized by the weakness and heterogeneity of its cooperation regimes.

The UN system, which has played an important role in the definition of the norms and strategies related to human rights and development, has lacked the political support from its member states – the major powers in particular – and consequently the financial resources necessary to contribute significantly to the socio-economic progress of poor countries. Over the past decade, the United Nations has mounted large world conferences on nutrition (Rome 1992), environment (Rio 1992), population and development (Cairo 1994), social development (Copenhagen 1995), women (Beijing 1995), or habitat (Istanbul 1996). The atmosphere at these conferences was more serene than in the past thanks to the absence of the major ideological rifts of the Cold War era. Nonetheless, their final recommendations formed a long list of proposals that governments could not or did not intend to respect. Moreover, the financial resources committed by states to achieve the objectives set up within these conferences have remained very limited.

The United States have constantly sidelined the United Nations from vital development matters: the price of raw materials, debt, trade, financial and monetary matters. They consider the United Nations should play a marginal role in economic and social areas even if they do attach some importance to humanitarian affairs, particularly regarding the flow of refugees, which comes under the UNHCR mandate. European Union countries' governments and public opinion have not really resisted this policy. The heterogeneity of UN membership, the complexity of its structure and its cumbersome decision-making process can explain the rich countries' indifference to this system. Furthermore, conference diplomacy – where representatives of each government expose their points of view and painstakingly produce the long list of often unrealistic and contradictory recommendations – is a strikingly unsuitable negotiation procedure for defining consistent development strategies. The practice of consensus for adopting a set of recommendations has resulted in further weakening the significance and weight of UN decisions. For these reasons, UN organizations contribute little to international social regulation.

They are certainly not in a position to carry out effectively their mandate to defend the social and economic rights of poor peoples.

Since the collapse of the Bretton Woods monetary system at the beginning of the seventies up until fairly recently, the IMF and the World Bank have been of little help in facilitating coordination of rich countries' macro-economic policies – to guarantee stability in exchange rates, avoid financial crises and encourage the development of poor countries as well as resolve the haunting problem of their debt. Instead of improving the situation, these institutions often contributed in the past to the social crisis of developing countries by supporting policies that condemned millions of human beings to a life of misery and grave violations of human rights. At the same time the development strategies recommended by these institutions were not being successful either. As a rule their policy triggered a high level of unemployment and increased inequality. A recent study on Latin America by the World Bank highlights this paradox: over the past years countries in the region have gone to great lengths to comply with IMF and World Bank directions, carrying out macro-economic reforms and major structural changes. They have taken steps to liberalize their economy, to open their markets to international competition, reducing their customs tariffs on average from 50 per cent in 1985 to 10 per cent in 1996, to reduce or eliminate their budgetary deficit, to modify their monetary policy, to liberalize their financial market and reform their banking system, to limit considerably their inflation rate and reform their social security system. Inflation is practically non-existent now and yet all this progress and resulting growth has done nothing to alleviate the glaring social injustices or reduce the number of poor. By the early 1990s the number of poor people had soared to 150 million. Yet according to the Bank another effort had to be made, particularly by reducing workers' social protection to facilitate lay-offs and by reducing employers' social security contributions.[14]

As a matter of fact the IMF and the World Bank continue to propose development strategies which take no account of human rights as proclaimed by the United Nations and the treaties ratified by states on the subject. The incoherence of World Bank projects in this respect has become unquestionable. In fact, its proclaimed principles and ideals in favour of social progress – particularly for family planning, basic health care, education, housing and employment or environment – are often undermined by the nature of the structural adjustment policy it recommends or imposes. Inspired by neo-classic conceptions, these measures are implemented regardless of the economic specificities of the different indebted countries, or even of the social conditions in the countries concerned. The debt burden of many poor countries is still exorbitant, whereas the liberalization of African economies has in no way slackened the region's drift away from the main poles of production and trade.

Moreover the IMF, under the aegis of the American Treasury Department, urged developing countries to liberalize movements of capital when they did not have the institutional means to assume this deregulation. During the autumn of 1997, the IMF was unable to do anything to prevent a series of competitive devaluations between the newly industrialized Asian countries. It nonetheless granted important loans to the governments of Thailand, Indonesia, and South Korea, while imposing austerity measures on the same governments. These measures were strongly criticized, even by the most ardent supporters of the free-market economy. In exchange for loans, the IMF imposed measures on these countries' governments similar to those which had been applied in indebted countries during the eighties, whereas such measures were unnecessary in this context and contributed to aggravating the monetary crisis. The IMF also demanded that these governments lift or reduce their restrictions on foreign investors' rights regarding national companies; this deregulation was bound to favour foreign banks and corporations. The structural adjustment measures recommended by Bretton Woods organizations have always been selective: they never aimed measures at rich countries' trade and monetary policies. These shortcomings reflect both their dependence on great economic powers and their technocratic working methods.

As we have seen, the World Bank appears today very interested in "good governance" involving respect for law, justice, and constitutional norms and procedures which render governments accountable for their actions. In 1993 the Bank established an Inspection Panel to provide an independent forum for private citizens who believe that they or their interests have been or could be directly harmed by a project that it finances. Moreover it recently suspended granting a loan to Indonesia by way of a sanction for a corruption affair involving a bank in Bali, but also for the central government's refusal to respect referendum results in East Timor.[15] Yet this interest has not prevented James Wolfensohn from paying tribute to President Putin at the time of the war in Chechnya.

It should be added that all too often international institutions escape some of the basic principles of "good governance," in particular the check-and-balance mechanisms necessary for the functioning of democratic institutions. They are the seats for negotiations that often take place in the greatest secrecy under the aegis of the major economic powers supported by business circles. They avoid control by national parliaments because of their technical nature and sometimes their decisions affect the fate of millions of individuals with large-scale social and ecological consequences. They have expanded their programmes and policies in the last decades without becoming accountable to those whom they directly concern. As Philip Alston, Chairman of the Committee for Economic, Social and Cultural rights, stated in 1998: "The IMF decides on the economic future of entire populations without being accountable to them in any way." Besides this it demands "complete transparency on the monetary policy that states intend to elaborate while the Fund itself continues to prepare its structural adjustment measures in the utmost secrecy."[16] Globalization has resulted in increased segmentation of the roles played by international institutions. Thus the WTO has been given a far-reaching mandate regarding the liberalization of goods and services. It has received wide-ranging competence for developing this regime of liberalization. It has a dispute settlement body, which appears to be functioning efficiently for the time being. Protection of the environment, respect for human rights and social rights, and the objectives of sustainable development are all subject to respect of the WTO obligations. In fact, no international institution exists with such extensive legal and judicial means necessary to impose enforcement of its sector-based aims.

The acceleration of liberalization generated by the implementation of WTO objectives might well result in a widening of the social rift unless states and international institutions take measures to correct markets' adverse effects. The constitution of the WTO contains no clause on social protection apart from a vague reference in the preamble to the relations between the easing of restrictions on trade and full employment. States cannot ban importation of products manufactured by children because the WTO condemns discriminatory treatment on the basis of national production methods, with the exception of work done by prisoners.

The WTO Ministerial Conference, held in Singapore from 9–13 December 1996, released the Organization from all competence in social matters, proposing that ILO assume its mandate in this respect – an elegant way of giving in to pressure from developing countries and transnational corporations who refuse to address this matter. Not without reason, governments of Southern countries consider that the increased interest on the part of OECD countries for the social dimensions of development or the environment is a protectionist strategy. They particularly believe that the low level of their social protection mechanism is one of their comparative advantages. In the North and South alike, supporters of the neo-liberal-inspired economic model are hostile to the idea of establishing social protection norms at the international level. They fear that the setting up of some sort of an international social regulation system would raise labour costs, favour public debt and lead to an increase in interest rates. Increased trade will encourage economic growth in developing countries and this growth will lead to a rise in their imports from OECD countries and improved working conditions. The ILO secretariat defends the idea of a mechanism sanctioning violations of certain of the Organization's fundamental clauses such as the banning of forced labour, child labour, freedom of trade unions and discrimination in the workplace. Some member states, however, including the United States, have not signed the Organization's conventions in these areas. This is why, in November 1997, the ILO's Governing Body proposed obtaining a consensus on a Declaration by the International Labour Conference reaffirming the essential principles of these conventions. This only goes to show how difficult it is now to implement vital norms on the international protection of workers.

The role of non-state actors

It is widely accepted nowadays that non-state actors contribute to economic and social regulation. Private corporations contribute to rule making or to the setting of all kind of standards, for example in telecommunications, food, medicine, finance, insurance, labour, or environment. Private enterprises are often considered to be more efficient, less bureaucratic and more sensitive to the requirements of change. The irruption of private actors in the public sphere could also account for governmental shortcomings. Yet integrating transnational corporations into governance structures implies enhancing the status of their contribution to political order or at least their economic and social role. They also contribute to deregulation in the economic and social sphere. Some transnational corporations, especially multinational oil companies, have also recently been accomplices to human rights violations. The civil wars or repression in several African or Asian countries (Myanmar notably) would not have lasted so long nor been so far-reaching without the collusion of the transnational corporations which exploit these bankrupt states' petroleum resources. In any case, the delegitimization of nation states through the action of transnational corporations and capital flow is not necessarily an expression of good governance. It is not always conducive to a better protection of human rights.

The irruption on the political scene of NGOs and all sorts of local and regional networks of associations is also a long way from resolving the question of procedure for democratic political participation. Human rights organizations and even development NGOs have little direct access to the WTO and the IMF whereas they have more and more representatives within international fora whose political influence is limited. They form nevertheless heterogeneous coalitions to protest against the policies pursued by OECD countries under the aegis of the organizations, expressing in this way the emergence of a new transnational public space.

Consumer movements can also contribute to demanding new codes of conduct by transnational corporations for the protection of the environment, or even for the protection of specific social rights.

In human rights matters NGOs are most of the time used to protesting against violations of individual liberties and serious breaches of human dignity perpetrated by governments, but they have not yet developed a concerted strategy to challenge private corporations which turn out to be accomplices to these violations. Moreover NGOs would be wise to devote more energy to pushing through reform of international institutions by again raising the issues of sovereignty and legitimacy, namely who is entitled to give the orders, according to which mode, submitting to which control body and within the framework of which political participation structure.

A programme for change

Progress in the implementation of human rights will not ensue from new legal international instruments, or from lofty rhetoric about individual liberty and democracy, but from the mobilization of political forces willing to fight mass poverty and to improve governance at the national and international level. Misery and social polarizations all over the world are today a major obstacle to the realization of human rights. They contribute to insecurity and violence, sometimes to civil war, which are an absolute hindrance to the the rule of law. There can be no stable political order either where there is no respect for the most elementary conditions of equity, justice, and social integration.

The scope and gravity of worldwide social problems necessitates in particular the development of new systems of regulation and a better control of present institutions. It is obvious that the state is no longer the sole authority which should be held accountable for violations of human rights, especially of economic and social rights. By strengthening their cooperation systems and sharing their sovereignty within the framework of regional integration structures, states should be in a better position to bear their responsibilities in fighting unemployment and developing new social protection systems. In any case, states will have to take measures to curb the concentration of economic power that can be seen in the spheres of banking and transnational corporations. They will have to harmonize their monetary policies and their social demands regarding these corporations and to restrain short-term movements of capital.

It seems particularly necessary to set up a new financial architecture. Solutions will have to be found quickly to the phenomenon of the poorest countries' massive debt. The IMF's mandate should be enlarged, so that, as John Maynard Keynes proposed at Bretton Woods, its stabilization and adjustment programmes are not directed exclusively against indebted countries.[17] In any case, the IMF should be more sensitive to people's standard of living and abandon its obsession with the stabilization of the financial market and the fight against inflation in order to enhance responsibility for employment and sustainable development.[18] It is becoming urgent to integrate social policy into development strategies. The progress of poor countries cannot be measured with the yardstick of criteria such as capital flow and easing of trade restrictions or the competitivity of their economies in the world market.

The beneficial objective of easing restrictions on the goods and services trade will have to be subject to the requirements of political order and the common good. Developing countries will have to take measures in order to regulate short-term capital movements that can trigger major socio-economic crises. They should resume policies aiming at the protection of their infant industries. They should promote the establishment of a world investment fund whose main function would be to assist the development of poor countries and which would be financed through a new international fiscal system such as the Tobin tax. The WTO, or any other organization, should be mandated to supervise transnational corporations whose oligopolistic structure is a threat to competition. Human rights have little chance of progressing on a universal basis in a world where governments have to give in to the interests of transnational corporations and private financial institutions or to the erratic constraints of speculative movements of capital. When capitalism is not regulated it finally destroys all principles of political and social organization. This is why the promotion of human rights is a political struggle which should be pursued not only at the national level, but also within the public space of international society.

Notes

1. During World War II President Roosevelt's State of the Union message on 11 January 1944, stressed that, "true individual freedom cannot exist without economic security and independence. 'Necessitous men are not free people.' People who are hungry and out of a job are the stuff of which dictatorships are made. In our day these economic truths have become accepted as self-evident. We have accepted, so to speak, a second Bill of Rights under which a new basis of security and prosperity can be established for all – regardless of station, race, or creed. Among these are: the right to a useful and remunerative job in the industries, shops, farms, or mines of the Nation; the right to earn enough to provide adequate food and clothing and recreation; the right of every farmer to raise and sell his products at a return which will give him and his family a decent living; the right of every businessman, large or small, to trade in an atmosphere

of freedom from unfair competition and domination by monopolies at home or abroad; The right of every family to a decent home; the right to adequate medical care and the opportunity to achieve and enjoy good health; the right to adequate protection from the economic fears of old age, sickness, accident, and unemployment; the right to a good education." This political philosophy clearly inspired the Universal Declaration of Human Rights after the war, as well as the European welfare states.

2. These are part of the Maastricht guidelines on the Violation of Economic, Social and Cultural Rights drawn up by a group of experts in 1997. See "The Viability of the United Nations Approach to Economic and Social Human Rights in a Globalized Economy," *International Affairs* 75(3), 1999, pp. 563–598.
3. "Human Rights, Democracy and Development," *Human Rights Quarterly* 21, 1999, p. 631.
4. *Human Rights Tribune* 6(1), 1999; see also on the Web Third World Network.
5. *Le Monde*, 7 September 1999.
6. "HRW Briefing Paper on Supermaximum Prisons," see www.hrw.org/reports/2000/supermax.
7. William F. Felice, "The Viability of the United Nations Approach to Economic and Social Human Rights in a Globalized Economy," *International Affairs* 75(3), 1999, p. 589.
8. See UN Doc, E/CN. 4SUB. 2/RES/2001/21; E/CN. 4/SUB. 2/RES/2001/14; E/CN. 4/SUB. 2/RES/2001/5.
9. UNCTAD, *Trade and Development Report 1997*, Geneva, 1997.
10. E/1997/17.
11. "Culture et démocratie," *Rapport mondial sur la culture*, Paris, UNESCO, 1998.
12. "A Proposal for a Comprehensive Development Framework," January 1999, www.worldbank.org.
13. "The Role of International Financial Institutions in Judicial Reform," *CIJL Yearbook*, VII, January 1999, pp. 31–50.
14. Shahid Javed Burki and Guillermo Perry, *The Long March: A Reform Agenda for Latin America and the Caribbean in the Next Decade*, La Banque Mondiale, Washington, 1997; see also Nancy Birdsall et al., *Beyond Trade Offs*, Washington, Inter-American Development Bank, 1998.
15. *Le Monde*, 22 September 1999, interview with Jean-Michel Severino, Vice-President of the World Bank.
16. E/C 12/1998/SR 20, 30 June 1998.
17. Norman Girvan, "A Perspective from the South," *New Political Economy* 4(3), 1999, pp. 415–419.
18. Robert A. Blecker, *Taming Global Finance: A Better Architecture for Growth and Equity*, Washington, Economic Policy Institute, 1999, p. 117.

6

Global accountability: Transnational duties toward economic rights

Henry Shue

It is bad luck to be born into a family that is too poor to feed one. But the fact that a quarter of all children are born into such families is not bad luck but bad organization.

Thomas W. Pogge[1]

Global institutional reach

Most ordinary people whom I have encountered are thoroughly decent and instinctively kind, except when they find themselves in a desperate situation in which they have little choice but to turn all their energies into an effort to save themselves. No doubt I have led a fortunate life and not encountered the worst, but I do not believe that the extraordinary levels of perennial misery in the poorest states of the world are primarily the result of heartlessness on the part of the better off. The explanation, I think, is more complicated; and it is importantly a story about opportunities not seen and accountability not felt – more blindness than heartlessness.[2] "It's tragic, but it is really nothing to do with me." No doubt this belief is usually self-serving, and perhaps self-deceptive, but it is typically sincere as well. It is also false. Which is another way of saying that we bear more transnational duties toward economic rights than most of us think we do – and that our vision is blocked by a misleadingly simplistic, and hopelessly dated, picture of the opportunities available in the world.[3]

We see no past connection between ourselves and the underdeveloped brains of malnourished children: we did not ask them to be born, we did not fire their fathers from their jobs, we did not steal the food from the mouths of the babies. These details are true: we did not do those things (we would not do those things). There has been no direct connection, in the vast majority of cases. We did not make the babies, and we did not make them malnourished. But social institutions, political and economic, formal and informal, seen and unseen – and the fundamental underlying purposes and procedures embedded in and guiding the specific institutions – provide powerful levers of opportunity for influencing the fates of even distant strangers. Great opportunities lie in, for instance, what Andrew Hurrell and Ngaire Woods call "the meta-rules," and what Christian Reus-Smit calls "the constitutional structure of international society," which control who, or what, decides what the rules are, and what kinds of rules can be made, for dealing with the material conditions we face.[4] But I am getting ahead of the story.

We need, first, to survey the moral landscape and its openings for effective action. The suggestion that we bear transnational duties toward economic rights can be challenged at many junctures, and I cannot, in this chapter, take up all the challenges. First, and most fundamentally, it can be argued that we bear no transnational duties toward such rights because there simply are no such rights. This first challenge entails treating the Universal Declaration of Human Rights (UDHR) and even the expression of the relevant parts of it in conventional international law in the form of a multilateral treaty, the International Covenant on Economic, Social and Cultural Rights (ICESCR), as, not a genuinely binding commitment morally (nor, perhaps, even legally because of the wiggle-room provided by phrasing like "progressively"), but merely some unholy combination of aspiration, on the part of the poor, and hypocrisy, on the part of the rich. This challenge is not groundless, even if unpersuasive, but I simply leave it aside here. I assume here that a child too young to provide food for itself has a right to receive food from others; this is not self-evidently true, but true all the same and embodied in a deepening international consensus. If a child has a right, someone somewhere has a duty to provide the food. But the bearers of the duty may be, most notably, the child's parents. The duty certainly might not be transnational. It may not even be national – if there is a hungry child in the urban depths of Chicago, am I the one who should provide it with food? Why me? I do not even know its name. And a fortiori a child born amidst the endless, to-me invisible civil war in the Sudan. Why me? I do not know that child's name either – I do not even own a map of the

Sudan on which I could look for its village, if I knew the village's name.

Yet this is ultimately a silly and misleading kind of example.[5] Affluent adults and hungry infants are not adrift in space. We all are embedded in a tangled jumble of social institutions, quite a few of which, like global capital markets, reach easily around (and around and around) the world. Of course a random individual like me has no private connection with a random infant somewhere – this is statistically most improbable. But the absence of private connection is also immaterial if there are deep social connections through the institutional structure of the international system in which all human individuals live.

If there clearly were no economic rights – not even the most basic subsistence rights like the right of a helpless child to nourishment – we would have no potential duties to discuss.[6] But even if there seem to be such rights, we still have a lot to talk about. For the second, more persuasive challenge to transnational duties is not a total dismissal of all economic rights but the contention that all the relevant duties fall locally or nationally. Any child may have a right to adequate nourishment, but the duties to see that it gets it fall first on its parents, then on its village, and then perhaps on its state. But such duties, it is often said, do not reach across oceans. This second challenge, then, is the one more worthy of discussion: "rights, yes; but duties that are transnational, no."

This second challenge can rest on either (or both) of two quite different grounds – grounds of thoroughly dissimilar kinds – which it is important to distinguish analytically, even though both grounds are sometimes invoked together (and are not ultimately completely unrelated). Most shorthand labels are misleading, and those I am about to introduce are no exception. However, in order to have a brief means of reference I will call them, respectively, the thesis of principled communitarianism and the thesis of causal ineffectuality.

Principled communitarianism

Those whom I am calling principled communitarians reject transnational duties toward economic rights because they consider such duties incompatible with higher priority duties owed to fellow members of more limited communities. Their argument is positive in the sense that it emphasizes the significance of, in Michael Walzer's words, "communities of shared value."[7] Nothing is said to denigrate the importance of distant strangers or their rights, but the fulfilment of duty begins, and then very nearly ends, 'at home.' Burdensome duties end 'at home' only because the special character of one's relationships with and responsibilities toward fellow members of the same community effectively exhaust the resources and capacities that anyone can reasonably be expected to devote to the performance of duty.[8] This in no way implies that other communities and the individuals who find their identities within them are of less than equal importance or worth. It reflects the de facto division of moral labour that is thought to be unavoidable if relationships within a community are to be deeper than relationships across communities.

And, as my use of Michael Walzer as exemplar of this view indicates, the issue is not between "Asian values" and "Western values." It is not that "Asians" value the community, and "Westerners" value the individual. On the one hand, Michael Walzer, British theorist David Miller, and American philosopher Richard Miller are each proponents of a version of principled communitarianism, without being "anti-individualist."[9] On the other hand, many Asians are passionately committed to the rights of individuals, without being "anti-communal." As Yash Ghai has observed, "some government leaders speak as if they represent the whole continent," when in fact (a) countries in "Asia" – largely a Western construct, in any case – differ greatly from each other and (b) many ordinary citizens in otherwise diverse cultures, especially those being repressed by the authoritarian governments in question, are desperately concerned about the rights of individuals.[10] Similar points can be made about "Islamic rights," much of the recent impetus for which came from repressive Middle East governments, not ordinary Muslims.[11] In short, on both sides of any meaningful East/West or Muslim/Christian divide, one will find both proponents and opponents of principled communitarianism. The disagreements within each camp are philosophical, not cultural – and not susceptible of any resolution brief enough to offer here.[12] We must return, however, to some of the important issues raised by principled communitarianism below in "Division of moral labour."

Causal ineffectuality

The thesis of causal ineffectuality is of a quite different kind. The heart of this thesis is the contention that, even granted everything that can accurately be said about international interdependence and about "our global neighborhood," or planetary village, the effects of any one person's life, especially the life of an ordinary person, must fade out before they touch more than a tiny fraction of the world's other people.[13] It may be that my life can be like a pebble dropped into a pond, sending out, for good or ill, ripples ranging out distances many times the size of the pebble. Yet, in a "pond" the size of this planet, the ripples still fade out long before they touch everyone, or even very many. And I cannot be responsible to, or for, those whom I have not touched.

Here is the picture invoked by the thesis of causal ineffectuality. The thesis weds an empirical sub-thesis and an ethical sub-thesis. Empirical: I have not touched most of humanity. Ethical: (therefore) I bear no responsibility toward most of humanity – even granting that they have rights that someone ought to protect. That "someone" is simply not me. I know vaguely perhaps that some horrible catastrophe has been slowly grinding its way through southern Sudan, unreported by CNN, for decades, leaving starving (and enslaved) children in its wake. But, whatever distant ripples my life may have had, they neither reached the shores of Africa nor penetrated its deserts. I did not cause the Sudanese civil war, I do not understand it, and it is not my responsibility to end it – it is *not mine* to deal with.[14]

This simple picture is profoundly misleading, both ethically and empirically. Ethically, it assumes that all responsibility is backward-looking and corrective. My only duties are to clean up messes that I myself have made, or at least contributed to. Such a sadly negative and exclusively past-oriented account of our duties omits, I believe, much that is best and most admirable about human beings, including accountability for the future we create. The equally essential and misguided empirical contention I shall encapsulate as: I have not touched (and cannot touch) many strangers. I have already mentioned the essential reason this empirical part of the picture is misleading: it assumes mistakenly that individual persons are adrift in a kind of non-social space, when in truth we are deeply embedded in thick transnational webs of institutions – and the underlying principles that shape the institutions – which give some of us wider reach and greater leverage than isolated individuals would have had. I may not have privately touched many strangers, but the social institutions on which I rely for the life I lead, from the worldwide web to whatever brought the West Nile encephalitis to New York City, profoundly affect billions of my fellows. This institutional reach may be "indirect," or anyway socially mediated, but it is by no means less profound for that. When a commander orders troops into battle, he may directly kill no one, but thousands may die because he spoke one word, not another, and that word reverberated with authority down the chain of command. And those who are excluded from many institutional webs – and in that literal sense, untouched by them – are often, if anything, more profoundly affected by the *institutional exclusion*. That the commander chooses not to include your village in the area to be defended hardly means the institution he controls does not affect your life.

Global radical inequality

The net effect of the extent of the reach of, and the exclusion from, human institutions upon humanity as a whole might best be captured by an important concept introduced in 1977 by Thomas Nagel, global radical inequality, which he defined as consisting of three elements.[15] In 1998 Thomas Pogge tightened the concept of a radical inequality by adding two additional conditions that a situation must satisfy in order to qualify.[16] I shall use the concept in Pogge's refined sense, in which the first, second, and fifth of the following elements correspond to Nagel's original three:

Nature
1. Those at the bottom [economically] are very badly off in absolute terms. (*absolutely extreme*)
2. They are also very badly off in relative terms – very much worse off than many others. (*relatively extreme*)
3. The inequality is persistent: It is difficult or impossible for those at the bottom substantially to improve their lot; and most of those at the top never experience life at the bottom for even a few months and have no vivid idea of what it is like to live in that way. (*persistent*)
4. The inequality is pervasive: it concerns not merely some aspects of life, such as the climate or access to natural beauty or high culture, but most aspects or all. (*pervasive*)
5. The inequality is avoidable: those at the top can improve the circumstances of those at the bottom without becoming badly off themselves. (*avoidable*)[17]

That is, I shall follow Pogge in calling global inequalities that are absolutely extreme, relatively extreme, persistent, pervasive, and avoidable "radical inequalities." I believe, as he does, that our world is in fact characterized by a myriad of interlocking radical inequalities, and I shall presently explain more fully why. Nagel originally suggested that radical inequality (in his initial sense) is inherently objectionable – inherently demeaning – and that those at the top economically and politically ought to act to eliminate it, irrespective of its sources or causal explanations. I have always found the suggestion that radical inequality is, in effect, intrinsically evil very compelling, but Pogge has now made a suggestion that is far weaker and therefore far more difficult yet to resist.

In addition to specifying the concept of radical inequality further by adding the third and fourth conditions above, Pogge proposes that we consider a case of radical inequality which has a specific causal explanation embodied in the following three additional features:

Source
6. Everyday conduct of those at the top (economically) often strongly affects the circumstances of those at the bottom in a way that shows that both coexist under a single scheme of social institutions.
7. This institutional scheme is implicated in the radical inequality by avoidably

producing the poverty of those at the bottom, in this sense: it is not the case that every practicable institutional alternative would also generate such severe and extensive poverty.

8. The radical inequality cannot be traced to extrasocial factors (such as genetic handicaps or natural disasters) that, as such, affect different human beings differentially.[18]

Taken together, these additional three conditions assert that the radical inequality in the world is in fact produced by shared global institutions.

Pogge's main points are, then, (a) that those of us at the top of radical global inequality (e.g. US, EU, and Japan) are guilty of contributing to the coercive imposition upon those at the bottom of the shared institutions that (1) produced in the past, and (2) maintain in the present, the radical inequality; and, therefore, (b) that we have a purely negative duty to stop harming those at the bottom by ceasing to operate institutions that (1) have imposed, and (2) continue to impose, such extreme but avoidable conditions upon them. The duties are obviously transnational duties to stop imposing severe economic distress. Now, I think that Pogge's picture is generally correct, but I want in the end to emphasize its forward-looking aspect where he emphasizes its backward-looking aspect. I want, in other words, to emphasize the theses I have just labelled (a, 2) and (b, 2), not (a, 1) and (b, 1). But I will proceed by looking at each of the three additional features listed by Pogge in order.

The initial clause of feature (6) is, unfortunately, open to a misreading as referring to private connections of precisely the kind, Pogge saw clearly sooner than I did, that we should not be looking for.[19] Saying that "everyday conduct of those at the top often strongly affects the circumstances of those at the bottom ..." might be taken to be saying that, for example, if Sally makes her morning coffee from Kenyan coffee beans, Sally is thereby implicated in the corruption of, and the exploitation by, the Kenyan coffee cooperative which purchased the beans from the farmer at an artificially low price. But that would be first to fall into the misleadingly sketchy picture of unattached individuals floating in a social space, which Pogge is rejecting, and then to search unavailingly for some hidden immediate connection between the floating individuals. Does Sally's drinking Kenyan coffee contribute to Kenyan corruption and exploitation? Should she then drink, say, Rwandan coffee instead? What about Rwandan "ethnic" conflict? And so on. It is not, however, that evident private connections between individuals are data providing evidence of underlying social institutions, but that the individuals are connected in the first place only because of, and through, institutions. The institutions are the connection, which is social.[20]

In any case, the institutions should, Pogge and I agree, be the focus of attention. To stay with the example, Sally should not think that the issue for her is whether to drink Kenyan or Rwandan coffee. The issue is something much closer to whether to press efforts to change the IMF so that it will not be controlled by people who are so ideologically doctrinaire that they actually believe that it is reasonable to coerce nations into trying to repay oppressive external debt contracted by dictators who stole or wasted the borrowed funds, by exporting commodities with highly volatile international prices grown on land that could much better be used to grow food for local consumption. The issue is not whose coffee beans to grind; it is within which set of international economic institutions to live (and drink one's coffee). To focus on private choices about consumption and production is to miss the point. The point is to ask: what are the social institutions that determine which private choices are available? Why are these our choices? (Why does Rwanda export coffee and Belgium export computers?) And who or what is maintaining institutions that so ill serve billions of human beings?

The fundamental point of Pogge's feature (6), then, is that the richest and the poorest both live within "a single scheme of social institutions." Feature (7) next draws out the political and moral significance of the existence of only "a single" global scheme: this global economic scheme – the only one there is at any given time – is "avoidably producing the poverty of those at the bottom," which is carefully, if negatively, explained as follows: "it is not the case that every practicable institutional alternative would also generate such severe and extensive poverty." This is a perceptive and vital point, but one must be cautious not to read into it more than needs to be there. As fascinating studies like, for example, Kenneth Pomeranz's *The Great Divergence: China, Europe, and the Making of the Modern World Economy*, make abundantly clear, any full historical explanation of international inequality undeniably involves material as well as social factors, such as the location of the coal deposits that underlay the industrial revolution (and the beginnings of anthropogenic climate change).[21] If Pogge's contention were interpreted to be that radical inequality is fully explained exclusively by social factors like economic institutions – and that the natural distribution of coal and oil, the natural evolution of diseases, and other such material factors had no explanatory role to play – the contention would be utterly implausible. The statement of feature (8) might have been clearer on this point as it dismisses the explanatory significance of "extrasocial factors ... that, as such, affect different human beings differentially." Certainly, it is true that material factors take on human significance only as humans – usually, acting socially – express preferences and adopt purposes. If humans had no preferences or purposes that involved the consumption of energy, the presence or absence of coal deposits would be of no consequence.

However, given the apparently universal human desire for greater material production fuelled by increasing amounts of energy, it is of great importance to the occurrence or non-occurrence of an industrial revolution whether, as in England, the deposits of coal were located near water that could relatively easily transport the coal to urban concentrations, or not, as in China.

There is no need, however, to deny that given only very minimal, standard, and widespread human desires, material factors are crucial elements in economies generally and in international inequalities in particular.[22] Pogge's basic point remains: for any given natural distribution of material factors, the selection of one alternative set of social institutions rather than another has profound consequences for human well-being and for, specifically, the distribution of wealth. Given the social role played by diamonds as jewellery, it is very important that Sierra Leone and Congo contain major deposits of diamonds; who is enriched and who is impoverished, or killed, because of these natural deposits depends, however, upon whether Belgian wholesalers have any scruples at all concerning the sources from whom they buy smuggled diamonds, upon whether veto-wielding Security Council members are willing to pay for peace enforcement to end civil war in Africa, and upon many other matters controlled by social organization.

Our existing radical inequality is avoidably produced by existing international institutions. This does not mean that material factors are not also part of any complete explanation of the current situation. It does mean that, for any given initial natural distribution, be it resource or virus, alternative social institutions combined with this same natural distribution would have yielded different outcomes. Most important to me, it means that "it is not the case that every practicable institutional alternative would also generate such severe and extensive poverty" (Pogge's feature (7)). Given all the extrasocial factors as they are, a different social response will yield different outcomes for the current international distribution of affluence and misery. We are avoidably producing the existing radical inequality in the sense that we are failing to adopt alternative institutions that, in the face of all relevant material factors, can reasonably be expected to produce less extreme international inequality. Material factors do not dictate that this is the only possible world. We have options. We are, therefore, accountable morally for contenting ourselves with this arrangement with its radical inequality.

That international inequalities have in fact been becoming far more severe during the years of "globalization" is abundantly well documented.[23] One possible way to think about the situation is in terms of institutional levels that are fairly deep – what, as I noted earlier, Andrew Hurrell and Ngaire Woods call "meta-rules." In research extending over the last several years Hurrell and Woods have built a substantial case that "globalization" is making international inequality much worse.[24] They argue that the rich and powerful nations – those better-off absolutely in the beginning – have benefited relatively more from the process of globalization. This has obviously transpired for many reasons, but one very important reason is that the nations that were already rich and powerful when the process begin made the rules for the process: globalization has done relatively more for the rich and powerful because it was designed, by the rich and powerful, to do precisely this. They controlled the "meta-rules": the rules that determined the rules governing globalization, for example, intellectual property law. The initial political inequality, which provided control over the rules of the game, is yielding increasing economic inequality as the outcome of the game. To put the thesis of Hurrell and Woods in the terms employed by Nagel and Pogge, the radical inequality in power existing at the beginning of globalization has enabled globalization to be structured so that it makes the radical inequality in wealth progressively worse.[25]

Even if one were not convinced by this more specific explanation by Hurrell and Woods, all that is crucial is that, as Pogge suggests, the poverty and the wealth are occurring within a single scheme of shared economic and political institutions and therefore a change in the rules governing these institutions would have effects that would reverberate around the globe. The behaviour of the Leviathans like the IMF in aggressively enforcing uniform economic policies on every state to the full extent of their power to do so, strongly suggests that they at least believe the basic rules matter enormously. We live in a world whose basic ground rules are being centrally managed to the fullest extent that grossly unequal power allows. In this respect there is only one game on the planet, and any nation who wishes to "play," i.e. have a functioning economy, must play by the single favoured set of ground rules. The Treasury Secretaries and Central Bankers of the triumphant – and triumphalist – OECD nations are doing their best to be sure that Pogge's sixth feature applies: that the globe has "a single scheme of social institutions" at the level of the fundamental rules of the economic game. I am not arguing that it is either good or bad to have a single scheme. I am arguing, with Pogge, that it is of fundamental ethical significance that only one game exists, because this means that everyone is in the same game. I am further suggesting, with Pogge, that the specific rules of the single scheme now in force are far worse for the poor and powerless than some alternatives that appear perfectly feasible (and not even especially painful for the affluent).[26]

The issue, then, is not whether some individual choice of mine exacerbated the Sudanese civil war, or whether Sally's choice of Kenyan coffee is supporting the Kenyan dictatorship; in fact, there are few such private connections. The issue is that Sally and I are enjoying a stable, inflation-free prosperity, including salaries more than adequate to allow us to enjoy the coffee and other luxuries of our choice, guarded by the gray-suited centurions of the IMF, World Bank, et al., who do not want to take the pressure off Nairobi to pay its foreign debt for barrels of oil until it has sold enough coffee beans to do so or to put the pressure on the Sudan to stop the slave-trading and negotiate an end to the civil war. Sally and I – and you – are implicated, not by the specific private choices we make within the regime, but by our tolerance of – our lack of opposition to – or even our support for, this global economic regime that provides these choices, not others. So the thesis of causal ineffectuality is groundless.

The practical significance of this that I want to emphasize – and here I differ from Pogge – is that an opportunity of a very specific kind is opened up, namely an opportunity to avoid knowingly inflicting harm in the future.[27] That radical inequality is avoidable means that alternative futures are available. We are accountable for any future we now help to create. To choose to continue with social institutions that, in combination with the relevant extra-social factors, maintain radical inequality, when the opportunity is open to us to create institutions that do not yield radical inequality, is to choose knowingly to impose radical inequality in the future. Radical inequality is not necessitated by material factors – it results from the material factors plus the economic institutions created to deal with those factors. Those of us who have institutional options are responsible for the decision we face whether radical inequality, and consequent denial of even mere subsistence rights, persists. The open opportunity to do better entails responsibility if we choose continuing radical inequality and continued denial of economic and social rights. Irrespective of whether it is correct to say that the institutions have been imposed in the past, we will be imposing them in the future if we see available alternatives and choose not to take one.[28] But who exactly is responsible for what?

Division of moral labour

None of this, however, establishes that any particular individual has a transnational duty toward the economic rights of any other particular individual. To whom am I responsible? This is an incomplete question, and it can be completed in various ways. It is useful to see, as Charles R. Beitz has recently noted, that two related but distinct issues arise: (1) to whom must one justify one's action? and (2) toward whom does one bear duties to act (or, to refrain from acting)? Let us call these (1) the responsibility to explain and (2) the responsibility to act.[29] It may be in a particular case that, in answer to the second question, I owe you nothing material, except that I do owe you an explanation of why not, that is, an answer to the first question. It is possible that I show you no disrespect by declining to provide something that you need, but I would show you disrespect if I refused to offer you good reasons for declining, at least if you asked. Let us next explore this a bit.

It is here that principled communitarianism returns. It is possible to believe that one lives in a community such that the following two propositions are both correct: (1) one's relationships with the other members of the community, but with no one else, are deep and significant; and (2) one is embedded in a fabric of reciprocal duties with all the other members of the community, with no comparable duties toward anyone else. I shall call this a morally significant community. A principled communitarian sees a planet occupied by a large number of separate morally significant communities.

Philosophers have batted around artificial examples of such situations, like two islands in a river, one upstream from the other. Upstream can affect Downstream because, for example, Upstream can draw water out of the river before it reaches Downstream, and Upstream can pollute the river before it reaches Downstream. But Downsteam cannot, simply because of the direction of the flow of the river, do either of these things to Upstream. If we add the assumption that they lack boats and other means of transportation for moving against the current, we can describe a situation in which the members of Downstream have no responsibility at all toward Upstream and its members – ("ought" presupposes "can") and Downstream cannot affect Upstream because it cannot reach it. If it cannot affect it, it cannot be involved in deep or significant relationships with it. However, Upstream and its members have considerable responsibility toward Downstream and its members because the former affect the latter in such major ways. With regard to the pollution of the river, for example, if the pollution affects the well-being of the Downstreamers, the Upstreamers owe them, at a minimum, an explanation and justification for engaging in the pollution: the Upstreamers have a (1) responsibility to explain. To refuse to explain – to refuse to answer the question, "Why are you doing this to us?" – would be contemptuous of the Downstreamers, treating their well-being as so unimportant that no explanation for damaging it is necessary. If, however, the Upstreamers have no other acceptable choice – they cannot survive without the polluting activities, and storing the pollutants on their own island would be far more dangerous to themselves than dumping them into the river is for the Downstreamers – then they may have no (2) responsibility to act, no responsibility to do anything differently (except, perhaps, to minimize the pollution and to continue to look for a third option). Here too "ought" presupposes "can," and the Upstreamers have, by hypothesis, no better alternative they can take.

One general observation to be made about the real world is that it is indeed in fundamental respects like this hypothetical example. Rich states can force open markets in poor states, and otherwise disrupt their economies, but poor states cannot do the same to rich ones; and so forth. "Globalization" is extremely "asymmetrical." And it has not simply turned out to be asymmetrical, because the asymmetry – the radical inequality – is built into the rules that define and constitute the global economic game. The further that Anglo-American economic "liberalization" proceeds, the more it is the case that the rich states do what they can and the poor states suffer what they must.

It follows, then, that (1) the responsibility to explain is owed to everyone affected by the ground rules. And "everyone affected" is literally everyone. We all live in the shadow of a single unified scheme. I take the scheme to be asymmetrical globalization, in which the rich get richer and the poor get poorer. But if I am wrong about the content of the scheme, what matters still is that it is a single global scheme that determines which choices are available. For any minimum of respect for the individuals affected requires that they be given reasons why the scheme – however exactly it is to be described – is as it is. If one-quarter of all children are born into families too poor to feed them, the parents seem entitled to be provided with some explanation why this is so.[30] Is this unavoidable? A law of nature? Would it be possible for them to be nourished only if the rest of us starved? If not, why are matters arranged as they are now – that is, why are the current rules the rules all must play by?

Everyone whose prospects in life are profoundly affected by the ground rules of a single institutional scheme is entitled to an explanation of why the institutions are as they are. A priori one cannot be sure that the explanation is not that this is the best that can be done. Perhaps we are not smart enough – or do not have resources enough – to do any better. Perhaps some original sin has doomed us to live this way. But everyone affected, which in this case is simply everyone, is still owed a justification and the explanation for the way the social rules handle the material realities. And in fact, of course, any suggestion that this is as good as it gets would be preposterous.

Nevertheless, one conclusion that does not follow is that everyone is in some undifferentiated way obligated to everyone else. It does not even follow – yet – that anyone has any transnational duties even if everyone has economic rights. Obviously, some division of the moral labour involved in protecting these rights is called for simply in order to avoid chaos, and all the duties might fall at a national or local level, for all that has been said here. Perhaps the principled communitarians are correct in suggesting that multiple considerations converge upon a kind of charity-begins-at-home (not that the duties here are actually of mere charity) approach to the assignment of duties even where the rights are universal. For instance, even universal needs for food, clothing, shelter, education, and medical care are satisfied in diverse, culturally specific ways best understood by the members of the culture in question; ideally any corresponding duties are best performed by those with the most complete understanding. Further, some of the most distinctively human and most highly valued human connections – love, loyalty, devotion, intimacy – are possible only within relatively exclusive and relatively long-term relationships. Theorists often call these special relationships, in contrast with one's general relationship with all humanity. One need not deny that it is important that even if I encounter a stranger in the desert, we share a common humanity that may lead him to give me a drink of his water simply because I am thirsty (and human), in order to acknowledge the various and wonderful values possible only between parent and child, between lovers, between fellow veterans of distant battles, or between members of genuine communities of shared value.[31] Once again, ideally many rights are best fulfilled and protected, not dutifully qua rights, but out of the loves and loyalties that define such special relationships.

And yet we must also ask what happens when the ideal does not come to pass. Yes, it would be better if the parents fed the child and gave her the foods she loves, prepared in her favourite way, at the time she likes, in the company she enjoys, but what if this is one of the 25 per cent of the world's families who lack the food or the fuel with which to cook it? Yes, better if the education comes from teachers who share the tradition, love and cherish it, and who speak the language without foreign accent, but what if those teachers were shot during the ethnic cleansing? We may need to know the ideal arrangements in order to set our ultimate orientation – they may be the star that guides us for the long term. But here and now we need to know how people are supposed to climb out of the mire they are currently stuck in. The ideal plan has its use, but first we need the back-up plan for those who find themselves off the main trail.

We need assignments of default duties. This is why, even if principled communitarianism were correct, it could not be definitive. Many of the default duties are transnational even if the primary duties were national, local, or familial. Why? Partly because the ideal plan has in fact not been followed, and people are now stuck. If no back-up plan is executed, they will remain stuck. That is, even their most basic rights will remain unfulfilled. The price of having no back-up plan would be very high.

But why might some of these strangers' rights be my problem, even as part of a default plan? Why might I be part of some back-up plans? Various cases arise; the case I am concentrating on here is the one in which global radical inequality plays a vital role. The children have a right to food.[32] The primary duties for the fulfilment of that right fall upon parents and relatives, but they have no food and no jobs in which to earn money for food. The secondary duties toward the children's right to food fall upon their government, which should ideally perhaps stimulate the economy and create jobs, but the interest on the state's foreign debt is greater than the annual foreign exchange earnings from the primary commodities that are its only substantial exports. The international financial institutions insist that at least the interest on the debt be paid – one must obey the rules, they say, if one is going to play the game. Meanwhile, this game works for me: inflation is low in my state, and the purchasing power of my salary grows; the stock markets are high, and the value of my retirement portfolio also grows. The explanation of why the children are stuck without food is of a piece with the explanation of why I am doing so well. The children and I live within the same ground rules; the same scheme that serves me well serves them ill. I am not uninvolved – I am a beneficiary. Because I know this, I am responsible for either accepting the rules as they are or trying to change them. I have a duty to change them because they are making it impossible for children to enjoy their basic rights and impossible for those with responsibilities toward the children prior to my own to fulfil them. I am the next in line and the first now who might be able to act. So now it is up to me to make it possible for the others in the line of responsibility ahead of me to act in future. When they can, I need not. This particular default duty is, then, a duty to empower, or re-empower, the bearers of primary duties.[33] And while the whole story goes far beyond what I have been able to tell here, I hope to have supported at least one type of transnational duty toward economic rights.

Notes

1. For invaluable inconsistency spotting in the original, I am grateful to my commentator at the Princeton workshop, Amanda Dickens, and to the editors; and for his typically perceptive reading, Thomas W. Pogge. See Thomas W. Pogge, "A Global Resources Dividend," in David A. Crocker and Toby Linden, eds., *Ethics of Consumption, The Good Life, Justice, and Global Stewardship*, Lanham, MD and Oxford, Rowman & Littlefield, 1998, p. 531, n. 12.
2. Understanding of the relation between the seeing and the feeling is supremely important but, so far, beyond my grasp. Here I focus on the seeing in the vague hope that feeling might follow. For probing work on the psychological dynamics, see Kristen

Renwick Monroe, *The Heart of Altruism, Perceptions of a Common Humanity*, Princeton, Princeton University Press, 1996.

3. I suspect that the picture was often learned in contexts, like high school civics courses, which were intended to make us patriotic but only left us myopic.

4. Andrew Hurrell and Ngaire Woods, "Globalisation and Inequality," *Millennium, Journal of International Studies* 24(3), Winter 1995, pp. 447–470, at 460; and Christian Reus-Smit, *The Moral Purpose of the State: Culture, Social Identity, and Institutional Rationality in International Relations*, Princeton Studies in International History and Politics, Princeton, Princeton University Press, 1999, pp. 14–15.

5. I have not always been clear about this.

6. I gave one compatible but distinct set of arguments for subsistence rights in *Basic Rights, Subsistence, Affluence, and U.S. Foreign Policy*, 2nd edn, Princeton, Princeton University Press, 1996 [1980]. An excellent analysis of the variety of available arguments is in Charles Jones, *Global Justice, Defending Cosmopolitanism*, Oxford and New York, Oxford University Press, 1999, chs. 1 and 3.

7. This view is worked out in Michael Walzer, *Spheres of Justice: A Defense of Pluralism and Equality*, New York, Basic Books, 1983. A valuable critique appears in Charles Jones, ch. 7.

8. This may appear to be a kind of moral "fatigue." However, the point is not that duty-bearers happen in fact to run out of energy, as it were, but that they are in principle entitled to cease their duty-performance and turn their attentions, and energies, to their own lives. The next step here leads into deep waters concerning the limits of morality, valuably discussed by, among others, Samuel Scheffler and Liam Murphy.

9. Richard Miller would likely find the "communitarian" label especially uncongenial because his fundamental premises are a form of Kantian universalism explicitly presented as an alternative to David Miller's "particularism." This is an important and fascinating debate within what I am choosing to lump together as one broad church on the basis of the largely similar conclusions reached about the extent of transnational duties. See David Miller, *On Nationality*, Oxford and New York, Oxford University Press, 1995, esp. ch. 3; and Richard W. Miller, "Cosmopolitan Respect and Patriotic Concern," *Philosophy & Public Affairs* 27(3), 1998, pp. 202–224.

10. Yash Ghai, "Asian Perspectives on Human Rights," in James T. H. Tang, ed., *Human Rights and International Relations in the Asia Pacific*, New York, St. Martin's Press, 1995, pp. 54–67, at 54. Also see Yash Ghai, "Rights, Social Justice, and Globalization in East Asia," in Joanne R. Bauer and Daniel A. Bell, eds., *The East Asian Challenge for Human Rights*, Cambridge and New York, Cambridge University Press, 1999, pp. 241–263; as well as the following, all also in Bauer and Bell: Tatsuo Inoue, "Liberal Democracy and Asian Orientalism"; Abdullahi A. An-Na'im, "The Cultural Mediation of Human Rights"; Norani Othman, "Grounding Human Rights Arguments in Non-Western Culture"; and Suwanna Satha-Anand, "Looking to Buddhism to Turn Back Prostitution in Thailand." Further see Xiaorong Li, "'Asian Values' and the Universality of Human Rights," *Report from the Institute for Philosophy & Public Policy* 16(2), Spring 1996, pp. 18–23; and compare Chandra Muzaffar, "Ethnicity, Ethnic Conflict and Human Rights in Malaysia," in Claude Welch and Virginia Leary, eds., *Asian Perspectives on Human Rights*, Boulder, CO, Westview Press, 1990, pp. 107–141.

11. See Ann Elizabeth Mayer, *Islam and Human Rights, Tradition and Politics*, 2nd edn, Boulder, CO, Westview Press, 1995; and London, Pinter Publishers, 1995; and several items in the previous note. Also see generally Tim Dunne and Nicholas J. Wheeler, eds., *Human Rights in Global Politics*, Cambridge and New York, Cambridge University Press, 1999.

12. I cannot tackle them here. I made a very modest beginning in "Menschenrechte und

kulturelle Differenz," in Stefan Gosepath und Georg Lohmann, eds., *Philosophie der Menschenrechte*, Suhrkamp Taschenbuch Wissenschaft, Frankfurt am Main, Suhrkamp, 1998, pp. 343–377, English version available from the author. Also see Charles Taylor, "Conditions of an Unforced Consensus on Human Rights," in Bauer and Bell, eds.

13. The allusion is of course to the Commission on Global Governance, *Our Global Neighborhood*, Oxford and New York, Oxford University Press, 1995.

14. And one can add in, although one need not, the thesis of principled communitarianism, and, anyway, I have prior responsibilities here.

15. Thomas Nagel, "Poverty and Food: Why Charity is Not Enough," in *Food Policy, U.S. Responsibility in the Life and Death Choices*, New York, Free Press, 1977, pp. 54–62.

16. Pogge, pp. 501–536.

17. Ibid., pp. 502–503.

18. Ibid., p. 504.

19. See Thomas W. Pogge, "Cosmopolitanism and Sovereignty," *Ethics* 103(1), October 1992, pp. 48–75. That is, in his terminology, feature (6) might be misread as "interactional" in the sense he wants to avoid.

20. This is Pogge's own point; I am criticizing only his wording, "everyday conduct."

21. Princeton, NJ, Princeton University Press, 2000.

22. I am grateful to the editors for emphasizing to me the fact that one can argue for the critical importance of rules, norms, and institutions without in the least denying that material factors are also an important part of the whole story. What matters is that a change of rules would produce a change in outcomes.

23. See, for instance, UN Development Programme, *Human Development Report 1999*, Oxford and New York, Oxford University Press, 1999. The full text of every *Human Development Report* for 1990–1999 is available in an interactive, searchable format on *Human Development Report CD-ROM*, E. 99III. B. 44, New York, United Nations, 1999.

24. See Hurrell and Woods, "Globalisation and Inequality," as well as Andrew Hurrell and Ngaire Woods, eds., *Inequality, Globalization, and World Politics*, Oxford and New York, Oxford University Press, 1999.

25. Naturally I am here painting with a broad brush. For more detail, see Ngaire Woods, "Order, Globalization, and Inequality in World Politics," and Frances Stewart and Albert Berry, "Globalization, Liberalization, and Inequality," both in Hurrell and Woods.

26. I am grateful to Amanda Dickens for emphasizing the critical importance of its being in fact the case that at least one of the alternative institutional arrangements would actually yield less inequality. I cannot imagine that there is not at least one arrangement better than what we have, but she is correct that Pogge's avoidability thesis, which I adopt, is an empirical hypothesis.

27. Pogge focuses more upon the harm already inflicted in the past and thus on backward-looking negative duties, duties to correct for harm already done. I am exploring here an argument about forward-looking negative duties, duties not to harm (further). I am still committed as well to the positive duties defended in *Basic Rights* but share Pogge's conviction that negative duties alone would carry us far beyond where we are now.

28. This is an attempt to deal with an important question raised by Amanda Dickins.

29. I take the distinction between these two issues to be at the heart of Beitz's recent distinction between "social liberalism" and "cosmopolitan liberalism" – see Charles R. Beitz, "Social and Cosmopolitan Liberalism," *International Affairs* 75(3), July 1999, pp. 515–529. In social liberalism, as espoused by Michael Walzer and the John Rawls of "Law of Peoples," citizens of one state need not explain their conduct to citizens of another. In cosmopolitan liberalism, illustrated by the work of Thomas W. Pogge and Beitz himself, everyone ought to be in a position to explain all the arrangments to

everyone, although cosmopolitan liberals will divide over whether one has duties to act toward everyone. This internal division among cosmopolitan liberals is what Beitz earlier dubbed "continuous" vs. "discontinuous": see Charles R. Beitz, "International Liberalism and Distributive Justice, A Survey of Recent Thought," *World Politics* 51, January 1999, pp. 269–296, at 288.

30. Some will suggest that the parents owe the rest of us an explanation of their choice to have children. Do you owe me an explanation of how many children you had? What is your explanation? Might theirs be at least as good?

31. It is crucial not to jump to the conclusion that these communities are likely to be modern states, however.

32. Besides the more general discussion in *Basic Rights*, I have discussed this in "Solidarity among Strangers and the Right to Food," in William Aiken and Hugh LaFollette, eds., *World Hunger and Morality*, 2nd edn, Upper Saddle River, NJ, Prentice Hall, 1996, pp. 113–132.

33. I am again grateful to Amanda Dickens for seeing this more clearly than I had.

Conclusion: Human rights in discourse and practice: The quandary of international justice

Jean-Marc Coicaud

This book has attempted to address and answer a set of questions focusing on the imperatives of justice at the national, regional, and international levels. The examination of these imperatives of justice has been conducted through an analysis of rights, both civil and political, and economic and social. The fact that reflecting on justice at the present time should be done through an examination of rights, and more specifically on the nature and relations of civil, political, economic and social rights, should not come as a surprise. There are two good reasons for this. First, any search for justice is based upon identifying values which are viewed as so critical to the well-being and the character of being human, including relationships with others, that they end up being institutionalized as rights. Rights then become the basis upon which claims are made, as well as an horizon of justice to which public institutions try to conform. Second, as Michael Doyle and Anne-Marie Gardner note in the introduction of the volume, after World War II, the international community embarked on an unprecedented effort to map out the requirements of justice for all mankind, providing normative guidelines as well as goals. The core of this effort was a more ethical understanding and arrangement of relations between individuals and the institutions governing them. In this respect, two enterprises stand out: the one that led to the adoption of the Universal Declaration of Human Rights (UDHR) in 1948, and in the 1960s, the adoption of the covenants on civil and political rights, and on economic and social rights.

Against this background, the book begins with Doyle and Gardner setting the stage by asking if human rights and international order are compatible. Their answer is: "yes, within limits." In spite of widespread scepticism regarding the impact of ethics and rights upon the conduct of international relations, they argue that rights, and in particular individual rights, cannot be ignored at the international level. However, as Doyle and Gardner point out, acknowledging the impact of ethics at the international level should not lead us to overlook the normative and political complexities that this entails. The book is therefore more of an attempt to clarify the rights debate than to provide definitive answers.

Following Doyle and Gardner, Ruth Gavison and Claire Archbold explore the domestic dimension of the rights debate concerning the relationship between civil and political rights, and economic and social rights. While Gavison explores the theoretical dimension of the relationship, Archbold examines the various mechanisms for incorporating these rights in domestic law. She chooses to do so by looking into the incorporation of rights in the constitutions of Canada, South Africa.

Moving the reflection to the regional level, James Mouangue Kobila and Tetsuo Inoue assess the impact of rights initiated in the West (or in developed countries of the North) upon the non-Western world, including in particular two regions: Africa and Asia. These regions serve for the authors both as an illustration and a test of the applicability of the dynamics of rights in settings which do not neatly fit into the Western framework. Kobila, focusing on the North-South divide, takes note of the great disparity that exists between the situation in the developed world and the one in developing countries. In this respect, he argues that the weak formalism of civil and political rights in the daily political reality of African countries dramatically echoes the lack of economic and social welfare from which most of the population of the non-developed world suffers. This statement is not in itself surprising. It constitutes, nonetheless, an important piece of evidence and an answer to one of the questions posed by Doyle and Gardner in the introduction to the volume, as to whether individuals who suffer desperate material deprivation can still be fully sovereign. What Kobila tells us is that, in principle, they can. Nevertheless, the imperatives of survival which confront them and the societies in which they live remove civil and political rights issues far from centre stage. Without strong social and economic foundations, without, therefore, the imperatives of economic survival and economic integration taken care of, it is likely that the affirmation of civil and political rights will remain within the realm of the abstract.

Ironically, Inoue's approach to the regional dimension of the debate regarding the divisibility of rights seems to amount to an argument from the other side of the fence of history. Unlike Kobila, Inoue is less concerned with the inability to give significance to civil and political rights in situations lacking the minimum economic level of wealth, than with the problems associated with the pursuit, and achievement, of socio-economic rights ahead of, and even excluding as a priority, civil and political rights. In this context, his criticism of Asian values is not conducted in the name of an antagonism between West and East but rather as a plea that recognizing the importance of civil and political rights can be a way for Asia to reconcile with itself, its own identities and traditions.

Finally, what about the international dimension of the reflection on rights? Here, Pierre de Senarclens and Henry Shue take a clear stand. Each in his own way argues that the recognition of rights at the international level – the internationalization of rights – brings international duties. Shue examines the speculative dimension of the transborder duties springing from the recognition and institutionalization of rights. In this regard, he looks into the ethical and political duties associated with the kind of power that makes developed countries the main beneficiaries of the current international system. As such, Shue's position certainly echoes that of de Senarclens, calling for a better implementation of human rights through international organizations.

This is precisely where it seems appropriate, in this conclusion, to pick up the debate and try to push it further with reference to, as Doyle and Gardner posit in the introduction, and following a statement made by the United Nations Secretary-General Kofi Annan, "individual sovereignty."

There are multiple ways to consider the issue of individual sovereignty. Each of the levels examined in the book – the national, regional, and global levels – furnishes more than one approach to the questions this issue raises.

However, reflecting on the reality of "individual sovereignty," by assessing to what extent the international community is now committed to it, seems all the more appropriate considering the changes that occurred in the aftermath of the Cold War, throughout the 1990s. These changes brought the discourse and practice of human rights to the centre stage of international politics. Reflecting on the meaning and reality of individual sovereignty through this angle will take us beyond the dichotomy of the civil and political versus economic and social rights debate. It will bring us back to the theme of human rights and international order with which Doyle and Gardner opened the book, and therefore close the circle of thinking encompassed in this volume.

In order to assess the extent to which the international community is committed to "individual sovereignty," we will touch upon four main points. First, we will examine how the normative dimension of international order encompasses principles on the basis of which individual rights can be recognized and implemented as imperatives. Second, we will emphasize the limits of modern international solidarity and the consequences that it holds for the implementation and protection of human rights at the international level. Third, we will show that, as a result, the projection of international justice with regard to human rights, while made possible by legal obligations, relies more at this stage on moral imperatives. Fourth, and finally, we will try to give a number of suggestions to overcome the limitations from which human rights conceptualization and implementation continue to suffer today, and to extend the possibilities they contain.

Towards international solidarity and the recognition of individual sovereignty

In the aftermath of the Cold War, the redistribution of international power contributed to the demotion of traditional strategic interests and the exacerbation of local conflicts. Combined with the pressure exercised domestically and internationally in the West by progressive actors asking for the crises of the period to be addressed, this allowed the extension of a sense of international solidarity as a policy option. As such, the West began to give an enhanced sense of importance to human rights at the international level, as a way to fulfil and abide by an ethics of international affairs.

There was no need to start from scratch in order to motivate and justify international involvement in the local wars of the 1990s. It only required a slight readjustment of the focus of the fundamental principles regulating international relations, including an approach that was more sensitive to human rights and humanitarian considerations. Understanding this presupposes exploring how the principles of international socialization were agreed upon in the post-World War II era, identifying them and examining their qualities. It also entails looking into the regulatory role they play by serving as the structural standards of international law and the international system. This calls for analysing how the evolution of the distribution of international power can influence the interpretation and application of international principles, thus also influencing international ethics and the guidelines it provides.

The process of formulation of universal principles regulating international relations after World War II[1] was initiated in the United Nations in the late 1950s and reached its climax in 1962 when a Special Committee on Principles of International Law concerning Friendly Relations and Co-operation among States was set up. Its work lasted several years. On 24 October 1970, a Declaration on Principles of International Law concerning Friendly Relations and Co-operation among States in accordance with the Charter of the United Nations was adopted by consensus in the General Assembly.[2] Without pretending to be exhaustive, the Declaration listed the critical principles at the core of the rule of law at the international level, allowing a modicum of relatively smooth international relations. A wide range of factors was taken into account in the discussions and negotiations that determined which international pronouncements engendered principles of universal scope and binding force. Treaties, General Assembly resolutions, statements by government representatives in the United Nations and diplomatic practice were considered. Ultimately, the fundamental international principles that the Committee identified and agreed upon reflected the classical Westphalian structure of the world system based on equality of states as well as the new trends that emerged after World War I and particularly after World War II. The following major principles were endorsed: sovereign equality of states; non-intervention in the internal or external affairs of other states; good faith; self-determination of peoples; prohibition of the threat or use of force; peaceful settlement of disputes; respect for human rights; and international cooperation. The principles of sovereign equality of states, non-intervention – at least in its role as a precept designed to protect states from interference of the traditional type in their domestic affairs – and good faith are those principles strongly embedded in the classical pattern of international relations. Self-determination of peoples, the prohibition of force (except in self-defence), peaceful settlement of disputes, respect for human rights, and cooperation among states tend to be indicative of the post-Westphalian model, that is of the changes brought about in the international community by the new values that have emerged in the twentieth century.[3]

These universal principles play a socialization role in international relations. Their socializing function can be broken down into three principal aspects. Their first role is one of inclusion. International principles bring a variety of value-ideals into the international system. Recognizing and incorporating them is of crucial importance for the inclusiveness of the international system. This is a key element of the intersubjective dialogue among the actors of the international system. Recognition and incorporation are made mandatory by the fact that these value-ideals are viewed as valid by a significant number of strategic actors. These actors identify with the value-ideals and consider the endorsement of international principles as a condition of their own integration and participation in the international system. They consider them as an indispensable feature of the quest for and establishment of a workable and just international system. As such, fundamental principles appear to be components without which the international order could not exist, nor hope to fulfil its claims to represent a sense of justice and have legitimacy. For example, the principle of the sovereign equality of states is central to the legitimacy of the current international system.[4] The fact that respect for human rights is an important element of the democratic legitimacy dimension of the current international order provides another example.

The second socializing role played by universal principles is to serve the rule of law at the international level as they help to define it. Universal principles fulfil this function in two ways. To start with, they help to shape the normative framework of the international system. It is largely in connection with international principles that the normative and legal architecture of international order is envisioned and established, from its most general to its most specific characteristics. Norms, rules, regulations, and standards of socialized international relations are associated with these principles, directly or indirectly. In addition, fundamental principles, through the value-ideals that they represent, inscribe their recommendations into a forward-looking movement. Playing the roles of axiological foundations, guidelines and ends, they encourage a predictability of interactions within the dynamics of reciprocity of rights and duties. These are geared towards regulating the present and even more so the future of relations among international actors. By playing this role, they are at the core of the deliberations, decisions, and actions of those eager to take the rules of the game seriously.

The third aspect of the socialization function of universal principles is to enhance a sense of community on the international plane. In delineating the overall setting of appropriate international interactions, international principles define the parameters and expectations of behaviour that members have as part of the international community. In doing so, they outline the ethics of international affairs within the realm and the bonds of international community.

Having these socializing roles entails giving a strong normative determinacy to international relations. Normative determinacy is reflected in the paths that fundamental principles recommend and those that they reject. It is at work in the prescriptions of the norms, rules, regulations, and standards associated with universal principles, as they participate in the process of universalizing, particularizing, applying, and deepening the axiological and political significance and reach of universal principles. Normative determinacy can also be found in the consistency international principles call for and help to produce in the conduct of international actors.

However, besides introducing normative determinacy, fundamental principles leave room for normative indeterminacy. On the one hand, this normative indeterminacy is necessary to the application of principles. The application of fundamental principles is not a mechanical procedure, nor should it be. Principles cannot foresee the details of each situation.

This is all the more true considering that social reality is relatively open and indeterminate. Contingency constantly enters into its formation and development. Applying international principles therefore presupposes a process of interpretation to assess how unfolding events fit into the vision and ordering of the international system by fundamental principles.[5] Yet, the normative indeterminacy contained in international principles is a sign of an uncertainty as to how the international system should prioritize the values that they delineate. This kind of normative indeterminacy shows that fundamental principles contribute to establish a normative order that, while designed and destined to be coherent, is only problematically coherent. It is not entirely convergent. The relative plurality of value-ideals represented by international principles and their relations accounts for this situation. This is best illustrated by the relationships of compatibility and competition existing between fundamental principles.

The sense of compatibility among fundamental principles is critical for the existence and functioning of the international system as a whole. If compatibility were totally absent, the international system would be at stake. Compatibility among the principles ensures that the international system is moving in a clear direction. Compatibility also makes fundamental principles mutually reinforcing. Examples of compatibility can be found in the fact that prohibition of the use of force, peaceful settlement of disputes, and international cooperation express, defend and promote a similar philosophy of international relations and work together in the service of the regulation of the international system. Respect for human rights and self-determination of peoples are also technically quite compatible, although this is not automatic, as the hijacking of the principle of self-determination of peoples by nationalist agendas in the Balkans in the 1990s came to indicate.

The problem is that not all principles are compatible. This lack of compatibility fuels a sense of competition among the fundamental international principles. Take for instance the issue of non-intervention in the internal affairs of other states and that of respect for human rights. These are both values about which actors feel strongly. Nevertheless, they are apt to be at odds with one another, and thus in competition. Their application may entail the choice of one over the other, which is prone to generate difficulties and dilemmas, if not deadlocks. Tensions are all the more possible considering that it is not only among principles that there may be competition but also between interpretations of a principle. The conflicting interpretations of sovereignty that affected the sovereign equality of states in the 1990s is a case in point.[6]

The juxtaposition of relationships of compatibility and tension among fundamental principles echoes the various demands that are recognized and served by an international system geared towards socialization. In giving resonance to the major strategic value-ideals that shape international political culture, it reflects and feeds into the three regulating roles of international principles that we mentioned earlier regarding inclusiveness, rule of law, and international community. In this context, the dangers of conflicts among principles which are not fully convergent tend to be tamed by the normative priorities that emerge as a condition of socialization – and that the distribution of international power helps to identify and push forward. Indeed, while all of critical importance, universal principles are not entirely of equal status. There is a more or less explicit and entrenched hierarchy established among fundamental principles that gives preference to certain interpretations and applications of principles over others. This normative hierarchy indicates the value-ideals to which the international system attaches a prevailing significance. For instance, up to the 1990s the territorial reading of the principle of sovereignty was the predominant paradigm, making it difficult to launch and justify international interventions in the name of human rights and humanitarian considerations. This tone corresponded with the distribution of international power existing at the time, namely made of East-West confrontation and North-South tensions.

The fact that priorities among principles are established in connection with the distribution of international power has consequences for the evolution of the international normative hierarchy. Not surprisingly, it implies that the priorities manifested by the interpretation and application of principles and their relationships may vary with changes in the distribution of power. This is precisely what happened in the aftermath of the Cold War.[7]

As it evolves with the transformations affecting the structuring parameters and the identity of the international system, the ethics of international affairs is not set in stone. This means that the deliberations and decisions of international actors are dealing with a moving target. This was especially the case for the Security Council in the 1990s. In the "arc of interpretation" that its members leaned on to deliberate and decide – connecting principles, unfolding events and the various characteristics of the distribution of power during these years – they had to take into account the pressure generated by the changed international landscape. This made it imperative to embark on a reading of international principles keen on addressing human rights and humanitarian concerns.

The Security Council could not avoid human rights and humanitarian issues. The numerous resolutions dealing with them in the 1990s illustrate this point.[8] Most peacekeeping operations of the period had a strong human rights component, as the peace processes in Cambodia, El Salvador, Guatemala, and Haiti show. In addition, attention to human rights and humanitarian matters also led the Security Council and peacekeeping operations to challenge the principle of sovereignty and its traditional territorial understanding. This resulted in the mixture of humanitarian assistance and peace enforcement, although under different conditions in each case, seen in Somalia, Bosnia, and Kosovo. Carrying perhaps even further the human rights and humanitarian shift was the establishment of the international tribunals. The International Tribunal for the former Yugoslavia was given the broadest mandate of any international investigative body since the Nuremberg trials carrying on the authority to prosecute individuals responsible for four groups of offences: grave breaches of the Geneva Conventions of 1949; violations of the laws or customs of war; genocide; and crimes against humanity. It was also given primacy over national jurisdictions and the ability to issue international arrest warrants if national authorities were unwilling to cooperate or failed to serve the initial indictment of the accused individuals. Similarly, the International Criminal Tribunal for Rwanda was given the task of prosecuting Rwandan citizens responsible for genocide, crimes against humanity, and war crimes.

These developments were so novel that it led some to raise the question of the discretionary powers of the Security Council to engineer them.[9] Further, their likelihood in terms of influencing the future, as the progress made on the establishment of the International Criminal Court indicates, certainly attests to the extent of the mutation that took place in the 1990s when it comes to a sense of international solidarity triggered by human rights and humanitarian crises.

The limits of modern international solidarity and the protection of human rights at the international level

The context of the post-Cold War era extended a sense of international solidarity to individuals in ways stronger than before. But it remained constrained by the configuration of international affairs. Two main factors account for this situation. First, there is the structure of modern democratic solidarity itself. Second, in spite of the progress of multilateralism and internationalism before and during the 1990s, the international system remains largely nationally rooted, with state actors in competition.

In comparison to traditional solidarity, modern democratic solidarity is wider. Rather than being locked in narrow and exclusive social forms of memberships, modern democratic solidarity is wider because it is based on values which feed on and seek wide belonging and inclusion. The values of universality and equality at the core of modern democratic culture introduce a sense of sameness and connectedness that opens wide the gate of identification with others. It opens wide the gate of a sense of community that goes far beyond the boundaries of the immediate community in which each individual is born.

The inclusive democratic values of universality and equality, and freedom, while generating a sense of connectedness among individuals, produce as well, through the individual autonomy that they also encourage, a distance between individuals. The tension between connectedness and distance contributes to make what is modern democratic law: the bringing together of people and the recognition of a normative basis for mounting a legal challenge if necessary. Indeed, in order to relate in legal terms with someone, an acknowledgement of the sameness of this person is first necessary. Without this sense of sameness and connection, the other has no grounds for any claim. Calling for a claim to be heard requires the recognition of the sameness, of the fact that there is a world and a humanity that is common and shared. The values of universality and equality allow for this requirement. But they also accommodate a second characteristic required for making a claim. Litigation and challenge call upon a sense of otherness, of distancing from the same. While the other has to be understood within the realm of the same, this has to take place without having the sense of the same overwhelming and annihilating the dimension of the other. Otherwise the idea of challenge itself tends not to be thinkable. The existence of the other within the realm of the same, triggered by universality and equality and helping to generate individuation, makes the challenge possible, opening venues for legal claims. Ultimately, it does so not only at the individual level, but also at the national level, and increasingly at the international level.

This combination of the same and the other, the understanding of the other within the realm of the same which is critical to the dynamics and development of modern democratic law, gives democratic values a double power of inclusiveness: they encourage inclusiveness through their embracing character as well as through the normative foundations they offer to the possibility of mounting challenges and claims. In other words, the fate of the other becomes part of the definition of the same – including the self and its qualification as a "decent self"; in addition, the understanding of the other within the realm of the same also provides normative grounds to the challenge of privileges and injustice in the name of democratic values.

In this perspective, it is not surprising that over the years, the widening of the circle of inclusion and deepening of the benefits of solidarity associated with it, namely understood as the recognition and respect of rights, have been objects of struggles. Indeed, in spite of the declarations of principles, the beneficiaries of democratic universalism and equality initially formed quite an exclusive club. It is therefore around the boundaries of inclusion and exclusion that the battles for political, economic, and social justice focused throughout the evolution of modern democratic culture. The objective was not necessarily to get rid of all forms of exclusion, since functioning as competent members of society requires embodying positions shaped along lines of inclusion and exclusion.[10] At stake was mainly where and how to draw the line between inclusion and exclusion in the key areas and roles of society, in connection with the expectations viewed as legitimate by excluded peoples.[11] The movement towards an ever wider and greater realization of a sense of justice, fuelled by the very content of democratic values, became one of the defining vectors of modernity, at the national as well as the international level. In terms of the international plane and international law, the drive towards the universalization of rights has probably encountered even more adversity than the diffusion of democratic rights and the constitutionalization of society have at the national level.

The beginnings of modern international law were very much a self-serving exercise for the major European powers. Modern international law was used to endorse and justify the distribution and workings of evolving international power structures. Commercial and political interests were critical elements in the monitoring of the international system at "home" in Europe, on the seas, and in the relations of the European powers with the overseas lands and people being newly discovered.[12] To this day the economic and political interests of the most powerful countries have remained integral parts of the making of international law. Countries at the receiving end of international power must continuously address and accept this. At the same time, however, the unveiling of new worlds and their ruthless subjugation by European powers led some to reflect on international relations in a more inclusive and respectful manner concerning the treatment of the other. In the domineering West, voices emerged that criticized the subjugation of non-Western people. They sought to protect them by insisting that they should be recognized as members of the human community. What was humanly, ethically, and legally owed to them, in terms of rights, came to occupy, in various ways, a number of scholars of international law, such as Bartolomé de Las Casas and Pufendorf. The mechanism of recognition and inclusion could not be harmless. It was also a double-edged sword. The recognition of the human sameness in the other that brought protection, could as well require adjustments from the newcomers to the "human community," including religious conversion and abandonment of local cultural traditions. But it certainly put the West on the path of the universalization of human rights.

The inclusive aspect of international law remained timid and marginal for centuries, like small islands in the oceans of international law mainly dedicated to making state actors the primary bearers and beneficiaries of international law. It took a lot of twists and turns in the history of national and international politics to redirect the modern discourse of rights – including Locke's possessive individualism – that had at times been used to conquer and colonize the non-Western world. A fundamental evolution of its values and priorities was necessary for the discourse of rights to be used as part of the foundation and guidelines for the spectacular development, after World War II, of an internationalization of individual rights geared towards ensuring respect for all human beings.

Yet, there is another side to the story of modern democratic solidarity and the universal inclusiveness that makes it possible. This other side of democratic culture greatly contributed to limit the extension of international solidarity in the post-Cold War era. It amounts to the fact that while wider than traditional solidarity and becoming increasingly so under the dynamic influence of democratic values, modern democratic solidarity tends to be thinner. The intensity of solidarity among individuals provided by democratic solidarity tends to be lower than in traditional solidarity. As modern democratic solidarity widens outward, it thins inward. Indeed, the normative structure of universality and equality, while maximizing inclusion at the human community level, brings about a strong sense of individual autonomy which lessens the level of inward social solidarity, which increases inward social anomie. The independence given to the individual by democratic values put limitations on traditional social forms of bonding and belonging. What brings people together is also what pushes them apart. Furthermore, the values of universality and equality cannot impede a hierarchy of priorities from playing a selective and limiting role in the extension of solidarity. Just as universality and equality did not prevent social hierarchy from continuing to exist and have significance, universality and equality could not get rid of the idea of priority, of a hierarchy of priorities. How could it be otherwise considering, to start with, that making priorities and living by them is an essential requirement of human life, without which no direction can be given to and no sense can be made of the decisions and actions of individuals.

Moreover, although the circle of the human community ever widens under the influence of universality and equality, the ability to relate and share becomes more and more abstract and remote the further away from the centre. As a result, the concrete experience of democratic community, from the wide circle of humanity, tends to transform itself into a world of concentric circles in which priority is given to more neighbouring worlds and people. In terms of modern solidarity and the impact that it has on the recognition and implementation of individual rights, this

takes a particular toll at the international level considering the continuing national bent of international politics.

In an international system which remains largely nationally rooted, the
lower intensity of solidarity among actors, the high degree of individual
autonomy that tends to keep them apart and the concentric character of
the diffusion of solidarity, have a dramatic impact on the limitations of
international solidarity. As the widest circle of humanity, the international realm does not benefit from the level of identification and participation existing at the national level, at least in integrated modern societies. In addition, the mechanisms called upon at the national level to
keep the socially disruptive aspects of democratic values under check are
difficult to transpose on to the international plane. As, for instance, the
self-interest of international actors and the lack of an international culture or tradition continue to be defining parameters of the international
landscape, institutionalizing a sense of international public good and the
delivery of the services associated with it remains elusive. Consequently,
in spite of the democratic rhetoric of universality and equality of access
to rights, its international pulling power remains weak. It is weakened
further when contextual considerations enter into the calculus of international solidarity – and they almost always do.

For example, a selective component tends to favour those beyond
borders with whom the most internationally engaged nations feel closer
for reasons of geographical, cultural, or psychological proximity,[13] or of
economic interdependence. By the same token, those who are on the
edge or fall outside the contextual sense of shared identity (or "weness")
at the international level, are certainly less likely to benefit from a sense
of solidarity.

Justice in the international realm: on legal obligations and moral imperatives vis-à-vis human rights

In integrated societies – economically, politically, and socially integrated
– it falls on the political institutions and power holders to perform services in a satisfactory manner, within their recognized realms of responsibility as defined by the core values of the society. It falls on them to
recognize that their responsibilities and duties echo the imperative to
abide by and implement as much as possible the rights of the members
of society, and of society itself,[14] as shaped by the society's core com-
manding values. These services may vary with the differences in the core
values establishing the identity of any given society.[15] It is based on their
ability to perform their public duties that political institutions and leaders

are evaluated, judged, and held accountable. They are accountable legally, through what their constitutions mandate them to do. They are also accountable politically, in particular, through the participation and election processes.

A strong sense of ethics inhabiting and guiding political deliberations, decisions, practices and outputs is likely to facilitate and encourage social virtues, and reciprocity, among interacting individuals within society. The more political institutions and leaders take their responsibilities vis-à-vis society and its members seriously, the more members of society are themselves likely to keep close to their heart their social responsibilities vis-à-vis their fellow members, the political sphere, and the society as a whole. In a highly socialized national community, for political institutions and leaders as well as for individuals, doing the right thing when it comes to social interactions is not simply a matter of acting morally. It is not only a matter of respecting the rights of others,[16] of deliberating and making the right choice out of personal judgment and volition.[17] It goes beyond this. It is about acting upon the constraining, yet consensual, effects of key values recognized as the basis of the ethics of the society. It is about identifying with regulatory social norms of society. For individuals, it is about acting out of a sense of social virtues and obligations. As for political institutions, they act out of a sense of public ethics and public policy obligations, a state of affairs which justifies in the best cases the fact that they have at their disposal a variety of implementation and enforcement mechanisms. Ultimately, this opens the way to a constitutional vision and functioning of society.

The situation differs significantly at the international level. The current level of socialization of international life, no matter how progressive it may appear today vis-à-vis what it was decades ago, still remains low compared to highly integrated societies. One of the reasons for – and illustrations of – this is that, at the international level, there is no direct connection between international law and international organisations, on the one hand, and individuals and their rights on the other. Hence the ambiguous attitude of international law vis-à-vis human rights.

Democratic values and principles today represent enough of a cultural pressure for the importance of individual and human rights to be duly acknowledged in the body of international law. However, it still largely depends on states to look after individual and human rights, to ensure that they are properly expressed and enhanced nationally. States acknowledge this responsibility by membership of the United Nations, as the Charter of the United Nations recognises the importance of human rights, and by ratifying, if they do so, human rights international treaties and conventions.[18] But what happens when states do not respect their commitments? What are the legal remedies offered by international law to protect human rights in national jurisdiction? They are very few.[19]

To this day the legal obligations of states vis-à-vis human rights remain largely internally exercised. Already at the regional level, the legal remedies offered by international law are scarce. For it is mainly in Western Europe, with the European Court of Human Rights, that appeal possibilities exist.[20] At the global level, the situation is even more problematic. When human rights violations take on an international dimension, when they hamper the development of friendly relations between states "based on respect for the principles of equal rights and self-determination of people," it is possible to take some action. The coupling of human rights issues with matters of international peace and security generates an incentive. But short of this, it continues to be difficult to take action in favour of human rights at the global level. There is no immediate legal recourse based on international human rights treaties and conventions to force states to live up to their commitments at home.[21]

International law, when dealing with human rights issues, envisions and organizes neither an international right to intervene nor an international duty to intervene to put an end to humanitarian crises and massive human rights violations. The obligation and duty to intervene, in particular is not legally endorsed, even in cases of genocide. There is indeed nothing in the Genocide Convention that clearly recognizes and creates a legal obligation for states to intervene.[22]

If there is no legal obligation to intervene to prevent or stop humanitarian catastrophes or massive violations of human rights, where does this leave us? It leaves us to think that the public dimension of the international system is quite limited, that the international realm is far from being communal. It is still largely state-centric, with international competition among states and the preservation of an idea of self-contained national sovereignty still in tension with respect for human rights. As such, it also forces us to fall back on a sense of morality.

When international interventions take place, they are not, first and foremost, part of an international public policy endorsed and triggered by international law. Since acting as good international citizens in the fields of individual and human rights, as defined by current international law, does not make international solidarity legally mandatory, intervening to save strangers is largely a voluntary matter, based on a moral awareness or political considerations. As there is no clearly established legal hierarchy that puts the respect of human rights ahead of sovereignty, international humanitarian intervention tends for the intervening powers to be a matter of feeling compelled to do the right thing, of acting morally and exercising a sense of altruism. Moral awareness is all the more likely to serve as a motivation for action when intervention is coupled with political interests and gains.

However, justification for action and action itself only based on morality are weaker than when sanctioned by law. This is the case because of the lower degree of institutionalization and socialization of morality compared to law. Law is based upon the recognition and implementation of rights. Rights are themselves values, moral values, that are viewed as so important in terms of each individual's life and relations among individuals that they have to be made into rights. Values as rights receive the legal codification and endorsement that make them the rules as well as the horizon of realization of the social game. They become part of the rule of law that calls upon them being at least minimally respected. If not, the rule of law guarantees access to claims and challenges based on the force of law, as well as enforcement mechanisms when necessary. In this context, doing the right thing morally and abiding by the law work together. They have convergent and cumulative effects. Law offers a set of procedures securing the regular implementation and, if needed, enforcement of moral values, of a certain vision of morality.

On the other hand, when doing the right thing is mainly a matter of moral judgment, and a judgment somewhat at odds with established law, the status and implementation of this moral judgment appear problematic. It loses the social and political qualities and attributes associated with law. It loses the predictability of a socially negotiated and endorsed course of action. Choosing to do the right thing is apt to become unreliable and unpredictable. Whether it happens or not is largely a matter of choice. It is up to international actors, primarily state actors, to act morally. This may or may not happen. Taking a moral stand and acting morally is not automatic, especially when it goes against key features of the standard legal wisdom. It is precisely this largely voluntary character of acting morally, in favour of human rights in particular, at the international level, that has historically led and continues to lead to a low level of international morality and ethics, and therefore in turn to a low level of international socialization. In spite of the normative foundation, and the encouragement and endorsement that it receives from a number of fundamental international principles – associated with issues of human rights in one way or another – such a moral course is still an uphill battle. Furthermore, any moral stand at odds with established law tends to be followed by shallow implementation, largely because in this situation it is difficult to mobilize and rally the wide support of actors and institutions that come with law.

This is all the more the case when a moral action goes against the status quo. For instance, an international military intervention that is not supported by legal obligation but is based on moral considerations is likely to generate debates and questioning. Because the intervention is caught in conflicts of moralities and legitimacies at the international level, it is not covered by a course of action clearly envisioned and organized by international law. Hence, as there is no legal agreement on the issue of intervention, the moral stand called upon is prone to be embroiled in polemics. The plurality of points of view on humanitarian intervention and use of force in the 1990s, with some states favouring them and others opposing them, serves as a case in point. The lack of obvious legal justification in favour of intervention made the choice to intervene a difficult moral, and political, one.

How to balance the fact that an intervention might be needed to help the victims on the ground, with the danger that intervening might also put on a slippery slope the respect of the principle of national sovereignty of member states?[23] How also to balance the fact that sovereignty was never meant to be a shield behind which civilian populations could be killed with total impunity, and the protection that it offers against self-interested external interventions? These are some of the considerations that have to be weighed.

Such thinking and the dilemmas it entails show that, contrary to conventional thinking, international relations is not foreign to ethics and morality. As a matter of fact, the contrary is true. First, there is the relatively low level of international legal protection for individual and human rights. Second, there is the recognition of the protection of individual and human rights as of critical importance, although not yet to the point that upholding human rights could justify fully removing the double-edged protection offered to individuals by sovereignty.[24] These two elements account for the fact that morality has become today an increasingly important aspect of the thinking on and practice of international affairs.

It is largely in this context, along with political considerations associated with it, that the Security Council came to deliberate and decide on what to do about the unfolding crises of the 1990s. The international changes taking place in the aftermath of the Cold War, including the multiplication of crises and the feeling in public opinion that helping was both possible and necessary, engendered a moral and political pressure that it could not ignore. Thus the fact that the Security Council stretched Article 39 of Chapter VII of the Charter and the definition of a threat to peace to justify United Nations intervention in internal conflicts and humanitarian crises. These crises previously had been considered matters of domestic jurisdiction under Article 2(7) of the Charter.

Eventually, the deliberations, decisions, and their implementations ended up being cast in dilemmas that reflected, inside the Security

Council and on the ground in the areas of conflict as well as in the world at large, the extent and limits of international ethics. They reflected and projected the difficulty of reconciling and making sense of the partly compatible, partly competitive demands of the international system, of the various constituencies, identities, and legitimacies that now inhabit and shape it.

Human rights, moral communities, and democratic culture: Where do we go from here?

As a whole, the story of the 1990s sends an ambiguous message when it comes to human rights and the emergence of a culture of affirmation and respect of "individual sovereignty." On the one hand, when confronted with extending a sense of international solidarity and responsibility for non-traditional strategic reasons, the key international decision makers of the period, while advocating international engagement, favoured the national realm and its ends over the international realm. This certainly presents a sobering view of the reality of moral obligations to people beyond borders. Those committed to a full cosmopolitan agenda would no doubt bemoan this state of affairs. On the other hand, there is also a more positive way to look at the story of the 1990s. The mere fact that the Security Council addressed the conflicts of the period in terms of dilemmas was in itself a form of progress. It was a recognition that states' rights are not all that matter. In responding to the conflicts in ways that differed from the status quo, the Security Council, beyond trying to address the immediate demands generated by wars, also helped to shape and alter the future of the international system in ways more sensitive to individual rights. As such, it contributed to strengthen the idea that the moral community of the world as a whole should not allow the fate of the various communities and their members to be ignored. This brought a greater sense of reality to what had been so far a largely rhetorical exercise.

In the balancing act among the moral, political, and legal obligations with which the Security Council struggled in the 1990s, it recognized the growing obligations that the international community has to individuals beyond borders, whoever they are and wherever they are. To be sure, such recognition is far from being perfect since it takes place within the realm of selective universalism, cultural relativism, reactive and reparatory justice, and has to portray concerns for human rights in terms of traditional national interest to create the minimum incentive for action.[25] Yet, addressing the conflicts, albeit as a dilemma, is recognizing more than ever the growing legitimacy of the moral community beyond borders. It represents the growing recognition that the community of duties towards others does not stop at the border. The centrality of dilemmas in the Security Council deliberations showed in the 1990's that the moral community beyond the national moral community was now strong enough to force decision makers to think of international engagement for purposes of solidarity and responsibility in terms of trade offs.

This does not mean, however, that the battle in favour of human rights has by now largely been won. It will continue to be an uphill battle, as there is still much progress to make. And it is here that international organizations have a critical role to play.

The tradition has largely been to examine questions of justice, authority, and rights in a national setting. The internationalization of societies and the socialization of the international dimension that are underway require an adaptation of this thinking to the emerging political landscape. They also make international organizations important tools for international justice. For the United Nations, as for any international organization, the challenges to think through and implement human rights and individual sovereignty imperatives are to this day quite daunting.

In this context, addressing the demands of international justice and the rights associated with them requires that at least three challenges are successfully met. Embracing and adjusting international diversity without smothering it is the first of these challenges. This entails facing the fact that on the international plane, plurality is much deeper – in terms of cultural differences, levels of development, and aspirations – than it is on the national plane. The question is how to implement a multilateral culture without having it become a tool of Western extension and colonization. The problem also encompasses how to bring about an international order that is not, in its regulation of openness, a veiled monopolization of power. It involves ensuring that democratic values and mechanisms – including democratic rights – that are meant to be tools of empowerment at the service of justice do not become instruments of power. Solving this problem calls for looking for ways to further democratize the cultural, political, and economic hegemony of which the multilateral project is a part. Upon this depends the fact that access to and circulation of power will not be hampered by multilateral arrangements themselves.

It will also be necessary for international organizations to address the weak sense of international community. In order to overcome this weakness, stronger mechanisms of global identification, participation, representation, responsibility, and solidarity than the present ones will have to be imagined and implemented. However, strengthening the sense of global community must not be envisioned as the construction of a war machine against the national or even regional realms. For if the development of a legitimate international community cannot be reduced to the imposition of one cultural model, neither can it be based on the exclusion or elimination of existing forms of political association. Forms of synergy and complementarity among the various layers of contemporary politics have to be encouraged. In this context, the democratic qualities of national, regional, and international political arrangements constitute an asset, one that can be capitalized upon in negotiating and facilitating the establishment of an international common sense.

The third and final challenge for international organizations is handling the effects of the paradox of contemporary democratic culture. The increased sense of responsibility at the international level and the simultaneous proliferation of a democratic culture of individual entitlement at the national level that is apt to be allergic to solidarity is, indeed, a riddle for institutions committed to international socialization. What is to be made of these two trends, and can they continue to develop in parallel? Will the evolution of contemporary international democratic culture pursue the liberal quest of entitlement? Or will it follow a more republican path – in which modern democratic culture as a whole is historically and ideologically rooted – with greater sensibility to the global social and citizenship concerns that it could bring about? The future state of the discourse and practice of rights and international justice will largely rest upon the answers to these questions.

Notes

1. For a historical overview of the international principles at work before World War II, see Hedley Bull, *The Anarchical Society: A Study of Order in World Politics*, New York, Columbia University Press, 1995, re-ed., pp. 23–38.
2. Resolution 2625, XXV Session of the General Assembly, in *General Assembly. Official Records: Twenty-Fifth Session*, Supplement No 28, A/8028, New York, United Nations, 1971, pp. 121–124.
3. For a slightly different perspective on fundamental principles, see Bull, pp. 65–68.
4. One of the attributes of sovereignty is to minimize the effects of the unequal distribution of international power. It fits the democratic conception of law, including international law, as the art of attempting to make unequal powers equal. Incidentally, law in a hierarchical culture is designed to ensure that what is viewed as unequal in essence remains unequal by law.
5. On the question of interpretation in international law, see for instance Michel Virally, *Le droit international en devenir. Essais écrits au fil des ans*, Geneva, Presses Universitaires de France, 1990, pp. 120–121.
6. In the debates of the period concerning humanitarian interventions, two conceptual interpretations of sovereignty found themselves in rivalry. Some advocated a territorial understanding of sovereignty, basically associated with the view that nations are independent realms within which national political institutions are entitled to exercise almost unlimited and unchallenged power. Here, the autonomy of the state vis-à-vis the international plane was conceived of as largely non-negotiable, the principle of nonintervention in the internal affairs of other states coming as a reinforcement of this in-

terpretation of sovereignty. Others put forward an interpretation of sovereignty that emphasized its democratic dimension, insisting on the significance of individual and human rights. The principle of respect for human rights was called upon to support this reading. The former view tended to be favoured by the non-Western world, and in particular by developing countries already deeply penetrated by dominant powers or fearing such penetration. The latter was the preference of the Western democratic nations. However, these nations, especially the most powerful among them, tended to rein in their advocacy for democratic sovereignty whenever its effects infringed upon their own autonomy of decision making, as was for instance shown by the United States's reservations regarding the International Criminal Court.

7. Incidentally, this should not lead one to think that international transformation is a one-way process, only triggered by alterations in the material dimension of the distribution of power, which are then factored in at the international normative level. Value-ideals can themselves contribute to changes occurring in the distribution of international power. For example, if the craving for respect for human rights was not the sole element that brought about the collapse of the Eastern Bloc, it certainly had an impact. Ultimately, when a transformation in the distribution of power is important enough, it can account not only for the emergence of a new approach to the hierarchical relationships of principles, but also can encourage the changes of fundamental principles themselves. This entails then a systemic alteration of the values and modalities through which international socialization takes place. Indeed, the ability of international principles and international law to be relevant and handle change depends upon the balance between determinacy and indeterminacy, of which relations of compatibility and competition among principles are parts. Lack of balance on issues that are not central to the functioning of the international community can exist without major consequences. However, if there is no balance on critical matters, the outcomes are likely to be devastating. International principles, international law and the institutions associated with them run the risk of losing their regulating power with the undermining of their social validity.

8. See for example the list of selected resolutions dealing with human rights and humanitarian issues between 1990 and 1994 in *The United Nations and Human Rights 1945–1995*, New York, Department of Public Information, 1995, pp. 139–141. For the resolutions themselves and related documents, see pp. 402–495.

9. The Security Council's extension of its domain of responsibilities to new areas in the 1990s caused Mohamed Bedjaoui, the president of the International Court of Justice between 1994 and 1997, to examine the legitimacy of these self-appropriated responsibilities. He wondered whether it would be judicious to establish legal control over the acts of the Security Council. See Mohamed Bedjaoui, *The New World Order and the Security Council: Testing the Legality of its Acts*, Dordrecht, Martinus Nijhoff Publishers, 1994, pp. 47–53 and 127–130. For more on the issue, see also Jose E. Alvarez, "Judging the Security Council," *American Journal of International Law*, Washington, DC, The American Society of International Law, 90(1), January 1996, pp. 1–4 and 10–14.

10. On this question, see for instance Andrew Linklater, *The Transformation of Political Community. Ethical Foundations of the Post-Westphalian Era*, Columbia, University of South Carolina Press, 1998, pp. 117–118. The socialist utopias that made the elimination of all forms of exclusion their goals ended up paving the way for communist totalitarianism.

11. Although the agreement of both parties is essential for the negotiation on and implementation of the rules and substance of justice, the evaluation of the just or unjust character of a situation accords more weight to the excluded peoples' point of view than to the privileged ones. Being on the wrong side of the fence gives greater credence and validity to the justice claims they may have.

12. For a detailed account of the links between international legal arguments and justifications, commercial and political interests associated with the European expansion overseas and forms of colonization, including conquests and settlements, see Richard Tuck, *The Rights of War and Peace: Political Thought and the International Order from Grotius to Kant*, Oxford, Oxford University Press, 1999, pp. 16–50, 78–108 and 166–196.

13. In this regard, there may be much geographical distance between the old European and Far Eastern nations, but for some of them, there is significant cultural and psychological closeness.

14. Political institutions and leaders' responsibilities and duties are not only owed to the members of the community, but also to the community itself as a whole, as its continuation and welfare is key to the welfare of each individual. This goes back to the social nature of the human condition.

15. The nature and modalities of services vary with the defining values of the society. See for example the differences in what is expected from the United States political sphere compared to that of the welfare states of the Nordic countries. From these differences derives the fluctuation of boundaries between what is a matter of public responsibility and oversight, and what is not, what is a matter of private choice and morality and what is a matter of social ethics and public policy.

16. There is obviously more to morality than this.

17. This is not contradictory with the fact that the power of individuals to deliberate and reach a decision on their own, and the willingness of political institutions to encourage such a tendency, is one of the defining criteria of democratic politics. Individual autonomy and freedom require a public stand and its enforcement if necessary. Similarly to a market economy which, when not understood as pure anarchy, is not a starting point, but an end-product based on regulations, individual autonomy and freedom require, to be socially sustainable, an adequate organization of the public space. As a result, rather than leading to the full removal of one at the expense of the other, the high level of social ethics and public policy regulated behaviours in democratic societies only fuels the debate on the appropriate character of the evolving boundaries between the spheres of private and public concerns.

18. Treaties and conventions dealing with individual and human rights create legal obligations, as ratification by member states makes them part of their national legislation and leads, in principle, political institutions to be committed to ensuring their respect. See Paul Reuter, *Introduction to the Law of Treaties*, London, Pinter Publishers, 1989, pp. 73–78, and Anthony Aust, *Modern Treaty Law and Practice*, Cambridge, Cambridge University Press, 2000, pp. 75–99.

19. The yearly assessment of national human rights situations by the United Nations Commission on Human Rights is hardly a breathtaking breach of the wall of *domaine réservé* by which states historically sheltered atrocities from international scrutiny.

20. The Inter-American Court of Human Rights handles few cases compared with Europe – and the United States is not subject to its jurisdiction. See David P. Forsythe, "Introduction", in David P. Forsythe, ed., *Human Rights and Comparative Foreign Policy*, Tokyo, United Nations University Press, 2000, p. 10.

21. Article 1 of the United Nations Charter. See also on this question, the comments by W. Michael Reisman, "Sovereignty and Human Rights in Contemporary International Law," in Gregory H. Fox and Brad R. Roth, eds., *Democratic Governance and International Law*, Cambridge, Cambridge University Press, 2000, pp. 240–258.

22. On this issue, see William A. Schabas, *Genocide in International Law*, Cambridge, Cambridge University Press, 2000: "Perhaps the greatest unresolved question in the Convention is the meaning of the enigmatic word 'prevent.' The title of the Convention indicates that its scope involves prevention of the crime and, in Article I, State parties

undertake to prevent genocide. Aside from Article VIII, which entitles State parties to apply to the relevant organs of the United Nations for the prevention of genocide, the Convention has little specific to say on the question. The obligation to prevent genocide is a blank sheet awaiting the inscriptions of State practice and case law. A conservative interpretation of the provision requires States only to enact appropriate legislation and to take other measures to ensure that genocide does not occur. A more progressive view requires States to take action not just within their own borders but outside them, activity that may go as far as the use of force in order to prevent the crime being committed. The debate of this is unresolved, and is likely to remain so, at least until the next episode of genocide, if there is no insistence that the subject be clarified," pp. 545–546.

23. After all, there is no guarantee that the intervening powers will not take advantage of their presence on the ground to secure long-term gains. The reluctance of developing countries to take such a risk makes them all the more attached to the value of sovereignty.

24. It fits to speak here of "double-edged protection." While the principle of sovereignty is designed to protect a nation and its citizens from external infringement, and constitutes as such a right embedded in a moral value, national sovereignty is also called upon at times to offer protection to crimes within borders, to assure non-accountability to their authors.

25. This is especially true in the American context.

Acronyms

ANC   African National Congress
COSATU   Congress of South African Trade Unions
ECHR   European Court of Human Rights
GATS   General Agreement on Trade in Services
ICC   International Criminal Court
ICCPR   International Covenant on Civil and Political Rights
ICESCR   International Covenant on Economic, Social and Cultural Rights
ICJ   International Court of Justice
ILO   International Labour Organization
IMF   International Monetary Fund
MPNP   Multi-Party Negotiating Process
NGO   Non-governmental organization
OAS   Organization of American States
OAU   Organization of African Unity
OECD   Organization for Economic Co-operation and Development
TRIPS   Trade Related Intellectual Property Rights
UDHR   Universal Declaration of Human Rights
UNCHR   United Nations Commission on Human Rights
UNCTAD   United Nations Conference on Trade and Development
UNDP   United Nations Development Programme
UNESCO   United Nations Educational, Scientific, and Cultural Organization
UNHCR   United Nations High Commissioner for Refugees
WTO   World Trade Organization

Contributors

Claire Archbold, LL.B., Barrister-at-law, is a lecturer in law at the Queen's University of Belfast, Northern Ireland

Jean-Marc Coicaud, Senior Academic Officer, Peace and Governance Programme, the United Nations University, Tokyo

Michael W. Doyle, Special Advisor, Executive Office of the Secretary-General, United Nations, New York

Anne-Marie Gardner, Ph.D. student in the Politics Department of Princeton University. She is completing a dissertation on the international politics of self-determination

Ruth Gavison, Haim H. Cohn Professor of Human Rights, Faculty of Law, Hebrew University in Jerusalem

James Mouangue Kobila, Assistant in Public law at the University of Douala-Cameroun

Tatsuo Inoue, Professor of Philosophy of Law, Faculty of Law, the University of Tokyo

Pierre de Senarclens, Professor of international relations and political science at the University of Lausanne

Henry Shue, is a Senior Research Fellow in the Department of Politics and International Relations and a Senior Research Fellow of Merton College, University of Oxford. He was a founding member of the Institute for Philosophy and Public Policy at the University of Maryland and the first Director of the Program on Ethics & Public Life at Cornell University

Index

A-bomb, immoral possession of 7
Acheson, Dean, former US Secretary of
    State 4
Ad hoc courts 96–98
Afghanistan 99
Africa, civil war in 168
African Charter for Human and Peoples'
    Rights 3, 90, 91, 92, 93, 94, 95, 104,
    105
African Commission for Human and
    Peoples' Rights 91–93, 107
African National Congress (ANC) 66,
    67
    constitutional guidelines for South Africa
        66, 69
African-Americans 126
Age of rights 56–58
AIDS 100, 102
Albanian Kosovars 9
Alberta 63
Alberta Individual's Rights Protection Act
    75
Alston, Philip 155
American Convention on Human Rights
    1969 3, 143
American democracy 128
American Treasury Department 154
Amin, Idi 11

Amnesty International 3
    in Argentina 13
Annan, Kofi, UN Secretary-General 1, 3,
    180
Arab-Muslims
    norms 104
    societies 104
Armenian Orthodox minorities 127
Asia
    communitarian aspect 129, 130
Asian values 15, 16, 116–131, 163, 180
Asian people 117
Atlanta, citizens of 6

Balfour Declaration 1926 59
Balkans, nationalist agenda in 184
Barcelona Traction, Light and Power
    Company Ltd. 102
Beaudoin-Dobbie Report 63
Beaudoin-Edwards Committee 63
Benin 101
Bill of Rights 15, 80, 81
    document 79
Bosnia 186
Bretton Woods 152, 158
    monetary system, collapse of 153
British North America Act 1867 59, 70
Buddhism 126

Buddhist tradition 129
Bull, Hedley 4

Calder case 1973 62
Canada 15, 58–65, 98, 99
  acid rain in 6
  Citizens' Forum 63
  Human Rights Commissions 80
  Quiet Revolution in 59, 62
  Supreme Court Reference on
    Constitutional Amendment 62
Canadian Bill of Rights 57, 58, 59, 60
Canadian Charter of Rights and Freedoms
    1982 58, 60, 61, 62, 64, 73, 74–76
Canadian constitution making 61, 65
Canadians, French speaking 75
Carter administration 3, 141
Center on Budget and Policy Priorities
    142
Central and South America 105
Charlottetown 59
Charlottetown Accord 1992 63, 64, 69
Charter of the United Nations 182, 191,
    192
  Article 39, Chapter VII 194
  Article 2(7) 194
China 13, 99, 126, 168
  "great leap forward" 44
  neo-Confucian tradition 129
Chinese Communist Party 121
Christian West 12
Christianity 126
Churchill, Winston 7
CIA operation 13
CNN 164
Cold War 60, 141, 152, 180, 181, 185, 194
Colombia 145
Commission on Human Rights, Special
    Rapporteur 146
Commission on the Status of Women 1999
    146
Committee on Torture 3
Confucian and Taoist traditions 125
Confucian-Islamic Asia 126
Confucianism 126
Contras 13, 14
  US aid to 13
Convention against Torture and Other
    Cruel, Inhuman or Degrading
    Treatment or Punishment 1984 2, 3,
    143

Convention for the Protection of Human
    Rights and Basic Liberties 1950 91
Convention on the Elimination of all Forms
    of Discrimination against Women 3,
    143
Convention on the Rights of the Child 3,
    143
  committee on 144
Convention on the Suppression and
    Punishment of the Crime of
    Apartheid 143
COSATU 77
Council of Europe 79, 93
Covenant on Economic, Social and Cultural
    Rights 1966 140, 143
CP and SE rights
  enforceability of 45–50
  hierarchy between 39–40
Cuba 13

De las Casas, Bartolomé de 188
Declaration and Programme of Action,
    Vienna 146
Declaration on Principles of International
    Law 181
Declaration on the Elimination of Violence
    against Women 146
Diefenbaker, John, Canadian Prime
    Minister 60

East Asia 148
East Timor 1, 128
Eastern Bloc countries 101
East-West 15
  confrontation 185
Enlightenment, eighteenth-century 138
Eritrea 13
Euro-American economies 117
Euro-Christian culture 104
Europe, social democracy in 119
European Commission of Human Rights
    90, 91, 94, 96
European Congress 1948 91
European Convention against Torture
    143
European Convention on Human Rights
    1950 3, 57, 93, 96, 143
  Article 25 94
European Court of Human Rights (ECHR)
    74, 79, 94, 95, 96, 192
European powers 188

European Renaissance, humanism in 138
European Union (EU) 101, 152
  law courts 96

Former Yugoslavia 11, 13, 96, 98
  IMF demands 151
  International Tribunal for 186
French and US governments, pressure of
    144
French Revolution, history of 118
Fundamentalist Islam 12

General Assembly 137, 143, 182
  Resolution 44/25 143
General de Gaulle, Free French Resistance
    7
Geneva Conventions 1949 186
Genocide Convention 192
Germany v. United States of America 99
Ghana 101
Globalization and its Impact on the Full
    Enjoyment of All Human Rights
    (Sub-Commission Resolution) 147
Greek Orthodox minorities 127

Havel, Vaclav 4
Heaney, Seamus 82
High Commissioner for Human Rights 147
Hindu-Confucian civilizations 104
Hinduism 126
Hiroshima 13
Hobbesian model 6
Hobbesian problem 4, 5, 6
Hoffmann, Stanley 4
Honduran frontier 14
Honduras 13, 14
Human rights, nature of 25–33
Human Rights Commission 137, 147
Human Rights Committee 144
Human Rights Watch 3, 142
Hussein, Saddam 14

Incorporation of rights in Canada, South
    Africa, the UK, N Ireland 179
India 44
  constitution 47, 48
Individual sovereignty 180, 181–186
Indonesia 126, 154
Inter-American Commission 90
Inter-American Convention for Human
    Rights and Duties 91, 95, 96

Inter-American Court of Human Rights 79,
    95
Inter-American Declaration for Human
    Rights and Duties 91
Inter-American Development Bank 150
Inter-American system for human rights
    90, 93, 98
International Commission of Jurists 94
International Court of Justice 99
International Covenant on Civil and
    Political Rights (ICCPR) 2, 35, 46,
    61, 74
International Covenant on Economic,
    Social and Cultural Rights
    (ICESCR) 2, 32, 35, 74, 161
International Criminal Court (1998) 46,
    144, 186
International Criminal Tribunal for Rwanda
    186
International human rights 11–14
International Law for Human Rights,
    Article 60 105
International Labour Organization (ILO)
    155
  Conventions 12
  Governing Body 156
International Monetary Fund (IMF) 45,
    147, 153, 154, 156, 157, 158, 169,
    170
Iraq 14
  citizens 14
  government 14

Japanese-Americans 30
Jehovah Witnesses 38
Jews 127
Judeo-Christian West 126

Kantian image 41
Kissinger, Henry 6, 9
Koranic rule 104
Korea 149
Kosovo 1, 26, 186
  war in 4
Kuwait 14

Latin America 148
  countries in 141, 149
Lee Kuan Yew, Singapore 126
Locke, Joseph 12, 189
  view of constitutionalism 56

Machiavelli 5
  problem 4, 5
Malawi 101
Malaysia 126, 149
Mali 101
Mandragola 5
Manitoba, aboriginal peoples in 63
Marshall Pétain and the Vichy regime 7
Mauritanian government 94
Meech Lake Accord 1987 62, 63
meta-rules 161, 168
Métis, rights of 70
Mexico 149
Middle East governments 163
Millet system 127
Multi-Party Negotiating Process [MPNP]
  66, 67, 68, 71, 77
Muslim/Christian divide 163
Muslims 104, 127
Myanmar 156

Nagasaki 13
Nagel, Thomas 164, 169
Nairobi 170
Namibia 66, 101
Native Canadians 59
  claims 62
  land rights 62
  organizations 64
NATO 9, 26
Nazi leaders, trial of 26
New York City 164
Newfoundland, aboriginal peoples in 63
Nicaragua 14
Niger 101
Nigeria 101
Non-governmental organizations (NGOs)
  13, 93, 95, 142, 144, 145, 146, 156,
  157
Non-Muslim minorities 127
Non-Muslims 104
North American countries 98
North Korea 99
North West Territories 64
Northern Ireland 15, 81, 128
North-South 15
  divide 179
  tensions 185
Nova Scotia 63
Nozick, Robert 41–42, 26
Nuremberg trials 186

OECD countries 142, 150, 151, 152, 155,
  169
Ontario 63
Onuma Yasuaki 120
Optional Protocol of the Covenant on Civil
  and Political Rights 144
Optional Protocol to the Women's
  Convention 1979 146
Organization of African Unity (OAU) 91
Organization of American States (OAS)
  charter 91
Orientalism 124–126
Orientalist dichotomy 131
Ottawa 6
Ottoman Empire 127

Pakistan 99
Paraguay v. United States of America 99
Pinochet affair 46
Pogge, Thomas 165–170
post-Cold War era 186, 189
Post-War period 60
Post-Westphalian model 182
Post-World War II 181
President Clinton, State of the Union
  address 142
President Mitterand 142
Prince Edward Island 63
Protestant ethics 125
Pufendorf, Samuel von, international law
  scholar 188
Putin, and war in Chechnya 154

Quebec 59, 63, 64
  nationalism 60, 63
Quebecois 76

Ramsey, Paul, theologian 8
Regional commissions for human rights
  90–95
Rwanda 11, 96, 97, 98
  conflict 97
  government 97
  international court for 106

Saskatchewan 63
Security Council 96, 97, 144, 185, 186, 194,
  195, 196
  members 168
  Resolution 827 97
Serbia and Serbs 9

Shaping Canada's Future Together 1991
  63
Sierra Leone and Congo, diamonds in 168
Singapore 126
Social and economic (SE) concerns and
  oppressive regimes 43–50
Social and economic (SE) interests 33–39
Somalia 186
South Africa 15, 47, 58, 101, 102
  Bill of Rights 65, 66–68, 70, 76–79
    preamble 72–73
  Botha government 66
  Commission for Gender Equality 80
  Commission on the Restitution of Land
    Rights 80
  Confucian vision of society 72
  Constitution 48, 72, 73, 76, 81
  Constitutional Assembly 72, 78
  Constitutional Chapter on Fundamental
    Rights 65, 73, 78
  Constitutional Court 79
  duties and rights 77
  equality 77
  Human Rights Commission 80
  Kempton Park negotiations 72, 77
  Law Commission 66, 70
    Report 1989 69
  State of Emergency provisions 76
  Transitional Constitution 66
South African
  experiences 65–73
  Interim Constitution 71, s. 31
  social and economic rights 68–70
South America 102
South Asia and Pacific region 99–100, 102,
  104, 105, 108
South Korea 154
Soviet Empire 148
  disintegration of 141
Special Committee on Principles of
    International Law concerning
    Friendly Relations and Co-operation
    among States 181
State, Anarchy and Utopia 41
Statute of Westminster 59
Sufism 129

Tanzania 11, 97
Technical Committee on Fundamental
    Rights 66
Teheran Conference 1943

Thailand 149, 154
Tobin tax 158
Treaty of Maastricht 101
Treaty of Westphalia 3
Trudeau, Pierre 59, 60, 75
  government 62

Ullman, Richard 4
United Nations (UN) 14, 97, 98, 102, 148,
  152, 153, 182, 191, 196
  Charter 137, 138, 139, 140, 143, 145–146
    Article 2(7) 3
  Conference on environment 1992 152
  Conference on habitat 1996 152
  Conference on Human Rights 1993 146
  Conference on population and
    development 1994 152
  Conference on social development 1995
    152
  Conference on women 1995 152
  Human Rights Committee 79
  issues within 146
  membership 152
  'Paris Principles' 79
  Sub-Commission on the Promotion and
    Protection of Human Rights 147
  treaties 57
United Nations Commission on Human
    Rights (UNCHR) 99
United Nations Conference on Trade and
    Development (UNCTAD)
  1997 Report on World Trade and
    Development 148
United Nations Development Programme
    (UNDP) 149
United Nations Educational, Scientific and
    Cultural Organization (UNESCO)
    137
United Nations High Commissioner for
    Refugees (UNHCR) mandate 152
United Kingdom 15, 58
  Canada Act 1982 62
United States (US) 14, 98, 99, 101, 141,
  142, 145, 150, 152
  and Uganda 11
  and Japan 13
  Bill of Rights 48
  Congress 13
  Constitution 7
  government 142
  in Vietnam, war in 9, 11

United States (US) (cont.)
  social security system 123
  welfare-state liberalism 119
Universal Declaration of Human Rights
      (UDHR) 1948 2, 10, 12, 23, 37, 38,
      43, 46, 60, 89, 102, 137–138, 141, 143,
      161
  Articles 22–27 139
US Midwest, acid rain in 6
US Supreme Court 60
US, EU, and Japan, global inequality in
      166
USSR, constitution in 48

Victoria, Canada 59
Vienna Convention on Consular Relations
      99
Vienna Declaration 1993 57
Vietnam, North and South 11
Vriend v. Alberta 75

Walzer, Michael 4
Washington dominance 12
West Nile encephalitis 164

West-centric human rights records 123
West-centrism 15, 116
Western Europe 192
Western normative languages, manipulation
      of 117–124
Western values 163
Wolfensohn, James 150, 154
Wordsworth, William 4
World Bank 45, 153, 154, 170
  study on Latin America 153
World Conference on Human Rights 1993
      16, 102, 137, 141, 147
World War I 70, 182
World War II 30, 60, 100, 139, 144, 178,
      181, 182, 189
WTO 155, 156, 158
  ministerial conference 155
WTO Agreement on Trade-Related
      Aspects of Intellectual Property
      Rights (TRIPS) 147, 148, 149
WTO General Agreement on Trade in
      Services (GATS) 147

Yukon 64